About the author

A pharmacologist by training, Mark Greener is now a medical journalist and editor, experienced in writing for both lay and specialist publications, including *Health Which?*. He has written widely on the subjects of drugs, nutrition and health for medical, nursing and consumer magazines.

THE WHICH? GUIDE TO MANAGING STRESS

MARK GREENER

CONSUMERS' ASSOCIATION

Which? Books are commissioned and researched by
Consumers' Association and published by
Which? Ltd, 2 Marylebone Road, London NW1 4DF

Distributed by The Penguin Group:
Penguin Books Ltd, 27 Wrights Lane, London W8 5TZ

Typographic design by Paul Saunders
Cover design by Ridgeway Associates
Cover photograph by Tony Stone Images

First edition August 1996

British Library Cataloguing in Publication Data
A catalogue record for this book is available from the British Library

ISBN 0 85202 608 0

For a full list of Which? books, please write to:
Which? Books, Castlemead, Gascoyne Way, Hertford X, SG14 1LH

Typeset by Saxon Graphics Ltd, Derby
Printed and bound by Firmin-Didot (France)
Group Herissey
N° d'impression: 35082

The author and publishers would like to thank Jane Chumbley, Rose Greener,
Dr George Kassianos, Marie Lorimer, Dr Anne MacGregor, Elaine Pollard,
Ami Sevi and Professor Malcolm Lader

CONTENTS

INTRODUCTION

RICH or poor, man or woman, young or old, everyone suffers from stress. Stress leaves some people irritable and tense. For others stress has a more serious legacy. Directly or indirectly, stress contributes to heart disease, cancer, stroke (the leading three causes of death in the UK), asthma, irritable bowel syndrome, migraine – the list is almost endless. However, it is not only the body that suffers. Stress ravages the mind, contributing to depression, anxiety, insomnia and even schizophrenia.

Society as a whole is also a victim of our stress-ridden lives. Alcoholism, smoking and drug abuse impose an enormous economic burden over and above the tragedy of the lives destroyed by addictions, both legal and illegal. Clearly, managing stress is essential – for ourselves, our families and society at large. This book aims to help you control your stress.

The first chapter describes the nature of stress; explores why stress is sometimes good for health; and reveals how our personalities determine our reaction to the events around us – from daily hassles to major disasters – and therefore the severity of our stress. The book goes on to show you how to develop an individualised plan to identify the most pressing cause of your own stress. Then it explores how the challenges facing us change as we get older.

Later chapters review the physical and psychological toll of stress. Stress attacks your most vulnerable point. So if you are at high risk of developing heart disease, stress may increase your risk of suffering a heart attack. Sometimes we directly translate stress into physical disease – irritable bowel syndrome and migraine, for example. Similarly, stress can spill over into mental disorders, including anxiety and depression. However, it does not end there. Stress maintains and exacerbates the symptoms of a variety of diseases. It delays recovery, and in some cases, notably heart disease and some cancers, it can prove fatal.

Apart from offering a salutary reminder of what can happen if we fail to manage stress effectively, the chapters exploring the physical and psychological toll of stress offer specific advice on dealing with stress-related health problems.

The final chapter provides a directory of stress-beating techniques – from acupuncture to yoga. These can tackle specific diseases and bolster your stress defences. Many also provide effective first aid for generalised stress.

Managing stress is a voyage of self-discovery. By the end, you will have learnt more about yourself. You will have a clearer idea of where you are going and how you are going to get there. By managing stress, you will remain at the peak of your mental and physical powers. Stress pervades every aspect of our lives, so manage stress and you manage life.

CHAPTER 1

THE GOOD STRESS GUIDE

STRESS dominates modern life. Every month, magazine articles suggest ways to alleviate stress. Marital difficulties, work problems and family conflicts – all important stress triggers – are common coffee-time conversation topics. We eat, drink or exercise to relieve stress – with good reason. Doctors link stress with almost every illness, from cancer to heart disease to asthma. Even if stress doesn't cause a particular illness, it certainly makes you feel worse. So, each year, doctors write millions of prescriptions for antidepressants, tranquillisers and sleeping pills. However, doctors' best efforts often fail to get to the root of our problems. Drugs only paper over our mental cracks, often leaving us dissatisfied. In response, alternative and complementary treatments use everything from herbs to acupuncture to colour therapy to bolster our stress defences. Stress relief is now a multi-million pound industry.

Yet stress has a tarnished image. Stress adds spice to our lives. Indeed, without stress we wouldn't even bother getting out of bed in the morning. Successfully dealing with a difficult, stressful problem leaves you with a sense of achievement. Stress is even enjoyable – ask any sports fan.

So what is stress? Even doctors find it difficult to draw a hard-and-fast line between the symptoms of 'harmful' stress and those of a spectrum of other mental disorders, including depression, phobias, panic and anxiety. Indeed, these diseases may express the same fundamental problem: our inability to adapt adequately to pressures in the outside world.

Anxiety, for example, is a nagging worry that something awful is about to happen. However, anxiety isn't linked to anything specific. In contrast, fear has a specific cause. But when fear reaches an intensity out of proportion to its cause, it becomes a phobia. So you may fear being mugged while walking through an inner city area. If you are too terrified to leave your suburban house you have developed a phobia.

The boundaries between these mental states and their relationship to 'stress' are very blurred. We feel 'stressed out' when our jobs become too demanding. In some people, chronic stress triggers anxiety. In others, stress leaves them depressed. The death of your spouse, for example, increases your risk of developing depression by up to 1,500 per cent. And the relationship works the other way. Some phobias – especially those that restrict normal activities – cause considerable stress.

When the going gets tough

Stress increases arousal – and you need to be aroused to deal with modern life's trials and tribulations. As the pressure – stress by another, more acceptable, name – increases, your arousal rises and your performance improves. In other words, stress allows you to rise to the occasion and perform at the peak of your abilities. Indeed, many actors rely on stage fright – the theatrical name for stress – to give their best performance. Even fear is beneficial. Fear breeds caution and keeps us out of danger. Our ancestors were less likely to pick a fight with a warrior tribe that they feared. Even today, a healthy fear of being mugged keeps you vigilant – and so you are less likely to be attacked.

So the right amount of stress – despite its tarnished image – is good for your health. Too little stress leads to boredom and apathy, and undermines concentration. However, you can have too much of a good thing: over-arousal undermines your performance. You feel 'stressed out' when the demands placed on you outstrip your resources, strengths or time. At this point you should rest, but many of us begin burning the candle at both ends. This uses up your mental and physical reserves. So you push yourself harder and harder – and feel worse and worse. The body's warnings become more urgent. Perhaps you start losing sleep. Maybe you feel depressed and permanently on edge. Your

concentration may flag. So you work longer and longer
ing to catch up. Eventually, the smallest additional stress
breakdown. Doctors describe the relationship between arousal
and performance as the 'n' shaped curve.

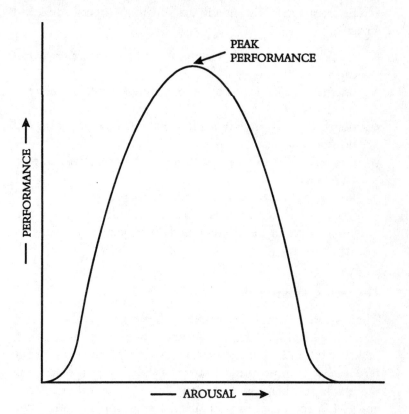

The 'n'-shaped curve showing the relationship between performance and arousal

What triggers stress?

Almost any event can cause stress. Some stress triggers are obvious – for example redundancy, bereavement, divorce, incurable
illness and moving house – but specialists are only now beginning
to realise the intense distress caused by some other events or situations. For example, doctors increasingly recognise the problem
of social phobia. Sufferers experience intense, debilitating anxiety
when they come under public scrutiny. In severe cases, sufferers
are unable to write a cheque or eat in public. Even holidays, the

very time when we should relax, can cause considerable stress – especially if the resort doesn't live up to its billing in the brochure. The emotional baggage we carry with us on holiday magnifies any stress. After all, holidays are supposed to be an escape from stress. Essentially, six situations trigger stress and anxiety:

- conflicting motives e.g. looking after a family as well as working outside the home
- internal conflict e.g. working for a company you feel behaves unethically
- unusual events e.g. arriving in a new job or a new town and not knowing what to expect
- unpredictable events e.g. exam results, appraisal or company take-over
- loss e.g. redundancy or the death of a spouse
- frustration at, for example, not being awarded the promotion you deserve or being stuck in a traffic jam and missing an appointment.

The value of control

These six situations share a common theme: we no longer feel in control. Feeling in control is a powerful weapon in the fight against stress-related problems. It also seems to be the critical difference between people who try to tackle their problems and those who feel helpless. So if your 'locus of control' is internal you feel in command of your situation, but if it is external, you feel the situation controls you. People with an internal locus of control find it easier to adapt and find solutions to their problems. Chapter two suggests some ways you can regain control of your life.

A company's most stressed-out employees tend to be those who work long hours, often for little pay, with little control over their working life: production line workers, check-out assistants and people performing routine clerical work, for example. Moreover, working on a production line or doing routine clerical work tends to be more boring than being in management. Boredom exacerbates stress.

In contrast, executive stress is fashionable – and profitable for stress management consultants. However, while senior executives work hard, they control their working life to a much greater extent than their subordinates. Moreover, an executive's workload tends to be more varied and interesting. Seniority also brings the financial rewards that allow senior executives to make the most of their leisure time.

The importance of feeling in control was underscored by a Swedish study which found that people who worked hard with little control consumed more tranquillisers than those workers with more control over their working life. But, as we'll see later, tranquillisers don't tackle the causes of stress.

Another study measured levels of cortisol, a stress hormone, in military pilots and their crews, such as navigators and radio operators. Before the flight, pilots and their crews showed similar cortisol levels – suggesting that they experienced similar amounts of stress and anxiety. However, after the flight, cortisol levels among crew members were higher than among pilots. This suggests that the pilots experienced less stress and anxiety than their crews, probably because they controlled the plane.

These studies highlight the difference between 'stress' and 'pressure'. A deadline for a report places the executive under pressure – a level of arousal you can cope with. Routine, boring and poorly paid work can cause chronic stress. Many people thrive under pressure. No one thrives under chronic stress.

The stress of uncertainty

Anyone involved in a round of redundancies knows the stress of uncertainty – a link underscored in a study of male students. The students listened to a voice counting to 15. The psychologists warned the students that on the count of 10 they might receive an electric shock depending on the card they drew from a pack containing 'shock' and 'non-shock' cards. For one group, the pack contained one shock card and 19 non-shock cards – a five per cent chance of receiving the shock. The second pack contained ten shock cards and ten non-shock cards – a 50:50 chance. The final pack contained 19 shock cards and one non-shock card – a 95 per cent chance of receiving a shock. Psychologists measured the students' arousal, which indicates their level of stress and anxiety.

Remarkably, the group with the five per cent chance of receiving the shock experienced the most stress and anxiety. The students with a 95 per cent chance of receiving the shock said they were reconciled to receiving it. The group with a 50:50 chance thought that the risk was high enough for them to expect a shock. They hoped for the best – but expected the worst. However, the people in the five per cent group knew that, logically, their risk of receiving a shock was low. But they couldn't be sure. This uncertainty triggered stress and anxiety.

This may suggest that being warned of dangers lying in the future reduces uncertainty and so alleviates stress. But in some cases being forewarned exacerbates stress – especially if the person tends to be apprehensive or anxious about life generally.

The stress of time

Trying to do more and more in less and less time is another common cause of stress. The economic climate means that employers increasingly expect more and more from their workforce. Despite modern technology, many people work longer and longer hours. To make matters worse, many employers exploit their workers' fear of redundancy.

However, we don't leave time pressures behind at the office. For example, many women now work outside the home. In 1973, 58 per cent of women worked. This increased to 66 per cent in 1992. The increase in the number of women working part-time is even more dramatic: up 30 per cent over the last 20 years. Many feel pressurised into being 'superwomen'. They want – or need – a career. But they also want to be good mothers and homemakers. Trying to fulfil these two demanding, and sometimes conflicting, roles – unless you've got an understanding partner or a well-paid enough job to afford a nanny and home help – leaves women tired, tense and stressed. They have little time to develop the interests that protect them from the ravages of stress. Using some of the time management techniques outlined in chapter two may help.

Working mothers highlight another common cause of stress: trying to bridge the gap between reality and expectation. No one can – or should try to be – the perfect partner, parent, house-keeper, lover and breadwinner rolled into one. Moreover, no job or marriage is perfect. The gap between our expectations when we start a new job or relationship and the reality commonly causes stress.

Micro-, mezzo- and macrolevel stressors

Clearly, stress triggers – the so-called stressors – come in many guises. But they break down into three groups: micro-, mezzo- and macrolevel stressors. Each level may contain the six stressful situations outlined on page 12. For example, traffic jams (microlevel), trouble with in-laws (mezzolevel) and not being able to find a job because of the economic recession (macrolevel) can all be intensely frustrating. Appreciating the differences between these levels can help you identify your stress triggers.

Microlevel stressors

Recent studies suggest that the slow, steady accumulation of everyday hassles may more accurately indicate your risk of suffer-ing stress-related illness than the number of dramatic events you experience, such as bereavement, unemployment or a new job. Such everyday microlevel stressors as delays on the train, traffic jams and minor family rows are the most common form of stress. But despite being so common their impact on physical and emo-tional well-being is poorly understood. However, the accumula-tion of everyday, even seemingly trivial, hassles undoubtedly undermines your physical and mental health. For example, the more daily hassles you experience, the greater your risk of suffer-ing a number of health problems, including the common cold and post-natal depression. Microlevel stressors also seem to main-tain and exacerbate anxiety disorders, such as agoraphobia.

Mezzolevel stressors

Mezzolevel stressors, the memorable life events, are less common but better studied than microlevel stressors. While chronic mez-zolevel stressors tend to have more impact on your physical and psychological health than short-lived events, even one-off events can damage your mental health. For example, a serious marital problem, divorce or separation increases your likelihood of suffering depression by 1,300 per cent.

Nevertheless, our response to adversity is partly determined by the amount of stressful baggage we carry with us. A minor hassle for one person may trigger a breakdown in someone reeling from the stress of getting married and the death of a parent. The 'Life Stress Scale' reflects this and assigns a value to certain stressful life events – including pleasurable activities such as marriage and Christmas. Your risk of suffering a stress-related illness depends on your score during the last year. Half the people with scores exceeding 200 develop health problems. Over 300 this increases to almost 80 per cent. However, it is important to realise that this scale may not apply to everyone. For example, the stress of taking out a mortgage depends on your financial circumstances.

THE LIFE STRESS SCALE			
Event	score	Event	score
death of a spouse	100	change in responsibilities at work	29
divorce	73	a child leaves home	29
marital separation	65	trouble with in-laws	29
jail term	63	outstanding personal achievement	28
death of a close relative	63	partner starts or stops employment	26
personal injury or illness	53	begin or end school, college or university	26
marriage	50	change in living conditions	25
being fired	47	revision of personal habits	24
marital reconciliation	45	trouble with boss	23
retirement	45	change in work conditions or hours	20
change in relative's health	44	moving home	20
pregnancy	40	changing schools	20
sexual problems	39	changing religious habits	19
new family member	39	changing social activities	18
business readjustment	39	taking out a small mortgage or loan	17
change in finances	38	change in sleeping habits	16
death of a close friend	37	change in number of family reunions	15
changing to a new type of job	36	vacation	13
change in number of marital arguments	35	change in eating habits	13
taking out a large mortgage or loan	31	Christmas	12
mortgage foreclosure	30	minor law breaking	11

Macrolevel stressors

We can also become stressed by pressures facing society. A few years ago many people felt anxious and stressed about the threat of nuclear war between the superpowers. Similarly, surveys suggest that morale in the USA fell dramatically after President John F. Kennedy's assassination in 1963. And admissions to mental hospitals rise during recessions in the US economy. It seems that the social, economic and political climate affects stress levels.

The fight-or-flight reflex

Despite acting on three levels, stressors cause a similar spectrum of stress symptoms, including feeling over-vigilant and on edge and suffering from muscle twitches, palpitations and restlessness. Many of these symptoms are produced by a cascade of biological changes, known as the fight-or-flight reflex.

The fight-or-flight reflex is controlled by the 'involuntary' or 'autonomic' nervous system that keeps us breathing and our hearts beating while we sleep. Normally, we cannot consciously control autonomic nervous system activity, unlike the actions of the voluntary nervous system. It is easy to decide to pick up a pen. It is harder to slow a rapid heart beat before giving a presentation. Nevertheless, yoga, meditation, biofeedback and a variety of other techniques described in chapter six may allow practitioners to exert some control over their autonomic nervous system.

The autonomic nervous system is divided into two – sympathetic and parasympathetic nerves – which have opposite actions. For example, sympathetic nerves increase heart rate, while parasympathetic nerves slow heart beat. The balance between the activity of the sympathetic and parasympathetic systems determines our level of arousal.

When you face stress or danger your sympathetic nervous system activity rapidly increases. This stimulates your adrenal glands – which lie on the top of your kidneys – to secrete more adrenaline, cortisol and other hormones into your blood. The combination of the increased sympathetic activity and the hormonal surge from the adrenal glands diverts your body's resources from your internal organs – such as your stomach – to your muscles.

Your body expects you to use your muscles either to fight or run away. So the amount of glucose and fats circulating in your blood increases to provide the energy you will need. Your breathing becomes deeper and more rapid to increase oxygen supply. Blood drains from the skin – which is why we go pale when scared. Your heart beat becomes stronger and more rapid – in some cases increasing from a resting rate of around 72 beats per minute to 180 beats per minute. Blood pressure also rises.

The combination of nervous and hormonal actions triggers changes in our bowel movements – which is why stress can cause nausea or diarrhoea. The salivary glands reduce their output, producing a dry mouth, while sweat glands increase production, resulting in a 'cold sweat'. The muscles surrounding the hair follicles contract, causing goose bumps, and the pupils dilate, creating a wide-eyed look. Hearing also becomes more acute.

Stress triggers the release of small proteins – known as endorphins – from the brain and from the adrenal and pituitary glands. Endorphins act on the same part of the brain as opiate pain killers – such as morphine and heroin – and have the same effect. Moreover, blood clots more quickly to limit the damage from an injury.

The fight-or-flight reflex evolved to get us out of danger quickly and with the least damage possible; we could then rest and refresh our reserves. This response was a life-saver when threatened by a rival tribe on the warpath. It is less appropriate when the threat is daily hassle from a patronising, over-demanding and unfairly critical boss. Your body is ready to fight – or flee the office. However, our veneer of civilisation prevents us from doing either – and the fight-or-flight reflex remains activated for long periods while we have no opportunity to rest and replenish our physical, emotional and mental reserves. The chronic activation of the fight-or-flight reflex produces many of the physical and psychological symptoms of chronic stress.

Adapting to stress

The fight-or-flight reflex, which we share with many other animals, was discovered in the 1930s when Hans Selye, a physiologist working at Montreal University, investigated the effects of stressors, such as infections or excessive heat or cold, on rats' hormonal responses. At first, the rats' adrenal glands enlarged and increased production of adrenaline and certain 'stress' hormones. However, Selye noted that over time, the rats became accustomed to intense stress. For example, their adrenal glands became less active and their biochemistry returned to normal.

Nevertheless, the rats' recovery was short-lived. If rats were exposed to the stressor for a further few weeks, the adrenal glands suddenly increased production again.

In other words, chronic stress dramatically changed the rats' hormonal balance, which irreparably damaged some of their internal organs. The rats, quite literally, died from exhaustion. Moreover, if the animals were exposed to a second stressor during the period that they appeared to become accustomed to the first, they quickly died. In human terms, the rats passed the peak and were on the downward slope on the 'n'-shaped curve (see diagram on page 11). Selye's experiments showed that animals can adapt to chronic stress – up to a point.

The holocaust survivors are living proof that humans can adapt to extreme stress. Less dramatically, doctors, politicians and environmentalists increasingly recognise that noise pollution can cause considerable stress. Noise pollution increases your risk of developing dizziness, headaches, gastrointestinal problems, ulcers, high blood pressure and a number of other stress-related diseases. Nevertheless, people living near a railway line or an airport become used to quite loud noises. But a crash near the house can mean that the sound of a train again causes considerable stress.

Learned helplessness

Some people adapt to constant stress by feeling helpless and apathetic. They come to believe that any attempt to alter their circumstances, no matter how hard they try, is futile. So they are less likely to take the necessary steps to resolve their problems, which exacerbates their stress. Psychologists call this type of adaptation 'learned helplessness'.

We all know the symptoms of learned helplessness. After failing an exam, failing to get a new job or failing in a relationship we become assailed by self-doubt. We may question our abilities, wonder if we'll ever succeed in our profession, or feel unattractive. Most of us recover by trying harder, moving to a job that better suits our abilities, or finding a more compatible partner.

However, learned helplessness can become entrenched in someone's personality.

> **JOE** lost his job as an electrical engineer and began, despite years of experience, to question his abilities. He became unable to apply for new engineering jobs that were well within his abilities, start his own business or even mend simple electrical faults around the house.

Joe's learned helplessness focused on his job. But learned helplessness can spill over into other aspects of life – undermining relationships with family and friends. A person may become withdrawn and apathetic and can start sliding into severe depression. This, of course, makes it even more difficult for sufferers to overcome their problems.

Assertive coping

Fortunately, few of us 'cope' with stress and anxiety by descending into learned helplessness. Nevertheless, we use a number of other psychological tactics, known as coping strategies, to adapt to stress. At the other extreme to learned helplessness, we can employ constructive coping strategies. Psychologists call these strategies 'assertive coping'.

Assertive coping helps us prevail over adversity, be it redundancy, terminal illness or financial problems. Chapter two helps you develop an individualised plan to tackle your problems through assertive coping, which breaks down into three broad lines of defence against stress.

Change your environment

In certain circumstances, you can change your environment to minimise stress and alleviate anxiety. However, the change has to be realistic. People with difficulties at work can change their environment by finding a new job or setting up their own business. But unless you're a very unusual person, assertive coping probably does not include dropping out and becoming a crofter in the

Scottish highlands or running a vineyard in France. It might seem a romantic idea, but you need special skills and the right temperament to make such dramatic changes work.

Change your behaviour
Be honest: often you make – or at least contribute to – your own stress. Perhaps you are bored and frustrated at work. So you don't make enough effort and your boss is always on your back. Perhaps you have few friends because you feel uncomfortable in social gatherings and seem aggressive or a wallflower. Perhaps drink or drugs are ruining your finances, undermining relationships at home and alienating the people best placed to help you. In these circumstances, changing your behaviour often resolves the underlying problem.

Change your response to stress
Sometimes you really are helpless. Perhaps your wife is dying from terminal breast cancer. Maybe you face daily racial abuse. Perhaps your mother is severely demented from Alzheimer's disease and no longer recognises you or her grandchildren. In these situations there is little you can do to resolve your predicament. However, changing your response to the situation may help you cope with the stress. Studies of concentration camp survivors suggest that people who do not blame themselves for their predicament are better able to avoid being overwhelmed by their situation.

Coping in the twilight zone

Between assertive coping and learned helplessness lie a variety of coping strategies that can tide you over an emotional or psychological 'rough patch'. However, allowing these behavioural patterns to become entrenched in your personality leaves you in a psychological twilight zone.

Unlike assertive coping, these strategies do not directly confront the cause of your stress. Rather, they alleviate the anxiety triggered by stressful and traumatic events by distorting reality or your self-perception. They allow you to cope from day to day without tackling the underlying problem. So you may rarely – or never – be happy. On the other hand, your distress is not obvious – as it may be if you develop learned helplessness or depression, for example. You suffer in silence.

Repression

Repression is possibly the most powerful of these defences. It involves banishing thoughts and desires that cause anxiety and stress from the conscious mind. For example, certain expressions of sexuality conflict with religious, social or moral codes. Some people 'resolve' this conflict by totally repressing their sexuality. Likewise, memories associated with guilt, anxiety or trauma can be 'forgotten'. However, the stress-provoking thoughts and desires remain lurking in the subconscious.

As a result, the repressed thoughts and desires may re-emerge from the subconscious and trigger stress symptoms – although the person is unaware of the cause of their distress. Alternatively, the repressed thoughts and desires may re-emerge in dreams, or when the person is under the influence of drugs or alcohol, or as irrational ideas. Psychoanalysis (see chapter six) delves into a patient's psyche to reveal and examine these repressed thoughts and desires. This may change the person's behaviour and alleviate stress and tension.

Denial

Denial is another powerful strategy to alleviate anxiety. People use denial to avoid accepting the reality of their situation – even when they face overwhelming evidence. For example, many alcoholics deny the damage wrought by their addiction. Alcoholics Anonymous* and other rehabilitation programmes succeed because, in part, they force people to face their addiction and deal with its consequences. Similarly, terminally ill patients may deny the truth until they can muster the emotional resources to face reality. Denial is similar to repression but focuses on current events rather than stressful events in the past.

Rationalisation

Rationalisation attempts to explain away stressful situations. So John, who was turned down for a job, convinced himself it was not all the advert made it out to be. Rationalisation also helps resolve inner conflicts. For example, someone fiddling his employer could rationalise his dishonesty by convincing himself that 'everyone does it, so why shouldn't I?'

Sublimation

Sublimation transforms a socially unacceptable trait into a more acceptable form. Some psychologists believe that many works of art result from sublimation. The artist transforms the energy generated by primitive urges into a more socially acceptable form. Similarly, sport may be a sublimation of aggression, and dancing a sublimation of sexuality. Freud even argued that sublimation converts people with a tendency to cruelty into surgeons, lawyers or teachers!

Identification

You attempt to overcome stress by imitating someone you admire. A young woman may identify with her more attractive and socially adept friend and attempt to take on some of her characteristics. However, people also identify with people who provoke stress. For example, an employee may identify with an overpowering boss. Identification with a certain group is a common way to deal with the stress of adolescence (see page 42). However, in extreme cases your personality can become submerged under the imitation.

Reaction formation

Jane worried she was still the dumpy, unattractive teenager whom everyone teased and who never had a boyfriend. She wasn't, but overcompensated by flirting and dressing provocatively. Jane coped by reaction formation – she grossly exaggerated a side of her personality to conceal her real problem.

Projection

Projection lays the blame for your stress and anxiety firmly at the feet of someone else. A classic – if cliché'd – example is the vicar who condemns promiscuity during his blood-and-thunder sermons, but who counts half the female congregation among his mistresses. Likewise, a woman who consistently accuses her faithful husband of infidelity on business trips may be concealing her urges. In other words, projection alleviates anxiety by attributing the stress-provoking thoughts and feelings to objects, events or people in the outside world. While this strategy can be effective, projection totally distorts reality – blaming someone else means that you don't take responsibility for your predicament.

Aggression

Aggression is another common reaction to stress, even among animals. When scientists placed two rats in a cage and gave one an electric shock, it attacked the other animal. Road rage is an example of stress provoking aggression: a driver reacts violently when another car cuts him or her up. Someone trying to mend a car may throw the spanners down in frustration. A child may throw a jigsaw into the air when she cannot get all the pieces to fit. This is 'directed aggression'- the violence is directed against the cause of the frustration. 'Displaced aggression' uses someone else as the scapegoat. You really want to hit your boss, but instead you kick the cat or pick an argument with your partner.

Withdrawal

Some people cope with anxiety and stress by retreating into a mental shell and hoping their problems will go away. They narrow their horizons until their lives are within limits they feel they can control. A strategic withdrawal can provide a breathing space to re-evaluate our lives, problems and priorities. But, taken to extremes, withdrawal can cut away the social supports that help us deal with stress and may lead to apathy, withdrawal and depression.

Regression

Some people deal with stress and anxiety by reverting to an earlier, less mature stage of development. After the birth of a new baby, for example, older children who were fairly independent may start bed-wetting or thumb-sucking again. Even adults may cry or chew their nails.

Risk-taking behaviour

These coping strategies relieve the anxiety caused by stress. However, they also act as warnings: something is wrong, which we need to face and change. But change means taking risks. And stress may alter our risk-taking behaviour.

Psychologists asked two groups of subjects to toss rings at pegs. The closest pegs received the lowest score, those in the middle were assigned an average score and those furthest away the highest score. Non-anxious people tended to throw rings at the middle pegs. They avoided the almost guaranteed success offered by the closest pegs. But they also avoided gambling for the high-risk, high-scoring pegs. In contrast, anxious people were more likely to aim at the closest rings, where they could be sure of scoring, or gambled for the high-scoring rings.

It's a long step from throwing rings at pegs to solving problems in the real world. However, in some people, stress may provoke two extremes of risk-taking behaviour: a very conservative approach to life or a high-risk strategy that often fails, but brings high rewards when it works.

Understanding your personality

Clearly, stress – and our reaction to it – is an intensely personal experience. One person's challenge may be the cause of another's breakdown. However, certain people seem especially vulnerable to the effects of stress. Part of the reason for this lies deeply rooted in your personality. Psychologists divide personalities into Type A and B (see box).

Type A people tend to be competitive, impatient, aggressive and ambitious. They move rapidly, talk fast and don't listen. They are

| ARE YOU A TYPE A OR TYPE B PERSONALITY? ||
Type A	Type B
very competitive	non-competitive
impatient	unhurried
goal-orientated	relaxed
aggressive	passive
restless, rapid movements	good listener
doesn't listen	talks at a
fast talker	reasonable speed

continually on the go – always doing something, even if it doesn't need doing. They never relax. So they often feel tired and fatigued. However, instead of listening to their bodies, they take fatigue as a sign of weakness and push themselves harder. Anger, hostility and aggression are common coping strategies among Type A people. Moreover, Type A personalities tend to be more likely to develop certain problems, such as high blood pressure and heart disease.

Type B personalities are the exact opposites. They are relaxed, calm and non-competitive. They move at a sensible pace and listen to you. In other words, the Type B person takes life as it comes. This lower level of arousal protects Type B people from severe stress. Most of us fall somewhere between these two extremes.

Our perception of stress also affects our reaction to it. For example, some people view the world in extremes. They expect perfection from themselves and others. A single mistake and they see themselves as a total failure. The gap between their expectation of themselves and reality causes stress. Other people view the world through a mental filter. They may, for example, forget all the good things that happen and focus only on the bad.

We also vary widely in our ability to cope with frustration. Disabled people often remain cheerful and live full and fulfilling lives despite the frustrations imposed by severe physical handicaps. However, some able-bodied people throw a temper tantrum if their dinner is not on the table the moment they get home from work.

In contrast, self-confidence, ambition, energy, commitment – to yourself, your family and work – and taking responsibility for your health all bolster your stress defences. Following the plan in chapter two should help you take control of your life. Many of the therapies described in the directory (chapter six) will help you maintain strong defences.

CHAPTER 2

CHANGING YOUR LIFE

TERMINALLY ill people soon realise that time cannot be squandered. They realise that they have little time left to fulfil their hopes, dreams and ambitions. Patients respond to the intense stress of impending death in different ways. They may quit their jobs to spend more time with their families. They may renew their interest in their careers. They may paint, write poetry or visit places they always wanted to see. But why wait until you face death to do these things? You can reduce stress by changing your life now.

1: Identify your problem

The first step is to understand your stress. But identifying the cause of your stress is often more difficult than it seems. Often we know that something is wrong but we have only a vague idea of why. We may be unhappy at work. We may feel unsatisfied with life generally. However, we rarely take the time to try to understand the cause of our distress. So on a blank piece of paper, write the following headings:

- What is the problem?
- Who is the problem?
- Where does the problem occur?
- Why does the problem occur?
- When does the problem occur?

If answering these questions does not reveal a specific cause for your anxiety, keep a diary for a fortnight. You can either keep the classic journal and record your thoughts and impressions each day, or you can simply note what you are doing or thinking about each time you feel tense, stressed or anxious. This can provide you with an insight into your problems. You might also consider counselling or psychotherapy. A trained outside observer can offer a new perspective that helps you get to the root of your problems.

Diaries can also help you tackle specific problems. So, if you want to cut down the amount of alcohol you consume, keep a record for a couple of weeks of when, where and how much you drink. Keeping a record means you have a target to aim at and should reveal ways you can change your habits.

Our quizzes on the next pages should also give you some insight into the severity of your stress and whether stress has begun to spill over into anxiety or depression. First, refer to the Life Stress Scale on page 16. How many events apply to you? How do they make you feel? Anxious? Depressed? The Life Stress Scale also provides you with some idea of your risk of developing a stress-related health problem, based on the number of major life events you have experienced over the past year. However, the scale does not account for the more common – and possibly more dangerous – everyday hassles. Moreover, not everyone who accumulates a score over 200 or 300 develops a stress-related illness. So how can you assess how stressed you are at the moment? One way is to count the number of stress signals you experience.

How many stress signals do you experience?

The wide variation in our response to stress – and our coping strategies – is reflected in the range of stress-related symptoms. The more of these stress signals you experience, the more serious your stress problem. However, the stress signals may change from moment to moment, so it may be better to note how many symptoms you experience over 24 hours.

Stress signals

- headaches
- muscle tension; stiff neck
- feeling isolated
- changed eating habits
- palpitations; rapid heart beat
- feeling scared
- sleep disturbances; insomnia
- fatigue
- crying for no reason
- breathing problems

- grinding teeth
- feeling of impending doom
- pallor
- inability to forget problems
- diarrhoea; constipation
- feeling pressurised
- nervousness; anxiety
- irritability; anger
- feeling jumpy; racing apprehensive thoughts
- procrastination; worry about making the wrong decision
- increased smoking or drinking
- being brusque, rude or sarcastic

- sexual problems; impotence
- losing interest in your hobbies or job
- poor concentration
- a 'lump' in your throat
- cold hands or feet; excessive sweating; a 'cold sweat'
- weak knees; dizziness; feeling faint
- excessively sensitive to outside stimuli
- muscle twitches and tics
- preoccupied with misfortune
- 'butterflies' in the stomach; nausea; indigestion/dyspepsia

Are you anxious or depressed?

Everyone is anxious at one time or another. But how do you know if your stress has triggered a more serious problem such as chronic anxiety or depression? Doctors commonly use the Hospital Anxiety and Depression Scale (see below) to distinguish the two conditions. However, remember that most depressed people also suffer from anxiety and that psychiatric conditions are notoriously difficult to self-diagnose. After all, you're using the same organ that is supposed to be ill to diagnose that something's wrong.

Complete both tests, ideally when you've had a 'normal' day rather than an intensely stressful or relaxing one. Check your score on **page 241**. If you score more than eight then you may be suffering from these problems. The closer your score to eight, the stronger your depressive or anxious trait. In other words, if you score six or seven, doctors may not regard you as suffering from anxiety yet, but you're well on your way. If you score eight or more you may want to consult your doctor, especially if you've had the symptoms for more than a month.

ANXIETY

1. **I feel tense or wound up:**
   Most of the time
   A lot of the time
   From time to time, occasionally
   Not at all

2. **I get a sort of frightened feeling as if something awful is about to happen:**
   Very definitely and quite badly
   Yes, but not too badly
   A little, but it doesn't worry me
   Not at all

3. **Worrying thoughts go through my mind:**
   A great deal of the time
   A lot of the time
   From time to time, not too often
   Only occasionally

4. **I can sit at ease and feel relaxed:**
   Definitely
   Usually
   Not often
   Not at all

5. **I get a sort of frightened feeling like 'butterflies' in the stomach:**
   Not at all
   Occasionally
   Quite often
   Very often

6. **I feel restless as if I have to be on the move:**
   Very much indeed
   Quite a lot
   Not very much
   Not at all

7. **I get sudden feelings of panic:**
   Very often indeed
   Quite often
   Not very often
   Not at all

DEPRESSION

1. **I still enjoy the things I used to enjoy:**
   Definitely as much
   Not quite so much
   Only a little
   Hardly at all

2. **I can laugh and see the funny side of things:**
   As much as I always could
   Not quite so much now
   Definitely not so much now
   Not at all

3. **I feel cheerful:**
   Not at all
   Not often
   Sometimes
   Most of the time

4. **I feel as if I am slowed down:**
   Nearly all the time
   Very often
   Sometimes
   Not at all

5. **I have lost interest in my appearance:**
   Definitely
   I don't take as much care
   I may not take quite as much care
   I take just as much care as ever

6. **I look forward with enjoyment to things:**
   As much as ever I did
   Rather less than I used to
   Definitely less than I used to
   Hardly at all

7. **I can enjoy a good book or radio or TV programme:**
   Often
   Sometimes
   Not often
   Very seldom

2: Deal with the serious problems

You should now have some insight into the type and extent of your problems. If you scored eight or more on either the anxiety or depression scale, you need to deal with these more serious problems before trying to tackle the cause of your stress. Severe depression or intense anxiety impair your ability to review and change your life. A short course of drugs (see chapter five) may alleviate the symptoms and provide you with a window of opportunity to tackle your underlying problems.

Once you have analysed your emotions and determined your stress triggers, you are on your way to developing an individualised anti-stress action plan. But have you got the time to change your life? Many of us already feel we're losing the time race without adding more to our plates. Deadlines loom ominously. We cannot cram any more into our day. We flit from task to task. On a day-to-day basis, time pressures cause more stress than almost anything else. The vast number of time management books is testament to that. So the first step in changing your life is to ensure that you have enough time to put your new life plan into practice.

Time management: not just for yuppies
Almost everyone can benefit from applying some time management principles. Time management is not just part of yuppiedom. It allows you to get more out of life. You can use the time you save to relax, exercise, spend time with the kids or do your share of the housework.

ERIC wanted to go jogging, but could never find the time. He solved it by blocking one hour off in his diary each Monday, Wednesday, Friday and Sunday. Eric did not let anything – other than a work or family crisis – impinge on that time. Eric looked on time management as part of the self-discipline he needed to exercise. And it took willpower, especially on the cold winter evenings, not to be waylaid by the demands of work, spouse and children.

Try these strategies to help you win the time race:

- Every Sunday night or Monday morning, list the tasks that you need to accomplish during the week. Before you stop work each night, use this master list to write down the tasks you must accomplish the next day. Then prioritise your list and tackle the tasks in this order.

- Break larger tasks into smaller, more manageable chunks.

- Allow at least an hour of your working day for unscheduled interruptions.

- Don't let the list become your master. It's a tool to control stress – not to raise the pressure. You cannot plan for the unexpected. If you find that you've not completed everything, then re-write the list.

- Think before saying yes and learn to say no. Even if you are self-employed it's better to turn work down than to do a bad job. Nevertheless, just saying no presents many people with a problem. They either feel guilty about turning down work or pressurised into saying yes – even if it compromises their social life or increases their stress levels. They gradually accumulate more and more work and more and more outside commitments until they have no time for themselves. Assertiveness training can help you say 'no' without causing offence.

- Avoid procrastination. We all have tasks we hate. However tempting it is, avoid putting off your pet hates. There's nothing worse than doing a job you detest under pressure of an imminent deadline.

- Eliminate time-wasters. We routinely perform many tasks at home and work simply because they are routine. Do you really need to clean the brasses each Sunday? Why not make it every other week? Do you really need to hold a review meeting every Monday morning? You may not realise that you're doing something simply because it has always been done that way. For a few days, list each task you perform as you change jobs rather than relying on memory. Then review the list and ruthlessly eliminate time-wasters.

- Can't you delegate? Can't the office junior do the routine filing? Can't your children wash the car or mow the lawn? You may have to pay for the privilege, but at least it frees more leisure time for you. Look at each task on your master list and ask yourself if someone else could do it.

● Ask your secretary or use an answering machine to screen calls.

● Remember that this is your life. Ultimately you are in control of your time and your life, so time management is really about controlling your life. Feeling in control helps alleviate stress. Time management techniques help you remain in control. Nurture this feeling.

● Take a longer term view. So try to separate your stressors: don't plan to change job, move house and have a baby at once.

One problem at a time...

Unless you are lucky, you'll find you have more than one problem. Deal with them one at a time. Often people fail to change their lives because they try to do too much too soon. Ideally, concentrate on one or two specific areas and don't set yourself too high a target. The changes should be small enough to fit into your everyday life. This may mean breaking larger problems into smaller ones. Succeed in these and you'll develop the self-confidence to tackle the larger problems.

JAN, a 40-year-old bank manager, identified three major problems. First, she was dissatisfied with her career and wanted to spend more time on her hobby as a semi-professional photographer. Secondly, she felt weighed under by her financial commitments – especially the huge mortgage that would not be paid off until the day she retired. Finally, she wanted to get fit. Her father had died of heart disease a week after his fiftieth birthday.

Jan decided to start with her fitness. She booked lessons at a gym and started jogging. She felt a great sense of achievement as her exercise tolerance rose steadily. Jan felt her career and financial problems were intertwined, so she concentrated on paying off her credit cards and loans one at a time and put her house on the market. She quit her job, and moved to a cheaper part of the country where she now splits her time between photography and helping local businesses with their tax, VAT and business finances. Her total income is less – but this is more than balanced by her lower outgoings.

Be realistic

We're good at making resolutions – especially after a few drinks on New Year's Eve – but we're generally poor at keeping them. You are not going to change your life unless you really want to. So make sure you are motivated – and that is easier if you concentrate on the present. Few people can motivate themselves to exercise, for example, on the promise of 'good health' in the future. If you want to exercise, concentrate on the immediate benefits, such as feeling fitter, looking better or not getting so out-of-breath. These are much more powerful motivators.

Set yourself clear, specific and achievable targets. There is no point in stating 'I want to exercise more'. You need to break this into stages. First, decide what type of exercise – running, for example – and if necessary find a club. Then decide you'll run further or longer each week. But these targets have to be achievable: you're not going to run the London Marathon after your second week of training. There is no point in wishing to be a striker for Arsenal if you're fat and forty. Don't waste your life on unattainable dreams.

Sort out your options

One of the major problems of stress is that we lose our sense of perspective. You've probably got more options than you think. If you want to change your job make a list of your experience and interests. Then write down the pros and cons of each career change you're contemplating. If you want to tackle your financial problems you need to sort out your income and outgoings and list your assets. Then you can decide how you can maximise your income and minimise your outgoings.

Not too fast

Change your life gradually. Attempting to change too fast too hard often leads to boom-and-bust. For example, rapidly increasing the amount of exercise you take can lead to injury or exhaustion. Likewise, dieters are more likely to keep the weight off if they lose it gradually rather than during a crash diet.

Stick with it

Overcoming stress usually means changing entrenched habits. These didn't develop overnight – and you cannot expect to change them overnight. You're bound to have relapses and set-backs. So accept any setbacks and keep going. Gradually the changes will become part of your behavioural patterns. It's also important to ensure that you don't become bored. So if you're trying to get fit by swimming try jogging or tennis. You could also swim at a different pool a week for a few weeks or take a different route while jogging. Other people beat boredom by setting themselves challenges.

Keep a sense of balance

If you work out or play computer games to relieve the stress caused by over-working, don't let that activity become your obsession. You'll just be swapping one addiction for another. Try to keep a sense of balance.

3: Bolster your defences

Change carries an emotional cost. On the Life Stress Scale (page 16), revising personal habits scores 24 points, two less than starting or leaving school, college or university and one more than trouble with your boss. So bolster your stress defences with some the techniques in our directory (see chapter six).

CHAPTER 3

THE THREE AGES OF STRESS

STRESS respects neither social standing, sex nor age. It affects the affluent and the poor, men and women, and haunts us from the cradle to the grave. Nevertheless, we face different challenges at different times of our lives. Understanding the three ages of stress helps us appreciate the cause of our – or our loved one's – distress.

Stress in children and teenagers

Childhood days are supposed to be the happiest of our lives. But for thousands of people they turn out to be the most miserable, and the effects of a miserable childhood can last a lifetime. During childhood, the mental and emotional foundations that support us for the rest of our lives are laid down. Strong foundations support a child through a lifetime of trials, tribulations and tensions. Weak foundations leave a child emotionally and mentally vulnerable – usually for the rest of their lives.

It may threaten our idealised view of childhood, but stress and other psychological problems are common in children. Around one in ten young people experience a psychiatric or psychological problem that lasts for at least a year. In inner cities, the figure increases to one in four. Moreover, the problem seems to be getting worse. For example, increasing numbers of children are diagnosed as suffering from serious depression. Doctors now estimate that around two per cent of school children and five per cent of adolescents suffer depression. Partly, the rise shows that we are better at recognising our children's torment and less readily dismiss childhood stress as 'just a stage they're going through'.

Stress may affect a child's psychological, emotional and even physical development. One study found that by seven years of age children who experienced certain persistent stress-related complaints – such as frequent and chronic bed-wetting – were 0.77cm shorter than their less anxious peers. It may not sound like much, but it's a visible manifestation of the child's inner turmoil.

Furthermore, a recent study found that children who experience a number of stressful life events during the first two years of life are almost twice as likely to develop diabetes before their 15th birthday as their less anxious peers. The stressful life events included parents separating or being seriously ill or injured, or hospitalised; the death of a parent, sibling, grandparent or a close friend; or moving house more than twice.

The family's structure also plays a part. Children from families where members have rigidly defined roles were 50 per cent more likely to develop diabetes. The link between stress and diabetes may be another example of the effect of stress on the immune system (see page 75).

The scars that last a lifetime

Untreated, many children are unable to grow out of their problems. A 20-year study found that GPs diagnosed psychological problems in 11 per cent of boys and 6 per cent of girls aged between 10 and 14. By the ages of 18 to 19, girls were more likely to have developed psychological problems: 24 per cent of females compared to 13 per cent of males.

Distressed adolescents often grow up into distressed adults – and their children are more likely to be disturbed. We pass on some of the risk in our genes. Children with parents who suffer mood disorders are more likely to suffer depression. Having one depressed parent doubles a child's chance of developing depression before adulthood. If both parents suffer depression, the child is four times more likely to develop depression. However, this isn't the whole story. Assume that one identical twin develops depression. The other twin is more likely to develop depression than the general public – but depression is not inevitable. If genetic factors were the only cause, both twins would inevitably develop depression.

Clearly, environment also plays a part. Childhood psychiatric illness weakens the personality's foundations. This undermines an adult's ability to form secure, lasting relationships or act as a role model for children. Poor relationships exacerbate stress and so increase the risk that any children will develop psychological problems. So some families with a legacy of stress and other mental problems can become caught in a cycle of distress. However, these are sweeping generalisations. Many people endure traumatic childhoods without passing the effects on to their children.

Does your child suffer from stress?

Children suffer from their own set of stress signals (see the box). The more of these stress signals your children exhibit, the more likely they are to be grappling with a problem or feeling anxious or worried. Stress can leave children isolated. They may find articulating their feelings difficult, and when they finally manage to tell their parents what is bothering them, they may be told 'don't be so silly'.

The stress of any life-event, good or bad, is magnified among children who have not developed the coping strategies – or perhaps the cynicism – that adults rely on. Without help, either from parents or professionals, some emotional problems lead to serious disturbances and mental illness as adults. The Helping Parents helpline* offers practical advice and counselling to parents and children. Parentline* also offers counselling and support to parents, while Childline* provides a similar service to children.

Stress signals in children
* aggression and bullying * antisocial behaviour * anxiety and phobias * bed-wetting * changes in appetite * doing badly at school; school refusal * eating problems * excessive disobedience * excessive obsessions * inhibitions * poor self-confidence * sleeping problems; excessive tiredness * smoking and drug-taking * social withdrawal; not having any friends * suicidal thoughts and talk * temper tantrums * truancy and delinquency * unhappiness

---

The death of a parent, grandparent or another relative can cause children considerable stress. Faced with bereavement, children often run the gamut of emotions from sadness and anger to disbelief. They may become obsessed with death and ask when they, you or another relative will die. It is best to answer the barrage of questions honestly and openly. This helps children express their grief. Bottling up their feelings can lead to illness, failure at school and disturbed relationships. However, if your child's behaviour is grossly abnormal or if the problems drag on, consider seeking professional help.

EMMA'S father died in an industrial accident. Emma, an intelligent seven-year-old, understood that her father was dead. But she couldn't understand why. She couldn't accept that her father's death was an accident and became convinced that 'someone killed my daddy'. Emma's mother – Rachel – was also grief-stricken and felt isolated. Both sets of grandparents lived at the other end of the country and could only visit occasionally. Emma's questions kept reopening Rachel's emotional scars and the questions usually went unanswered. So Emma became more confused and scared. She stopped eating and refused to go to school. She would sit brooding in her room, then exploded in temper tantrums. During a visit, Emma's grandmother persuaded Rachel to seek help from a child psychotherapist. The child psychotherapist helped Emma reveal her confusion and feelings and understand that no one had killed her father. She is eating again and doing well at school now.

Bullying

Bullying is a common cause of childhood stress and is more serious than the usual playground squabbling. While it can seem trivial to an adult, protracted bullying can destroy lives. Some people carry a lingering resentment towards the bullies, the school, their parents who failed to help, and authority generally for the rest of their lives. In a few cases, the torment is so intense that the child runs away or commits suicide. If your child is being bullied, you need to tackle the problem. However, children are often reluctant to admit that they are being bullied. If you suspect anything, try to talk to your child and, if necessary, the school.

Bullying rapidly destroys a child's fragile self-confidence, so you might have to help your child regain self-esteem by, for example, joining clubs outside school. If the bullying is especially severe and widespread, join clubs several miles away. This reduces the risk that someone else from the school attends, and gives the victim a chance to form new friendships. Teaching some bullied children to defend themselves with judo, karate or boxing can elevate their self-esteem and allow them to confront the physical threat. Even children who hate sport often enjoy the martial arts – and it may never come to giving the bully a bloody nose. The self-confidence fostered by the martial arts often allows children to walk away. Your local library has details of the local clubs.

Martial arts can overcome physical weakness. However, do not encourage your children to fight back unless they are able to defend themselves. Victims of bullying are usually physically weak. Loosing a fight further reduces children's confidence in themselves – and you.

The Helping Parents* helpline offers advice to parents and children on bullying, school phobia and other problems. Children can also phone Childline* about bullying or any other problem.

When children need professional help

In the UK, around a quarter of a million children suffer from psychological disorders severe enough to require professional help. However, that help is in short supply. Perhaps 90 per cent of children who endure serious behavioural and emotional problems or suffer physical or sexual abuse do not receive professional help.

Children often find expressing disturbing thoughts or feelings very difficult. Psychotherapists help children to make sense out of events they cannot understand – such as divorce, a parent's death or being taken into care – and express their anxieties and fears. Around three-quarters of distressed children benefit from sessions with child psychotherapists, although treatment usually lasts a year or two. The Association of Child Psychotherapists* can help you find a local practitioner. GPs, teachers, social workers, health workers, child guidance clinics and child psychiatrists may also refer a child to a psychotherapist.

Using drugs to treat childhood psychological problems is controversial. However, it's more common than you might expect. In one survey, three-quarters of GPs and almost 70 per cent of consultant child psychiatrists had prescribed either tranquillisers, sleeping pills, antidepressants or other psychoactive drugs to a child under the age of 17 years during the three months before the study. In some cases GPs prescribed psychotropic drugs without talking to a consultant child psychiatrist, which may or may not have been appropriate (see chapter five).

In some cases prescribing antidepressants to children is totally justified – if the child is suicidal, for example. However, in some cases, antidepressants are prescribed for conditions better treated without using drugs. Prescribing antidepressants to a child is useless if the family as a whole is having problems, for example. Moreover, psychoactive drugs can impair a child's growth, learning and behaviour. In the longer term, prescribing pills to children may encourage them to reach for the tablets rather than struggling to solve their problems. Pills can help alleviate suffering. But – for both adults and children – they are rarely the whole answer.

Coping with teenagers

Living with teenagers is a time of stress and conflict for the entire family. Teenagers struggle with sexuality, responsibilities and independence. They may face drug abuse, racial harassment and unemployment. Parents have to come to terms with their children not being children any more. Stress is inevitable.

However, you can take some measures to limit it:

- Treat teenagers like adults, and talk calmly. Nothing winds teenagers up more than having someone preach to them.
- Answer any questions – especially about sex – openly and honestly. Remember that teenagers may have completely different views from you about drugs, fashion and the environment, for example. You can discuss these, but respecting their position can prevent disagreements becoming conflicts.
- Try to build confidence. Being a teenager is hard enough without being constantly criticised for the way you dress and behave – unless the latter is clearly dangerous.
- Set rules – but don't expect teenagers to obey. Challenging rules is one way teenagers exert their independence. However,

if some rules – for example, a curfew – are especially important, try trading off less important rules if they stick to the
curfew.

● Try not to overreact. You were a teenager once. Remember
how it felt? Remember how your parents reacted? Your
records probably irritated your parents as much as your son's
latest CD.

● You'll be the role model for how your children deal with their
teenagers. Aim to be a positive – rather than a negative – influence. The perfect parent and the perfect teenager don't exist.
So don't blame yourself when you fail to live up to your own
standards.

Examinations

As if the mental, physical and emotional impact of adolescence
are not enough, teenagers have to cope with the stress of sitting
exams that determine the course of the rest of their lives. Most
teenagers recognise the importance of exams. They are unlikely to
need you to remind them that they need to do well. You can help
most by keeping the family away from their room and by offering
support. Naturally, you want them to do well. But you should be
realistic, and if the worst happens support your child and offer
practical advice. Failing exams can shatter a teenager's confidence.
However disappointed you feel, your child probably feels worse.

TONY passed his 'A' levels – but not well enough, and he lost
his place at veterinary school. Instead of trying to help, his
father – a vet – made Tony feel guilty about the time and
money invested in his education. He said Tony's mother was
ashamed of having a failure for a son and that he could not
expect them to bale him out of his inevitable life on the dole.
Then Tony's father did not speak to his son for six weeks. The
father's reaction probably says more about the pressure Tony
had to endure than any lack of academic ability. In any case,
failing exams isn't the end of the world. Exams can be re-sat.
Sights can be lowered. Tony studied animal physiology instead
of becoming a vet. He was awarded a doctorate and is now a
leading academic. His father is speaking to him again!

Drug abuse

It's a fact of life. Teenagers try drugs – both legal and illegal. Many people start smoking in adolescence to alleviate the stress of being a teenager. Most older adolescents drink alcohol. Many teenagers flirt with soft drugs such as cannabis and Ecstasy. Few teenagers become addicts or suffer any long-term effects. So you need to keep the risks in perspective to allay your anxiety if nothing else.

Long-term drug abuse, thankfully, is still relatively rare. Nevertheless, drug addiction causes considerable physical and mental harm and contributes to suicides, violence and accidents. Moreover, while many people take drugs to escape stress, they often make matters worse. Drug abuse – especially in poorer inner city areas – fuels poverty, crime, prostitution, homelessness and the spread of sexually transmitted diseases including AIDS. While most drug users do not become addicted, no one can predict who is likely to remain a recreational user. Addiction is complex, influenced by more than a drug's effects on the body. Personality, age and street culture all play a part.

Solvent abuse

While drugs such as Ecstasy, crack and heroin hit the headlines, the true damage to our teenagers' health is wrought by alcohol, nicotine and solvent abuse. Over 100 people – usually teenagers – die every year from solvent misuse. Around one in ten children, usually between the ages of 13 and 14, experiment with solvents. However, most don't sniff for long. Only two per cent of children sniff for a few weeks or months and just one per cent become long-term abusers. But don't underestimate the dangers of solvent misuse. Solvents are toxic to the heart – an effect that can prove fatal. Children can suffocate on the plastic bags used to inhale the vapours, or they can choke on their vomit since many solvents are powerful emetics. Re-Solv* publishes leaflets and booklets about solvent abuse.

Watching for problems

Since the 1960s experimenting with soft drugs has been part of being a teenager. Most soon stop. A few go on to develop long-term problems or addictions. The box highlights some of the warning signs, but do not consider them in isolation. Moreover, drug problems can be very difficult to spot – so don't jump to conclusions – and are even harder to deal with. If you think your son or daughter has a drug problem, try discussing it in a non-judgmental way. Part of the appeal of drugs is that they are an act of rebellion almost guaranteed to upset the older generation. And remember that many teenagers use drugs – legal or illegal – as an escape from their problems or family conflicts. So try to regard drug addiction as a disease. In many ways it is.

Treating addiction

Signs of a drug problem
* aggression * anxiety and depression * apathy * changes in appetite * changes in lifestyle, e.g. new friends * clammy skin * headaches * insomnia or drowsiness * irritability * memory loss * nausea and vomiting * over-excitement * palpitations * poor concentration * strange behaviour, e.g. paranoia, disorientation, hyperactivity * slurred speech * spots around the mouth and nose (typical of glue sniffers) * sweating * tremors * watery eyes and nose

---

Treating addiction involves overcoming the compulsion to take drugs, managing withdrawal and maintaining abstinence, thus attacking the problem from all sides. Addicts' urine is often monitored for traces of drugs. Addicts undergo education, group therapy and psychotherapy. Diseases that increase the risk of relapse, such as alcoholism or depression, and drug-induced disorders are treated. For example, long-term cocaine users may experience heart disease, seizures and strokes. Intravenous drug abusers can contract AIDS and hepatitis B.

Treatment does not end once the addict has gone through withdrawal. Drugs produce changes in the brain that persist after withdrawal. Moreover, addicts often face social and medical problems as well as employment difficulties that greatly increase the chance of a relapse. Professionals, such as doctors and nurses, are more likely to be cured than addicts with poor education and no prospects.

Clearly, managing addiction is a challenge and no programme can guarantee success. However, in-patient programmes are between two and four times more successful than out-patient clinics, partly because addicts are removed from the circumstances that feed their addiction. Usually 30 to 50 per cent of addicts enrolled on a programme abstain for a year. A further 15 to 30 per cent avoid compulsive use.

Methadone maintenance for heroin addicts is the best known drug rehabilitation programme. By being supplied with methadone, addicts don't need to buy heroin from street dealers or resort to crime to fund their habit. Apart from getting methadone, addicts are counselled and educated. Since the programme's introduction after the second world war, the success rate has gradually improved. In the early 1970s, only around 40 per cent of addicts completed the detoxification programme – half the rate in today's leading centres.

The Standing Conference on Drug Abuse (SCODA)* represents drug services and people concerned about the impact of drugs in the community. Release* and the National Drugs Helpline* offer advice and support on all aspects of drug abuse. Families Anonymous* is a self-help group for the relatives and friends of drug abusers.

Anorexia and bulimia

Teenagers are usually highly sensitive about their appearance. If they feel that they do not conform to their ideal body image, their self-confidence can suffer. In some cases, this misplaced body image leads to anorexia or bulimia.

Eating disorders seem to be becoming more common. Scottish figures, for example, suggest that rates of anorexia have risen three- to four-fold since the 1960s. Partly this reflects our increasing recognition of eating disorders. Partly it reflects society's emphasis on slimness: most anorexics diet obsessively before developing overt anorexia (see box). However, there seems to be a genuine increase in the number of cases.

Dieting is common among adolescents and not every teenager that diets becomes anorexic. Nevertheless, anorexics seem to lose control of their eating habits during a diet. Studies suggest that certain factors predispose people to this loss of control. For example, up to 95 per cent of anorexics are young women. Childhood obesity, family conflict, coming from a higher social class and going to dancing and gymnastics classes – pastimes that encourage

---

Symptoms of anorexia
* being lower than the minimum normal weight for height and age
* an intense fear of being fat or gaining weight * obsessive thinking about food and compulsive calorie-counting * a disturbance of the perception of body size: anorexics feel fat even when underweight * female anorexics usually find their periods cease and fertility declines dramatically

---

a lithe shape – may increase the risk of anorexia. Anorexics also tend to have certain personality traits. For example, they tend:

- to be high achievers
- to have an earlier onset of periods, which means that they confront the problems, challenges and stresses of adolescence at an earlier age
- to be perfectionists, meticulous and obsessive
- to have rigid mental views, be socially inept, avoid risk, and conform to authority
- to set unrealistically high standards for themselves
- to concentrate on and over-emphasise the importance of their failures – they either totally succeed or totally fail.

Bulimia is easier to hide than anorexia. As a result, nobody knows how many people suffer from bulimia – although it is probably three to four times more common than anorexia. Some estimates suggest that up to 90 per cent of young adult women experience some symptoms of bulimia – such as binge eating or being over-concerned with their body image – but full-blown bulimia probably affects less than five per cent of young women. Only four per cent of bulimics are men.

Bulimics eat vast quantities of food, then get rid of it by vomiting, using laxatives or over-exercising. In extreme cases, bulimics eat around 6,000 kilocalories a day (more than treble the necessary amount) and binge and vomit up to 30 times a day. Bulimics, like anorexics, have a morbid dread of fatness. However, there are important differences between the two eating disorders. Anorexics may starve themselves to death, but bulimics do not lose weight. Furthermore, bulimics tend to be in their twenties rather than their teens.

Bulimics' and anorexics' personalities also differ. Many bulimics have a demanding, manipulative mother and a distant father with high expectations, especially about his daughter's appearance. Bulimia also tends to affect assertive women. Some psychiatrists believe that bulimia expresses depression, anxiety, sexual problems and stress in our food-obsessed culture. For example, 94 per cent of bulimics feel guilty, 80 per cent complain of poor concentration, 69 per cent habitually worry, 68 per cent feel on edge and 62 per cent avoid anxiety-provoking situations. Bingeing and vomiting may help bulimics cope with anxiety and depression. Bingeing is associated with guilt and anxiety; purging brings relief.

However, bulimia isn't necessarily for life. A study followed a group of bulimics for ten years. Just over half recovered completely, while 39 per cent still experienced some symptoms, but only nine per cent continued to suffer full-blown bulimia. The study found that younger people are more likely to recover than those developing the disease later in life. Women from a higher social class and those marrying or cohabiting are also more likely to recover. This underlines the value of support from family and friends when you're trying to recover from serious stress-related diseases such as bulimia. Women from families with a history of alcohol abuse were also more likely to recover. Maybe these women witnessed a successful recovery from alcoholism and resolved to seek treatment.

You cannot tackle bulimia or anorexia on your own. You need specialist help. However, that help is in short supply. Just one in ten bulimics receives treatment, which ideally combines drugs, behavioural therapy and an eating plan to deal with the underlying problem. Some antidepressants – the selective serotonin reuptake inhibitors (see chapter five) – may help when depression triggers binge eating. Around half of bulimics taking an antidepressant show reduced bingeing. Nevertheless, most still eat abnormally.

Psychotherapy helps sufferers face the cause of their poor body image and lose their morbid fear of being fat. Problem solving and behavioural therapy reinforce the positive aspects in their lives. Cognitive therapy reduces binge eating among bulimics by about 90 per cent, with about two-thirds remaining in control for longer periods. However, bulimia is more than binge eating and cognitive therapy reduces the use of laxatives, purgatives and alleviates depression and anxiety. Recovery takes time. It takes between one and five years for a person suffering from anorexia to reach and stay at a reasonable weight. In the meantime, patients follow a meal plan: this helps anorexics regain weight and bulimics to break a binge-purge cycle. Coming to terms with their problems is the only way patients can beat anorexia and bulimia. Contact the Eating Disorders Association* for further information.

Suicide

As with adults, suicide is the ultimate condemnation of society's care of young people. European figures show that depression – one of the strongest predictors of suicide risk – has increased markedly among young people over the last decade (see chapter five).

So what drives a child to attempt suicide? In Coventry, between 1982 and 1990, between two and three in every 1,000 children aged between 12 and 15 years tried to poison themselves. Asian teenagers were slightly more likely than Caucasians to attempt suicide. Girls from both ethnic groups were also at higher risk. However, among younger children Caucasians were more likely to poison themselves than Asians – although in younger children, distinguishing accidental from deliberate poisoning can prove difficult.

The similar incidence of Caucasian and Asian teenagers attempting suicide suggests that adolescents of all races face similar problems. Family problems, depression, delinquency, family violence and experiencing loss all make children more likely to hurt themselves. Racial harassment, tension between generations regarding dress, religion and relationships outside the family may exacerbate the problem among Asian youth.

Racism

Children feel the effects of racism at a young age. This may be one of those times when you cannot do anything about the cause of the stress – at least in the short term. However, it may help if you can get your children to change their response to racial harassment. It's hard, but both children and adults need to try to avoid being provoked – especially if the abuse is verbal rather than physical. You are a role model for your child. Condemning racists as ignorant imbeciles below your contempt may help. But this doesn't mean you should accept racism as inevitable. Working in your local community to build bridges between the races may help dissipate your anger towards racial tension and, in the long term, tackle the root of the problem.

The African-Caribbean Mental Health Association* offers advice on mental illness tailored to black people.

Stress in adults

Adults may be more likely to suffer the ravages of stress than either teenagers or elderly people. This seems somewhat surprising given that teenagers are angst-ridden, hormonally driven and extremely insecure, and elderly people face death, isolation and illness. Nevertheless, some stress-related diseases, such as depression and alcoholism, are most common among younger adults.

Partly this reflects the fact that elderly people have a lifetime of experience which they can use to combat stress. But pressures facing the baby boom generation differ from those faced by their parents. Increasing urbanisation, crime, racism, disintegrating traditional family roles, social isolation and the pace of technological change all conspire to increase the pressure. Some scientists even speculate that changes in nutrition and pollution could contribute to the rise in stress-related problems, such as depression, alcoholism and drug abuse.

Changing occupational patterns may also play a part. More than 45 per cent of students studying for business and social administration degrees are now women. This compares to ten per cent in 1973. But better educated women don't always land better jobs. In the USA, fewer than five per cent of senior executives are women. In the UK, the figure is under two per cent. Of the UK's three million managers, perhaps a fifth are women. Among the million senior managers, fewer than four per cent are female. To make matters worse, employers do relatively little to alleviate specific causes of stress among their female employees – childcare, career-break strategies and so on.

At the same time, women's increasing role in the workplace puts men under stress. Men are no longer guaranteed their traditional roles of husband, father and provider. Some, by choice or circumstances, stay at home, look after the children, cook and do the housework. Unfortunately, these men often endure the ridicule of family and friends. Moreover, few companies offer paternity leave. Indeed, most companies expect their employees to work longer and longer hours, but spending more time at the office means less time with your partner and children. This conflict between work and family can cause considerable stress, and leave workers feeling guilty and confused.

Unemployment increases your risk of developing physical and mental illness. But waiting for the axe to fall can be as bad for your health as unemployment itself. A study of middle-aged British civil servants underlines this. Members of a department facing privatisation reported more ill health than their colleagues in secure employment. However, their illnesses did not result from changes in behaviour, such as smoking or drinking more or exercising less. Job insecurity is a time of great stress and anxiety for the workforce under threat and this seems to translate into physical illness – or at least feeling unwell (see also later in this chapter).

Women and stress

Women face different problems to men; partly, this is biological – men don't have a hormonal menopause, for example. Women also express their emotions in different ways. Women are more likely to suffer from depression; men tend to abuse alcohol and drugs.

Women are often stressed because of society's prejudices and discrimination. For example, professional women experience more headaches, depression and physical ill health than their male colleagues – especially if they are junior or middle managers. Compared to men, women managers tend to experience more conflicts between work and home, career and marriage, and career and childbearing. We have already seen that role conflicts are a major cause of stress. Women managers may be more likely to resolve conflict using positive coping strategies than their male colleagues. However, many still resolve conflict using Type A behaviour – which predisposes them to heart disease and high blood pressure.

Have a peaceful pregnancy

Pregnancy is often stressful for the mother-to-be and her partner. You worry about the baby being healthy, about making it to hospital in time, about the labour being protracted and painful, as well as the expense, and you worry whether your figure – or your relationship – will ever be the same again. Despite these worries, you should try to relax.

Relaxation during pregnancy can prove difficult – especially if you are on edge because you have had previous miscarriages, you are worried about money, or your relationship is under pressure. However, you can help yourself have a peaceful pregnancy:

● plan: e.g. how you will make it to hospital; how you will cope financially

● avoid stressful situations: avoid arguments at work; try to avoid travelling on public transport during the rush hour; use flexitime if you can or chat with your boss about altering your hours

● avoid travelling by air, especially if you have had a miscarriage – air travel, apart from any physical effects, can be intensely stressful

● learn about your options: everyone worries about their baby being healthy. Although there are no guarantees, a number of tests are available that may put your mind at rest – your midwife will be able to provide details

● devote some time to yourself each day

● exercise – you can swim, walk and exercise in many other ways during pregnancy. Your midwife can provide guidance on the safest way to exercise. Some swimming-pools and fitness centres run special sessions for pregnant women.

Post-natal depression

Having a baby is one of the most enjoyable yet stressful times in a woman's (and her partner's) life. As anyone with children can – and given half a chance probably will – tell you, nothing prepares you for the emotional, psychological and social impact of a new baby. Leaving work and coping with the relentless demands of a tiny infant can leave new mothers isolated and frustrated. Not surprisingly, some feel irritable, anxious and depressed. Both parents may have to endure sleepless nights. While a tearful few days is a normal part of childbirth, severe depression certainly is not.

Up to 80 per cent of new mothers suffer the 'baby blues', usually between three and ten days after giving birth. The hormonal and emotional changes may leave new mothers tearful, moody, anxious, confused and unable to sleep. On the other hand, ten per cent of new mothers feel elated and mildly manic soon after giving birth.

Between 10 and 15 per cent of new mothers suffer post-natal depression (the symptoms described on page 121). A third of these women suffered depression at some time before having their baby. The stress and hormonal changes surrounding childbirth trigger a relapse. Adverse social circumstances can exacerbate post-natal depression. A quarter of teenage mothers living in deprived inner cities suffer post-natal depression. However, half of all cases of post-natal depression go undetected – and untreated. One problem is that post-natal depression may develop up to two years after delivery, which means that doctors and women may not always link the depression and childbirth. Untreated post-natal depression can have devastating consequences on the mother, not to mention her child and family.

Post-natal depression may, for example, undermine the mother-child relationship and can impair the child's physical, emotional and intellectual development. By four years of age, children of mothers who suffered from post-natal depression score about 12 IQ points lower than those born to non-depressed mothers. The children are also more likely to develop behavioural problems. Post-natal depression seems to have a greater impact on boys than girls: boys exhibit more behavioural problems, for example. Later on, children of mothers with post-natal depression are more likely to suffer depression themselves.

In extreme cases, a few women develop post-natal psychosis. A mother suffering this may want to commit suicide, kill her baby or may believe her child is deformed. Women who have suffered from mental illness in the past are more likely to develop post-natal psychosis. Unmarried mothers are also at higher risk, as are those whose child was born by Caesarean section. Many women feel a Caesarean section is an 'abnormal' birth and forget that it is a major operation. Fortunately, post-natal psychosis is rare. It develops after only one or two in every 1,000 births.

Psychiatrists aim to lift the burden of post-natal depression from the shoulders of mothers and their children. Psychotherapy may help uncover the cause of the low mood, help women regain their self-esteem and put mothers back in control of their lives. Therapy usually means including the whole family, especially the partner (around a quarter of new fathers also develop depression).

The partner's role underlines the value of a secure family environment. Women who feel isolated and unsupported are especially likely to develop post-natal depression. Moreover, women suffering from post-natal depression often experience intense fears – about cot death, for instance. Your GP or health visitor can help you keep your fears in perspective – so don't suffer in silence.

You can also help yourself minimise the stress. You are more likely to develop post-natal depression after your first child, so read some of the many books available to get some idea of what to expect. Once the baby is born, put yourself and your child first.

- Ignore the housework or get your partner to do it – you are more important than an immaculate home.
- Arrange for a babysitter so you can devote some time to yourself.
- Share night-time tasks with your partner.
- Get treatment if you need it. If you don't get help, you're not only hurting yourself, you're hurting your baby. You can take some antidepressants even if you are breastfeeding without any risk to your baby.
- Breastfeeding reduces the levels of stress hormones released when you confront stressors and hassles.
- Many women feel isolated after giving up their job to look after a baby. A phone call from your partner at lunchtime may make all the difference.
- Don't return to work too quickly. Give yourself time to recover.
- Counselling, psychotherapy and even just talking to your health visitor may help. Stressful life events including bereavement and marital difficulties can exacerbate post-natal depression. You may want to get specific help for these problems.
- Contact the Association for Post-Natal Illness* and the National Childbirth Trust* for further advice and support.

Pre-menstrual syndrome

Pre-menstrual syndrome (PMS) has attracted controversy since it was first described in 1931. Doctors still argue about the symptoms of PMS. They argue about its cause, its treatment – even about whether PMS really exists as a 'disease'.

Between 50 and 90 per cent women experience mild symptoms – such as irritability and fatigue – in the week leading up to their periods. However, PMS significantly disrupts quality of life for up to ten per cent of women.

PMS symptoms (see box) tend to develop as progesterone levels increase between days 14 and 28 of the menstrual cycle. The symptoms are relieved by menstruation and are absent or very much reduced during the post-period week. However, women with PMS do not have abnormal hormone levels, and it is a mystery why some women are 'hypersensitive' to normal hormonal changes. Once a woman believes that she will suffer PMS each month she becomes more aware of the symptoms around that time whether they are linked to menstruation or not. A group of students were told that they suffered from PMS, when they did not. The women reported water retention, pain, changed eating patterns and changed sexual habits for seven to ten days before their period. Their moods, however, did not change.

As PMS overlaps with a number of other disorders, the timing of symptoms is crucial. Most doctors ask women to keep a dairy of their symptoms for at least two cycles. This reveals that 40 to 50 per cent of women complaining of PMS have the true syndrome. Many others suffer from pre-menstrual exacerbations of another problem. While in some the problem has no relationship to the menstrual cycle, they convert stressors – such as marital problems, depression or anxiety – into physical symptoms.

Advice and support are the first step in treating PMS. Many women feel frightened and confused by their symptoms. Helping them understand the cause of the problem often takes the edge

---

Common PMS symptoms
* breast tenderness * bloating * clumsiness * craving for food, especially carbohydrates * depression * feeling out of control * headaches * irritability * tension * tearfulness * tiredness and lethargy

off the symptoms. It is essential to get to the cause of the problem. Many women would rather blame PMS than admit to problems at work or at home – an example of projection (see page 23). Being treated for a medical condition means that they don't face the reality.

Among women with true PMS, cognitive therapy may change the patient's response to symptoms. This limits the monthly impact of PMS. Many women report benefiting from alternative treatments, such as B6 or evening primrose oil. Vitamin B6 may help emotional symptoms and breast tenderness. Foods rich in B6 include meat, fish, nuts, bananas, potatoes, bran and dairy products. You could try supplements – but doses over 200mg daily may cause side effects. Evening primrose oil and other sources of gammalinolenic acid – such as medicinal borage and starflowers – may alleviate breast pain in 60 per cent of women. Some women also find that gammalinolenic acid reduces depression and irritability. However, doctors are split about the effect of gammalinolenic acid on other PMS symptoms.

Doctors may prescribe a number of other treatments for PMS, such as diuretics for water retention. Antidepressants may also be effective but are taken throughout the cycle. Some doctors give progesterone by various routes. At high doses, progesterone is a sedative and tranquilliser. Results with progesterone are mixed: some women benefit – although others feel worse.

Oestrogens prevent ovulation. Theoretically, the contraceptive pill should relieve PMS. However, again women vary widely in their response. In around three-quarters the pill alleviates PMS. Others show no change, while some report worsening symptoms. Different preparations suit different women and finding the right pill is a matter of trial and error. However, most PMS treatments act on hormones. Hormone implants and patches – as used in hormone replacement therapy (HRT) – offer another option.

If these fail, specialists may resort to more potent drugs, including danazol and a group of drugs called LHRH analogues. Both prevent ovulation and alleviate PMS. However, danazol causes a number of disfiguring side effects including acne, weight gain, facial hair and a deepening voice and is only used for very severe PMS. LHRH analogues induce a temporary 'medical' menopause that lasts for up to six months. Side effects are similar to those seen during the menopause and include sweats, flushes, vaginal dryness, and so on. Furthermore, LHRH analogues are expensive and tend to be used only in women who have tried and failed to respond to other treatments.

Clearly, there is no magic bullet to relieve the stress of PMS. So try to help yourself first:

- Keep a record of the type, frequency and severity of symptoms alongside the dates for your periods to determine if you really suffer from PMS.
- Reflect on your life (see chapter two) to see if there are any other possible causes for your symptoms.
- Limit your stress – follow some of our suggestions in chapter six.
- Consider alternative therapies – many PMS sufferers benefit from homeopathy, aromatherapy or herbalism (see chapter six).
- Take care of yourself – eat a healthy diet; drink less alcohol and caffeine; stop smoking; take regular exercise.
- If these fail, talk to your GP or contact the National Association for Premenstrual Syndrome*.

The menopause

The two or three years around the menopause – the end of periods – can be intensely stressful. Hormonal changes during this time, which is also called the climacteric, cause a variety of symptoms (see box). For example, 80 per cent of women suffer hot flushes and a quarter experience sweats. More disturbingly, declining bone density increases the risk of developing osteoporosis and women are also more likely to suffer a heart attack or stroke. Declining oestrogen levels underlie many of these symptoms. However, women who have undergone a hysterectomy that has left their ovaries intact become menopausal, on average, four years earlier than women who have not had their womb removed. Up to a third of these women do not experience vasomotor menopausal symptoms, such as hot flushes and sweats, so oestrogen levels are not the end of the story. Some GPs offer an annual screening that measures blood levels of follicle stimulating hormone. This detects early hormonal menopause and means that women are in a better position to discuss their treatment with their GPs.

Using HRT to increase oestrogen to pre-menopausal levels relieves the hot flushes and sweats and helps prevent heart disease, osteoporosis and strokes. Taken for five to ten years around the menopause, HRT halves your risk of a heart attack or hip fracture and reduces the risk of stroke by a third.

Menopausal symptoms
* anxiety * aching joints * cystitis * dizziness * faintness * genital dryness * headaches * hot flushes * insomnia * irritability * itchy skin * loss of confidence * loss of interest in sex * mood changes * memory loss * palpitations * painful intercourse * poor concentration * sweats * vaginal dryness and bleeding * weakness

---

Women who have undergone a hysterectomy can take oestrogen HRT alone. Women with intact wombs must also take progestogen (progesterone), for 10 to 13 days each month to protect the womb lining (the endometrium). Oestrogen increases the thickness of the endometrium – which may predispose you to cancer. In post-menopausal women, oestrogen taken on its own increases the risk of developing endometrial cancer between two- and three-fold, according to a study of over 23,000 women followed for an average of almost six years. Adding progestogen induces withdrawal bleeds, which sheds the endometrium and eliminates the increased risk of endometrial cancer. HRT is generally safe and the side effects partly depend on the formulation (see below). Taking HRT for more than ten years may increase breast cancer risk. However, this is greatly outweighed by the reduced risk of osteoporosis, strokes and heart disease.

Women can now choose from a number of HRT formulations.

Tablets
These are the most widely used oestrogen formulation, have been available for over 30 years and are simple to take. However, the oestrogen dose in a tablet is relatively high and, as a result, nausea is a common side effect. Some patients take preparations continuously, others for 21 days, followed by a seven-day break. More recently, a 'continuous combined' formulation was launched,

which delivers a daily dose of oestrogen and progestogen. After four to six months, during which breakthrough bleeding may occur, withdrawal bleeds usually cease. However, continuous combined HRT can be used only by women who have not experienced a menstrual period for at least a year.

Implants
First used in the 1960s, implants release oestrogen directly into the blood stream over three to six months. Women using implants do not have to remember to take a pill or replace a patch. However, implants are inserted into the fat under the skin, which necessitates using a local anaesthetic. Implants are also hard to remove, which makes curtailing their action difficult if you develop side effects.

Vaginal creams and pessaries
These alleviate vaginal and urinary menopausal symptoms. However, they tend to be messy and the amount of oestrogen passing into the blood varies widely. Using vaginal creams and pessaries for two to three weeks is relatively safe. However, oestrogen in vaginal creams and pessaries is unopposed by progestogen, so repeated courses are not recommended for women with intact wombs. If symptoms persist, they should consider another type of HRT.

Gels
Gels are applied to the skin and release oestrogen directly into the blood. However, gels need to be applied every day, but not before a bath or shower, as bathing may wash away the gel. They can cause red, irritated skin.

Skin patches
These are usually changed twice weekly, but some new patches can be replaced weekly. Patches mimic the pattern of oestrogen release from the ovaries. However, some women experience side effects including skin irritation, sore breasts, weight gain, nausea and headaches. The patches may also fall off – especially if you get sweaty – and even (rarely) stick to your partner in bed.

Helping yourself

The undoubted long-term health benefits of HRT mean that women should discuss its advantages and disadvantages with their doctor as they approach their menopause. But HRT is not an elixir of youth, so take some other steps to limit the impact of 'the change':

- If you cannot sleep, follow the suggestions on good sleep hygiene (see page 170).
- A healthy lifestyle including eating a healthy diet, taking regular exercise, not smoking and limiting excess alcohol consumption reduces the impact of the menopause.
- Boost your self-esteem by getting a job or studying for some qualifications with the Open University* or as one of the growing number of mature students. Your library will have details of most further education colleges and universities.

Hormonally driven mood swings may be exacerbated by life-stressors, such as bereavement or divorce. The relaxation techniques outlined in the directory (chapter six) protect against the stress surrounding the menopause. A few women suffer depression during their menopause. Consult your GP if you develop any symptoms of depression (see chapter five). But perhaps most importantly you should maintain a positive outlook on life. You will probably spend almost as much time as a post-menopausal woman as you did in your childbearing years. The menopause doesn't close the book on your life – it starts a new chapter.

The Women's Health Concern* offers advice and support tailored to women's problems. *Understanding HRT and the Menopause*, also published by Which? Books, covers this subject in greater detail.

Sex and stress

Sexual problems are a common cause of stress. Take impotence: physical factors such as injury, alcoholism, diabetes and multiple sclerosis are responsible for about three out of four cases of erectile dysfunction – a consistent inability to attain and maintain an erection. The rest have largely psychological causes, such as performance anxiety.

Impotence is an extremely common problem: in the USA over half the male population recently admitted that they experience some degree of impotence at some time. Erectile dysfunction becomes more common as you age (see diagram), and may herald serious diseases including diabetes, cardiovascular disease and prostate disease. Despite this, fewer than one in ten men with reversible causes of erectile dysfunction are treated.

Impotence and age

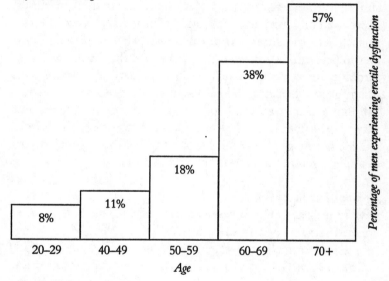

Lifestyle factors

An unhealthy lifestyle can cause impotence. Atherosclerosis – hardening of the arteries – may clog up blood vessels supplying the penis, in the same way as vessels supplying the heart become blocked before a heart attack. This stops the penis filling with blood and so prevents erections. Following a healthy lifestyle can improve a man's sex life. One study found that after taking up aerobics, middle-aged men kissed and cuddled their lovers more often than another group who exercised just by walking. The exercising men also had sex more often and had better orgasms. Another study found that middle-aged swimmers had sex twice a week, 40 per cent more than their lazier counterparts.

Psychological factors

Worrying about your performance in bed can also cause impotence or premature ejaculation. Failing repeatedly during intercourse causes stress, anxiety, frustration and apprehension. The man may become preoccupied with thoughts of failure.

Groin muscles need to relax to allow blood to engorge the penis and maintain the erection. Anxiety increases muscle tension, blocks the blood flow into the penis and so prevents erections. Psychosexual counselling is especially effective for men suffering from performance anxiety, most of whom complain of short-lived or flaccid erections rather than a total absence of erections. Therapy reduces performance anxiety by encouraging couples to perform intimate acts that don't need the man to be erect. Stroking, caressing and touching dispel anxiety and the erection often follows. Sex aids, such as vibrators, may also help re-establish intimate contact. You could try using the morning erections when the bladder is full. Psychosexual counselling can also help if you are having problems coming to terms with your sexuality, for example if you're a transsexual or a transvestite.

Aphrodisiacs that work

Few traditional aphrodisiacs really work. Spanish fly – the crushed remains of a beetle – irritates the urethra, which some people find erotic, but it's highly toxic and is more likely to kill you than turn you on. A bowl of oysters isn't going to turn a couch potato into Casanova. But oysters and other seafoods are rich in zinc, and men who do not eat enough zinc may find their sex drive falls and that they have low sperm counts.

In moderation, alcohol usually improves your sex life. It relaxes you and reduces your inhibitions. But too much and you may be unable to do much about your amorous ambitions. Too much drink can also make you so uninhibited that you don't practise safe sex. Nevertheless, a bottle of wine shared between two can work wonders.

Some drugs for impotence are available. Yohimbine, for example, is extracted from trees and plants growing in Africa and the Americas. Traditionally, witch doctors brewed these plants as teas, which they claimed increased emotions and enhanced sexual feelings. Then in the 1980s doctors found that yohimbine helped up to 80 per cent of impotent men to get erections. However, some of the studies produced mixed results. Doctors have more success with drugs such as papaverine, prostaglandin E1 and phentolamine which the man injects directly into his penis. Impotent men carry such a psychological and emotional burden that they are willing to inject themselves.

Other techniques to counter impotence include vacuum devices, compression bands, inflatable bags implanted into the penis, and surgery to open blocked blood vessels. The Impotence Association* runs a helpline staffed by trained personnel, and *The Which? Guide to Men's Health* covers more information on this subject.

Female 'impotence' is less well studied – probably because it's less obvious. Lubricants available at pharmacies can help if sex is painful because of a dry vagina. Again, stroking, caressing and sex aids aid intimacy. Psychosexual counselling can untangle the psychological and physical causes of underlying sexual difficulties. The British Association for Sexual and Marital Therapy* can put you in touch with a therapist.

Stress at work

We spend most of our waking lives working – often with people we dislike, in jobs we hate, for little appreciation and even less money. Then we come home to a mound of unpaid bills. The stress sometimes becomes so great that people simply run away from the rat race. The National Missing Persons Helpline* estimates that 38 per cent of people who go missing are aged between 31 and 50 years. Another 25 per cent are aged between 19 and 30 years. Most are men and many go missing following financial or work pressures. Most of us are not driven to such dramatic displays of distress, although stress is part of our daily routine.

A company's most stressed-out employees tend to be those who work long hours, for little pay and who have little control over their working life – production line workers, check-out assistants and people performing routine clerical work, for instance. In contrast, senior executives work hard, but their workload is varied and brings financial rewards. However, it is control that separates the boss's stress from that of his or her subordinates. So put yourself in control.

Beating bullying bosses

You know the type: the bosses who run you down in front of your staff. The bosses who cancel your holiday at the last minute – not because they need to but because they can. The bosses who humiliate you after a presentation. The good news is that you can beat bullying bosses. The bad news is that it takes guts – you need to confront your boss.

First, accumulate your evidence. Note examples of times you felt bullied. Reflecting on these at home helps you determine whether you really are being bullied or whether you are using projection (see page 23) to cope with a job that is poor for other reasons. Next arrange a meeting with your boss. Make sure that it is in private – bullies rarely back down in public. Remind him or her of the situations you feel were unacceptable. Tell your boss that you are not prepared to take abuse any longer. State that if you are going to be dressed down it should be in private, not in front of the rest of the staff. In some cases, bullies may be genuinely unaware that they have caused offence.

But this approach can backfire. It may make matters worse. You then have to decide how far to take things. You could go over the head of your boss – most companies have a complaints procedure. You could try to beat bullying bosses at their own game and humiliate them in front of other people. But in some cases you will have no option but to look for another job. But whatever you do, don't put up with it.

Relocation stress

Increasingly, employers demand a mobile workforce, yet relocation can exert a high financial and mental price. Children are uprooted from schools, friends and clubs. Either you or your partner may have to quit a job. A new job would need a very attractive salary to compensate. Until you find your way around the social life in your new location, you and your partner can be thrown together. So it is not surprising that moving house and changing jobs rank highly on the list of life stress events. In an attempt to compromise, some people try commuter marriages – working away during the week and coming home at weekends is increasingly common. But commuter marriages put considerable stress on the marriage and undermine relationships with children.

Against these stressors, you need to balance the advantages of relocation: your improved future prospects; a more interesting job; the chance of getting a job; the extra money; the opportunity to start over in a new town; better schools. So deciding whether to relocate is not easy. You might like to divide a piece of paper down the middle and write the advantages of relocating in one column and the disadvantages in the other. These aren't going to be of equal importance. Losing your place on the pub football team is likely to be far less important than improving your child's educational prospects. Nevertheless, it should give you an idea of whether the advantages of relocation outweigh the disadvantages.

Life on the dole

In chapter one we saw how, when Joe lost his job, he descended into learned helplessness. He was unable to apply for engineering jobs that were well within his abilities, start his own business or even deal with simple household electrical faults. Spending some time on the dole is a fact of life for an increasing number of experienced, well-qualified people. The days when entering a profession was a passport to a lifetime's employment are gone. For older people, being on the dole carries an undeserved stigma and can be tantamount to an enforced early retirement. While most of us don't descend into Joe's abyss of despair, unemployment is intensely stressful.

Apart from the financial problems, unemployment exerts a toll on your health. Government studies which have followed more than half a million people since 1971 suggest that death rates are 37 per cent higher among men who were unemployed during 1971 and 1981. One in five unemployed men suffered from a 'neurotic' disorder compared to a tenth of those in full-time employment. Among women, the mental toll of unemployment was even higher: 38 per cent of unemployed women suffered 'neurotic' disorders compared to 16 per cent of those in full-time employment. Five times as many unemployed women suffered from depression as those working full-time.

Being made redundant can be a shock – even if it's expected. The shock can be so great that some people follow their normal routine. They get up at the same time, catch the same train and come home at the same time. This can carry on for weeks. Others drink or lie in bed. But the best way to avoid being overwhelmed by redundancy is not to blame yourself for your predicament. You are hardly to blame for the recession, so remain positive. You can find another job. It may not be easy. It may mean learning new skills. It may mean moving to another part of the country. But remain positive that you will find a job and try to remain active.

Lack of money is usually the most pressing problem. Sort out your new income and expenditure. Find ways to economise and determine which benefits you're entitled to. Write to your creditors to let them know you are now unemployed and try to negotiate lower payments. Some creditors may accept interest payments and give you a holiday from paying back the principal.

After looking at your finances, look at yourself. List your work experience, qualifications and interests. Then set your long-term 'life objectives'. Then set yourself shorter term goals that help you attain these objectives. Finally, list specific tasks you have to accomplish in order to achieve the short-term goals. Want a job in international sales? Your short-term goal may be to get an MBA or learn another foreign language. The specific task is to find out what courses, grants and loans are available to help with education and setting up a new small business.

In other words, view unemployment as an opportunity. Even if you apply for every job going, you will still have plenty of free time. So if finances allow, decorate the house or take up a hobby. If they don't, catch up on your reading or start exercising. Here is the ideal opportunity to plan the rest of your life and make the career switch you always wanted to make. Unemployment can be productive.

Divorce

When you get divorced, as with bereavement, you lose a fundamental part of your life, so it's not surprising that divorce ranks second only to bereavement on the Life Stress Scale (page 16). But divorce is increasingly part of modern life. If it happens to you, you need to face the realities of your divorce and move on.

Deciding that a marriage has failed is difficult. Many people endure years of misery, despair, even violence before coming to that conclusion. However, other couples become entrenched in domestic civil war, the origins of which are forgotten, but in which neither side is willing to back down. In these circumstances, marriage counsellors and reconciliation services help both sides compromise. But both partners have to want the marriage to work, be willing to give and take, and modify unreasonable behaviour. Relate[*] offers counselling for partners throughout the UK. You may also want to consider specific counselling if, for example, sexual problems, drink or drugs are causing you marital difficulties. Marriage counselling can help you smooth out the rough patches that many marriages go through.

Usually it is difficult to decide who is at fault when a marriage breaks up. In most cases, neither you nor your partner is really to blame. Some people even justify infidelity: 'if only he'd spent more time with me, I wouldn't have been unfaithful.'

The person who leaves the marital home often feels guilty. Both partners feel rejected and rake over the ashes of the romantic hopes and ideals they held at the start of the marriage. Divorcees tend to mourn their failed marriage. These feelings can drag on for years before the person comes to terms with the end of the marriage. So try not to feel guilty or hate your ex-partner. You have a new life to get used to: one with financial problems, one of isolation, one of feeling rejected, one playing a new role as a single person or a single parent.

The last role is particularly tough. Divorce can have a devastating impact on children, leading to psychological problems, delinquency and poor school performances. However, an amicable divorce, where parents manage to remain on good terms after the separation and where the partner without day-to-day care of the children – rightly or wrongly, usually the father – is involved as much as possible, seems to go some way to ameliorating the stress of divorce. So make sure contact arrangements are fair and clear.

Some children blame themselves for the divorce. Children must explore their feelings and understand that they are not the reason that their parents don't love each other any more. They also need reassurance that they haven't lost the love of either parent. Clearly, children shouldn't become caught in a 'tug-of-love' between the two parents. And they shouldn't be asked to take sides. There rarely are any.

Families Need Fathers* and BM Families* help children maintain a good relationship with both parents.

Loneliness

Loneliness isn't only the divorcee's prerogative. Many people have been lonely for years because they never found Mr or Ms Right, or because they were caring for elderly or invalid relatives, or because they are married to a career or because their partner died. The answer to loneliness is simple to give but harder to put into practice: get out there and meet people.

Apart from making your social life more varied, meeting people is good for your health. A large number of studies involving thousands of patients suggest that social isolation increases the risk of dying from a multitude of causes. Indeed, social isolation is as deadly as smoking or increased cholesterol, especially for women. Studies suggest that socially isolated men at any particular age are up to three times more likely to die than more social men of the same age. This increases to four times among socially isolated women. Similarly, married cancer patients seem to fare better than their single peers. Social isolation also increases your risk of suffering a number of diseases including heart disease and depression. Patients should make the most of self-help groups.

Almost every town now has a singles' club. Your library or local paper will have details, or you can contact the National Federation of Solo Clubs*. These clubs hold regular meetings, where you will be welcome. You could also try joining a local club for your hobby. You'll meet like-minded people, which always makes starting new relationships easier. Divorcees and single parents can also join Gingerbread*, which has branches nationwide.

If you still find it hard to meet people you could be suffering from social phobia (see chapter five) or you could be intensely shy. Doctors can treat social phobia. If you are shy, enrol on social skills and assertiveness training courses that help you speak to people and overcome the fear of rejection that underlies many people's shyness. Contact your local library or adult education centre for details of local courses.

Stress in elderly people

We live in an ageist society that values youth and beauty. The young and beautiful often view everyone over the age of 60 years as a latent Victor Meldrew. But elderly people face considerable stress. Many elderly people live in poor housing, while others cannot afford to heat their homes adequately. Children grow up and move away, removing an important source of social support. Retirement brings financial problems. Illness begins to limit an elderly person's movement and older people start living in the shadow of their own death and that of relatives and friends. They may have to move into a nursing home or care for a partner declining into the disability of Parkinson's or Alzheimer's disease. So you may expect stress, anxiety, depression and other stress-related problems to worsen as you get older. However, elderly people may be better prepared to deal with stress, anxiety and depression than the younger generation.

Do you get stronger as you get older? Your view of stress certainly changes as you get older. Elderly people tend to rate individual life events – such as bereavement, financial problems and serious illness – as more stressful than younger people, but they are less likely to report experiencing stress or stress-related health problems. This could suggest that elderly people are more reluctant to own up to suffering from stress, but our coping style also matures as we get older.

Elderly people tend to view stressors as unchangeable. Younger people tend to believe that stressors are problems waiting to be solved. This may reflect the different challenges faced at different ages. Younger people are usually stressed by problems at work – which they can change. Older people tend to be concerned with ill-health – which they are often unable to influence. Younger people are also generally more likely to use coping strategies, such as projection, denial and regression, that distort reality (see pages 22-4). By middle age you tend to evolve more mature coping styles, such as humour and sublimation, that are less likely to distort reality. Younger people use direct confrontation to solve problems. As you age you increasingly use indirect action. Older people also have a lifetime's experience to draw on. If you have coped with the death of a parent, that experience will help you deal with the loss of a partner. When it comes to the common stressors, you have been there.

However, these are only trends: elderly people also enter denial: the elderly man who still lays a place at the dinner table for his dead wife, the old woman who dismisses a huge cancerous tumour on her wrist as 'a touch of arthritis'. Stress also seems to rise again in very elderly people, reflecting, perhaps, the inevitable decline towards infirmity and death.

Depression

Between two and eight per cent of elderly people suffer from mild depresson and another one to five per cent from severe depression. Physical illness exacerbates depression. Up to 45 per cent of elderly people admitted to hospital experience depression. Furthermore, approximately five per cent experience dementia – a clouding of mental abilities.

Nevertheless, depression and other psychiatric disorders are under-diagnosed and under-treated in elderly people. One study suggested that only four per cent of elderly depressed people receive treatment – despite suffering from depression for at least six months. Part of the reason for this may lie in the attitude of elderly patients towards mental illness.

Over the last 50 years or so, society has become more psychologically minded. But older people may regard some of the emotional states that now fall under the medical umbrella as being 'not worth bothering the doctor with', simply part of the human condition or the will of God. However, there is no need to suffer in silence. Treating depression can dramatically improve the quality – and maybe even the quantity – of your life. Treatment does not necessarily mean drugs. Indeed, psychiatrists increasingly recognise that drugs prescribed for other disorders can cause, exacerbate and maintain depression. For example, some estimates suggest that up to one in ten cases of depression in elderly people may be caused by beta-blockers – a class of drugs used to lower high blood pressure. Provided the depression is not too severe you may benefit from counselling or psychotherapy. You can also receive specific counselling. If your depression is triggered by the intense stress surrounding bereavement, for example, contact Cruse[*].

Sleep problems

Up to half of elderly people and 65 per cent of those in nursing homes report suffering from insomnia. A poor night's sleep leaves you anxious, stressed and irritable, but insomnia's consequences can be more serious. One study surveyed over 700 patients aged at least 65. The researchers re-interviewed 524 of these two years later. Of the subjects who were not depressed at the first interview, experiencing sleep disturbances increased their risk of developing depression approximately threefold two years later.

So don't regard insomnia as trivial or an inevitable part of ageing. Most people, even if they have suffered from insomnia for years, can sleep better. The first step is to treat any underlying condition, such as the chronic pain of arthritis, that leaves you unable to sleep. Then try following our tips on good sleep practices (page 170). It is especially important not to nap during the day.

Taking sleeping tablets for a few days can help while, for instance, arthritis treatments work or you begin to work through the worst of your grief following a bereavement. Sleeping pills can alleviate the stress and anxiety that follow in the wake of insomnia. This offers you a breathing space to tackle the underlying cause. Long-term use – particularly of the older benzodiazepines – carries a number of dangers, even for young, fit and healthy adults. Elderly people seem to be especially vulnerable to some of these side effects. For example, many of the benzodiazepine hypnotics cause a hangover – you feel groggy and sleepy the following morning. This may further slow your reflexes and increase your risk of falls. As your skeleton naturally gets weaker as you age, benzodiazepines can increase your risk of breaking a bone.

Fitness for the over-sixties

Regular exercise helps you sleep provided you don't work out too close to bedtime. It also helps keep your heart, muscles and mind healthy. However, many retired people don't exercise – not because they can't, but because they don't believe in themselves. Older people often don't know their capabilities. As you age your perception of what you can achieve is often lower than your performance potential. Some people walk several miles a week well into their eighties and even beyond.

These people probably got into the habit of walking earlier in life. But it's never too late to start. Nevertheless, you should talk to your GP before you start exercising – especially if you have heart disease, breathing problems or any other chronic illness. Sometimes your GP may refer you to a physiotherapist who can devise an exercise programme that overcomes the limitations imposed by arthritis, for example.

Some aerobics and fitness clubs run special courses for elderly people. *Exercise for healthy ageing*, a booklet published by the charity Research Into Ageing*, suggests a number of exercises you can perform at home. Gentle exercise can make a dramatic difference to your well-being. For example, women aged between 75 and 93 years increased their thigh muscle strength by a quarter by gently exercising for a total of just three hours a week for 12 weeks. This is equivalent to setting the biological clock back by between 16 and 20 years.

Meditation

Meditation may reduce the ravages of ageing. A group of 50-year-olds who practised Transcendental Meditation* (see page 207) for at least five years showed better vision, hearing and lower blood pressure than non-meditators. The scientists concluded that meditators were biologically 12 years younger than non-meditators. Similarly, a study of nursing home residents found that meditators were less likely to deteriorate mentally and physically over the three years of the study. For example, meditators had better memories and lower blood pressure than non-meditators. By the end of the study, subjects had an average age of 84: despite their advancing years, all the meditators were still alive. In contrast, some non-meditators had died. Yoga (page 238) and tai chi (page 236) are similar in many ways to meditation and can keep both mind and body flexible.

Moving into a nursing home

Moving into a nursing home is intensely stressful. You are leaving the house you may have lived in for several years and entering a communal home with people you don't know, so you must ensure that your new home satisfies your needs.

So how can you pick a home? Nursing homes must register with the local authority, and social services inspect homes at least twice a year. So ask to see the social service reports of any home you are considering. The local authority social services department may also be able to provide details of local residential care. The district health authority holds lists of local nursing homes, which may be particularly useful if you're trying to find homes that offer specialist skills – caring for people suffering dementia, for example.

Age Concern* and Help the Aged* offer further advice on finding a home. While you are visiting a home look for obvious signs of neglect (see box). The Registered Nursing Homes Association* is the trade association for nursing home owners.

What to look for in a nursing home
* Is the home bright and cheerful? * Are staff helpful and professional? * Are there sufficient staff to cope with the number of residents? * Are residents active or slumped in chairs staring into space? * Is the menu appetising? * Are the home and gardens pleasant and well maintained? * Does the home have easy access to public transport, social services and healthcare? * Is any special equipment available? * Will the home allow you to decorate and personalise your room with some items of furniture, ornaments or pictures?

You may want to consider drawing up a legal contract between yourself and the owner. This should include when the fees are reviewed. Ask if you can stay in the home for a week or so before taking a final decision. You may have to pay, but you will get a chance to meet the other residents. You need to ask yourself one fundamental question: could this place feel like home?

Caring for an ill relative

Caring for an ill relative places the carer under considerable stress. Often the needs of the carer – who may also be suffering from his or her own set of health problems – are submerged by those of the patient. Not surprisingly, when the person finally dies, the gap in the carer's life can be huge. You can take several steps to help minimise the stress of caring for an ill relative.

For example, learn about the disease. This may reveal new ways you can help the patient. It also helps you understand the medical reasons for the care you are giving. It can also help you understand the patient's behaviour. This is especially important if, for example, the patient becomes aggressive or behaves in a sexually inappropriate manner. Contact and co-operate with your local nurses, GPs and specialists. Ask if any specialist services are available. Many areas now run specialist Parkinson's disease clinics and may have specialist nurses to deal with incontinence or pressure sores, for example. Contact the self-help group that focuses on the particular illness – many chronic diseases now have a support group that offers practical advice. Most libraries hold lists of local organisations and may have a directory of national organisations. Your GP or consultant may also be able to provide details of the local self-help group. SeniorLine* is Help the Aged's free helpline for senior citizens, their relatives, carers and friends.

Consider counselling. This does not necessarily mean formal counselling: many people find that sharing their experiences and gaining advice and support from a self-help group combats stress. The Carers National Association* and the Black Carers Support Group* can offer more general information and support.

Find time for yourself. Try to get out at least once a week. The social services may also be able to arrange residential care that allows you to go on holiday.

Remember the simple things. Check, for example, that the patient's hearing aid works and that spectacles have the correct prescription. Consider home modifications.

Caring for ill relatives is enough of a burden now, but it's a cause of stress that will inevitably increase as the population continues to age. US predictions suggest that neurodegenerative diseases including Alzheimer's disease, motor neurone disease and Parkinson's disease will overtake cancer as the second leading cause of death by the year 2040.

CHAPTER 4

STRESS AND DISEASE

EVERY day GPs see patients complaining of muscle tension, fatigue, indigestion, insomnia and headaches caused by excessive, prolonged stress. Stress also exacerbates asthma, eczema, and angina. But until relatively recently most doctors treated diseases of the mind and body as separate. Even asylums were built some distance away from general hospitals. Over the last 20 years, though, doctors have reconsidered the traditional split between mind and body. It is now clear that communication between the mind and the body runs both ways. Stress may trigger some diseases – and it can undoubtedly make you feel worse if you suffer from a physical ailment. So the next two chapters are warnings – what can happen to your physical and mental health if you don't control your stress.

Stress and infections

There is now no doubt that stress – including the stress caused by exams, bereavement, caring for chronically ill relatives, and marital problems – suppresses the immune system. People experiencing intense grief are more prone to infections, for example.

Your risk of suffering a stress-related illness depends partly on your accumulation of 'life events' in a year. For example, half the people with scores on the Life Stress Scale (see page 16) exceeding 200 will develop health problems. If the score is over 300 the risk increases to 80 per cent. However, enduring high levels of microlevel stressors – day-to-day hassles – also increases your risk of suffering a number of health problems, partly because stress undermines our immune defences.

Two-way traffic

We live in a sea of infectious agents, surrounded by bacteria, viruses, fungi and parasites. When one of these organisms invades, cells in the immune system release chemicals to eradicate the infection. These chemicals also activate nerves that in turn stimulate the brain. The brain feeds back on the immune system through nerves supplying the bone marrow, thymus gland, spleen, lymph nodes and other organs. This increases production of white blood cells – the main line of defence against infection. In other words, the immune system affects the brain and vice versa.

This 'nerve mediated immunity' is backed by the release of hormones from the pituitary and adrenal glands. For example, the pituitary gland releases growth hormone and prolactin during stress. Both partly control the immune system's ability to fight infections. Short-term stress also increases the numbers and activity of natural killer cells – the white blood cells that destroy invading bacteria and viruses.

Increased natural killer activity and the hormonal surge are part of the fight-or-flight reflex and protect us from infections after a possible injury. However, during chronic stress the levels of growth hormone, prolactin and natural killer activity decrease. The immune system's decline in activity may have evolved to protect us from the risk of developing autoimmune disease. But this deregulation leaves you vulnerable to infection. Low levels of growth hormone, for example, seem to reduce white blood cell activity and inhibit antibody production. Animals deprived of growth hormone are more likely to die after infection with salmonella and listeria. So chronic stress suppresses the immune system.

A definite link

Studies of medical students about to sit exams have confirmed that stress impairs immune function. For example, the number of circulating white blood cells fell compared to the levels a month before the exams. The decline was most pronounced in students enduring additional stressors or who were lonely. In parallel with this, students reported more symptoms of infections. The number of white blood cells also falls following bereavement and in severe depression, and stress is a well-recognised trigger for the reactivation of latent oral or genital herpes infections.

Even macrolevel stressors may undermine your immune system. American doctors saw an increased reactivation of latent herpes infections following the Three Mile Island nuclear accident. Similarly, herpes may reactivate following stressors such as marital problems and caring for a chronically ill relative.

The evidence that stress predisposes us to infection is now overwhelming. Consider a few examples:

- A study of 1,400 military cadets infected with the Epstein-Barr virus, responsible for glandular fever, found that cadets who were under stress because they were highly motivated but who were only achieving a poor academic performance were more likely to develop symptoms. They also spent longer in hospital if they developed glandular fever.
- Introverts seem to be more likely than extroverts to contract the common cold.
- Stress may contribute to the progression of HIV infection to full-blown AIDS.
- One study investigated a group of three- to five-year-old children. Those children showing the largest increase in heart rate and blood pressure when performing stressful tasks – such as copying a structure built with bricks – were considered 'reactive'. When reactive children were exposed to stressors – such as peer problems, changes in their routine or toilet problems – they were more likely to contract an infection than low reactive children. At other times, reactive children were less likely to become infected.
- The traffic between the immune system and brain runs both ways. In some patients, a latent herpes infection re-emerges shortly before the onset of depression. Some scientists speculate that the re-emergence of the infection triggers an immune response that feeds back to the brain. This changes the brain's biochemistry and produces depression.

And it seems that alleviating stress gives your immune system a boost. For example, having well-developed social contacts protects against reactivation of herpes infection.

Many of the effects of stress on the immune system are relatively small. However, small differences may be critical if the body is weakened. For example, stress-induced respiratory infections may be an inconvenience for most people. But they can be life-threatening for someone with severe asthma.

Immunological civil war

The link between stress, immunity and disease does not end with infections. In the so-called 'autoimmune' diseases, the immune system regards certain parts of the body as foreign protein and tries to destroy them. In rheumatoid arthritis, for example, the body mounts an immune response against joints, causing pain, swelling and inflammation. Why the immune system comes to regard the joint as 'foreign' isn't known. Nevertheless, many people report that stress exacerbates the symptoms. Indeed, some chemicals released by the immune system during acute stress seem to increase the progression of rheumatoid arthritis and may go some way to explaining the link between stress and this crippling disease. The Arthritis & Rheumatism Council for Research[*] and Arthritis Care[*] offer advice and support.

Studies suggest that death, divorce and severe illness may precipitate diabetes among people predisposed to the disease. For example, children who endure stress during the first two years of life are twice as likely to develop insulin-dependent diabetes than their peers. Insulin-dependent diabetes arises when the immune system destroys insulin-producing cells in the pancreas. Patients sometimes report that their first symptoms emerged during a time of stress. Stress also undermines patients' compliance with the regular insulin injections needed to control their symptoms.

Stress and cancer

The immune system does more than just protect us from infections. It also destroys cells that could develop into cancers. Each day, some 35 billion cells divide in a healthy adult – each producing a new cell. Invariably, some of these new cells are defective. Certain immune cells – natural killer cells, for example – act as a quality control system, selectively eradicating cancerous cells. So you might expect that chronic stress, which undermines the immune system, would predispose people to cancer.

Nevertheless, the jury is still out. Cancers usually take several years to develop from a cancerous cell to a diagnosable tumour. People smoke and sunbathe for many years before developing lung and skin cancer. Asking cancer patients to remember what their mental state was before and during the growth of the cancer is unrealistic. Furthermore, most cancers are rare. So huge numbers of patients would be needed to run a prospective trial where researchers follow a group of people for many years to see which diseases they develop and the associated risk factors. Targeting high-risk patients may provide some insight into links between stress, emotion and cancer. But the results may not apply to the general population.

The stress of a high-risk life
The link between cancer and stress may be uncertain, but being diagnosed as having cancer inevitably produces stress. You don't even have to develop cancer to suffer from its stressful effects. Being at high-risk of developing cancer is enough to cause considerable distress. For example, certain women are known to be at high risk of developing breast cancer, including: women whose mother or sister had breast cancer; childless women; those who had their first baby in their 30s; and those who had a late menopause.

Before undergoing mammography, women at high risk of developing breast cancer experience levels of acute stress that far exceed those among low-risk women. In one study, a quarter of high-risk women showed signs of psychological problems – around the same proportion as among women with breast cancer and over twice the rate in low-risk women. This stress is exacerbated if the woman is recalled. Eight per cent of women screened for breast cancer are recalled for further assessment. Many do not have cancer on more detailed examinations. Even among those who ultimately receive a normal result, many women at high-risk of developing breast cancer continue to experience distress.

Ironically, this may mean that women are less likely to examine their breasts regularly or go for mammography – despite being at high risk. Counselling can dramatically reduce the levels of distress experienced by women at high risk of breast cancer and keep their fears in perspective.

When you get the bad news...

To many people, cancer is a death sentence. Certainly, the statistics are stark. One in three people in Britain develop a cancer and one in four die as a result. Despite advances in drugs and surgery, deaths from cancers of the lung, breast, stomach, prostate and brain remain stubbornly high.

Relatives often try to protect patients from the truth. In one study, 47 per cent of relatives asked doctors not to tell the patient about the cancer. But ignorance isn't necessarily bliss. Most cancer patients want to be informed – even if that means facing bad news. A survey of people with advanced cancer suggested that 72 per cent wanted to be kept fully informed. A further six per cent wanted to know – but only when they asked. Only three per cent wanted to live in ignorance. In another study, 94 per cent of patients wanted as much information as possible – irrespective of whether it was good or bad.

Nevertheless, being told they have cancer throws some patients into an abyss of despair. For example, a third of women with breast cancer develop severe anxiety, a fifth become depressed and a third experience sexual problems. Tackling cancer's psychological toll is as challenging as treating the tumour – and just as important. Women with advanced breast cancer who endure more stressful life events have shorter survival times than less anxious patients.

However, some doctors may not recognise patients' suffering. In one study, physicians recognised depression and anxiety – which was severe enough to justify treatment – in only 20 per cent of women suffering from breast cancer. They fared little better in cervical cancer sufferers: the detection rate reached 25 per cent. Even in cancer wards with specialised psychiatry services, only 40 per cent of patients receive the help they need. So if you feel depressed, anxious or over-stressed discuss your feelings with the people organising your treatment.

Other doctors increasingly recognise the heavy emotional toll exerted by cancer. As a result, psychosocial therapies that aim to alleviate the depression, anxiety and stress surrounding cancer are now often a central part of cancer management. Patients may undergo group therapy to explore their feelings and emotions about cancer. They may be offered marital therapy if they feel their marriage is under strain. Alternatively, some patients enter individual therapy to deal with specific problems, such as excessive crying and refusing to eat. Grief therapy, increasingly used in breast cancer patients, allows patients to grieve actively if they feel they have lost their health, femininity, breast and so on, so that patients may emerge from psychotherapy with a more positive outlook. Counselling may even improve survival. People who feel less depressed, isolated and frightened are more likely to eat better, sleep more soundly and exercise more. They are also more likely to follow their doctors' instructions – which can involve taking unpleasant treatments. Contacting the appropriate self-help group may also be beneficial – see Facing the truth (page 82).

The stress of caring for a cancer patient

Cancer places a huge burden on relatives. They may have to watch their loved ones suffer chronic pain, lost dignity and distress. They may have to face the prospect of spending the rest of their lives alone. They may have to decide what to tell their children. Not surprisingly, around 12 per cent of cancer patients' partners suffer either anxiety or depression. Women seem particularly susceptible to psychological distress if cancer strikes their partners – or perhaps they are just more willing to admit to their feelings. However, the partner – male or female – of a depressed patient is three times more likely than the partner of other cancer patients to suffer depression.

Despite this mental torment, almost half of cancer patients' partners who suffer chronic stress, anxiety or depression do not seek professional help. Many would benefit from counselling, enrolling in self-help groups or consulting their GPs, who may prescribe tranquillisers or antidepressants to tide people over the worst of their distress. However, most partners of cancer patients find they are able to draw on reserves of emotional and physical strength they were unaware they had.

Cancer pain

For many cancer patients, pain – or the fear of pain – is the most distressing aspect of their disease. It may keep them awake at night, it may prevent them from eating – it may even drive some to suicide. Chronic pain, which can be caused by the tumour and its treatment, is common in cancer. In the early stages, perhaps half of cancer patients suffer pain. This increases to 70 per cent among terminal cancer patients.

Opioids, used to relieve pain for at least 4,000 years, remain the cornerstone of treatment. Up to 95 per cent of patients say that they can bear their pain, or that it goes altogether, after taking morphine. Despite this, the World Health Organisation estimates that 60 to 70 per cent of cancer patients, even in medically advanced countries, do not receive adequate pain relief. Cancer pain often goes unrelieved because illegal opioid abuse has tarnished morphine's medical reputation. In reality, using morphine for pain relief rarely causes dependence. A study of almost 12,000 patients who received narcotic painkillers found that just four went on to abuse drugs. Only one developed a major drug problem.

To gain the maximum benefit, morphine needs to be taken before patients begin to experience pain, but doctors may prescribe inadequate doses, too widely apart. By the time patients experience sufficient discomfort to request morphine they may be in severe pain. They then may require a large dose of morphine that causes mental clouding and other side-effects. One way round this is to use a syringe driver to deliver a constant dose of morphine and antiemetics (drugs that alleviate nausea and vomiting) over 24 hours. Modern drug delivery systems release constant low doses of analgesic that keeps pain at bay. For example, patches can deliver powerful painkillers (such as fentanyl) through the skin. Other formulations allow patients to take morphine as controlled-release tablets and suspensions every 12 hours. Analgesics may be prescribed with other drugs. Tranquillisers, antidepressants, relaxation and meditation may reduce anxiety and pain and help patients cope with side-effects.

Facing the truth

Oncologists – cancer specialists – now cure around 40 per cent of cancers. But many patients are eventually told that their cancer is incurable. Faced with this reality some patients run the gamut of negative emotions, including fear, uncertainty and anger. But you can talk to someone. Your hospital may offer psychotherapy or drugs to help you cope with the emotional impact of cancer. You may also find talking to a specialist nurse helpful.

However, it may be easier to talk to someone who is not directly involved with your care. You may find a counsellor helps. Patients' groups such as BACUP*, Cancerlink*, and Tenovus Cancer Information Centre* offer general advice and support for cancer patients and their families. There are also specialist groups for individual cancers, including Breast Cancer Care*, Hodgkin's Disease and Lymphoma Association*, Leukaemia Care Society* and Save Our Sons* (testicular cancer).

You may also benefit from complementary medicine. Cancer patients massaged using aromatherapy oils show fewer physical symptoms and report less anxiety, tension and pain. However, be very wary of anyone offering a cure for cancer. Tragically, some charlatans prey on people during this most vulnerable time.

Stress and heart disease

Cancer may be more feared, but heart disease remains the UK's leading cause of death. Each year, around 180,000 people die from heart disease – 105,000 prematurely. Heart disease kills a third of men and a quarter of women. A further two million suffer symptoms of heart disease, such as angina. More rarely, people die from stress-induced arrhythmias – disorganised heart beats – following conflicts with parents or neighbours, assaults, or even getting married or starting college (see page 92).

Traditionally, heart disease is almost a badge of success. In the 1940s, a doctor reported that many heart disease patients were self-made men who 'would rather die than fail, and frequently they did'. However, heart disease is egalitarian. Indeed, men in low-paid jobs or who are unemployed are three times more likely to die from heart disease than those in professional or managerial positions.

Moreover, over 76,000 women die each year from heart disease and about 900,000 suffer angina. Indeed, heart disease kills more women over 50 years of age than any other disease. Women in high pressure jobs are three times as likely to suffer from heart disease as their less stressed peers. Nevertheless, studies comparing heart disease rates among women found that, overall, working women were no more likely to suffer a heart attack than housewives. Married, divorced, widowed and separated women were more likely to develop heart disease than single working women, and working women were more likely to develop heart disease the more children they had. This was not the case among housewives. Tackling stress may therefore help you avoid becoming another heart disease statistic.

Taking a global approach

Over 250 factors – including infections, diet and depression – may increase your risk of developing heart disease. You need to tackle as many as possible. You cannot alter some heart disease risk factors – being male, having a family history of heart disease, being Asian, or getting older, for example. But you can reduce your risk from a number of other factors such as smoking, inactivity, high blood pressure, diabetes and high cholesterol. So exercise regularly and eat a healthy diet low in fat – especially animal fat – and high in vegetables. If you already suffer from heart disease, or if diet does not reduce your cholesterol levels adequately, you may need to take drugs that lower cholesterol.

Many heart disease risk factors are intertwined. Stress may make you smoke or eat poorly, or it may increase your blood pressure. Nevertheless, the risk from some of these factors greatly outweighs that from stress alone. For example, smoking more than 20 cigarettes a day doubles the risk of heart disease compared to non-smokers. Stopping smoking is the single most effective thing you can do to lower your risk of heart disease. Smokers' risk of suffering heart disease declines to almost that among non-smokers within five to ten years of stopping. So far as heart disease is concerned, there is no point in combatting stress if you still smoke.

Why hostility and anger harm your heart

Heart disease is caused when fatty deposits – known as atherosclerotic plaques – build up on the walls of the blood vessels supplying the heart. This narrows the blood vessels and starves the heart muscles of oxygen. The crippling pain of angina signals that the heart is not getting enough oxygen. The pain forces angina patients to slow down and, thereby, balances the oxygen supply and demand.

There are two types of plaques – stable and unstable. When blood pressure increases, the plaques come under considerable strain. Stable plaques can withstand the pressure. However, unstable plaques may rupture and expel their contents into the blood. This causes the blood to clot, which completely blocks the blood supply to the heart and the patient suffers a heart attack. Many people at high risk of suffering a heart attack – for example, those who have experienced a heart attack in the past – take a daily dose of aspirin, which makes the blood less likely to clot. But don't take aspirin without talking to your doctor first. There is a small risk that regular aspirin may trigger a haemorrhagic stroke (page 93).

Stress stimulates the fight-or-flight response. As we have seen, this involves a surge of adrenaline and an increase in the amount of fat circulating in the blood to meet the expected demand from the muscles. However, adrenaline makes blood more likely to clot and it narrows blood vessels. This response evolved to limit blood loss in the event of an injury. Now it increases the risk of suffering a heart attack.

Moreover, if the fat released into the blood as part of the fight-or-flight reflex isn't used up it is deposited as part of the plaque. The increase in fat doesn't only reflect a worse diet when you are stressed. A group of accountants kept a note of their eating habits for six months. During April – the busiest time of year for accountants – their cholesterol rose even though their diets did not alter greatly.

Argue your way to a heart attack

Chronic hostility – which scientists define as believing that other people are unreliable, immoral and potential enemies – increases your risk of suffering a heart attack, as do aggression, annoyance, irritability and suspicion. A recent study from Finland assessed plaque size and levels of cynical distrust, impatience and irritability, and the way 119 middle-aged men controlled anger. Atherosclerosis – hardening of the arteries caused by the plaque – advanced twice as fast among cynical, distrustful men and men who attempted to repress and control their anger, aggression and irritation.

While most studies involve men, hostility also harms women's hearts. One study compared women who express their anger by making sarcastic remarks, slamming doors or striking out with those who boil inside and withdraw from other people. Doctors measured blood pressure and heart rate during a mental arithmetic test (which causes considerable stress). The women who expressed moderate amounts of anger showed a less marked increase in blood pressure and heart rate than those who boiled inside or who blew their top.

Dealing with anger

People with Type A personalities (page 25) tend to be hostile and angry and seem to be particularly prone to high blood pressure. Their hearts may have the most to gain from stress management techniques. However, even short-lived increases in blood pressure put unstable plaques under pressure. So how can you reduce your hostility and anger?

- Think of the consequences: is it worth losing your temper at a child's tantrum or because you've been cut up at a road junction?
- Use visualisation. Imagine situations where you become angry. Imagine the situation in enough detail and you will probably feel anger and annoyance welling up inside you. So try to remain calm. Staying calm when you imagine a stress-provoking situation makes it easier to stay calm when you face the reality.
- Regular exercise alleviates anger. Exercise also lowers your risk of developing heart disease by lowering blood pressure, increasing the strength of your heart and burning up circulating fats.
- Take several deep breaths when you feel your temper rising. Counting to ten really can help.
- Meditation also helps you develop a calmer approach to life. Try to identify and change your Type A forms of behaviour (see page 25), such as time urgency, hostility and anger. If you want to know whether you suffer from time urgency, try taking your watch off at work one morning or afternoon when you don't have a meeting. Then see how tense you feel. Assertiveness training or time management may help.
- Take up creative leisure pursuits that provide a healthy diversion from the daily routine. Do something than cannot be rushed, such as yoga, pottery or gardening.

● Try some of the stress management techniques in our directory (chapter six).

After a heart attack

For many people the advice to control stress may be too late.
They may already have heart disease or even have suffered a heart
attack. However, tackling stress is just as important after the heart
attack. It could save your life.

Doctors split 461 male heart attack survivors into two groups.
During the first year, men in one group received visits from a
nurse when they reported feeling stressed. The nurses aimed to
deal with their problems. The second received only routine medical care. Men receiving routine medical care and who reported
high levels of stress were three times more likely to die and 1.5
times more likely to suffer another heart attack than those men in
the same group reporting low levels of stress. However, the
highly stressed men who received the nurses' help to deal with
their problems were no more likely to die or suffer another heart
attack than their less stressed counterparts.

It is also important to be realistic. You do not recover overnight
from a heart attack. So consider the improvement from week to
week rather than daily, and don't be downhearted about your
prospects for recovery – most patients recover within a few
weeks, even from heart surgery. By-pass operations and other
heart operations are becoming more common – surgeons now
perform some 18,000 heart operations each year. Most patients
take around six to eight weeks to make a full recovery, largely
because the chest muscles, bones and joints have to heal. Around
75 to 80 per cent of patients who undergo heart surgery return to
their jobs after around two to three months.

Nevertheless, heart disease can place a considerable strain on
the entire family. Relatives may need help from counselling or
should discuss their worries with a doctor.

Depressed mind: depressed heart

Excessive tiredness and fatigue – common stress-related symptoms – seem to increase your risk of suffering a heart attack.
Between 30 and 60 per cent of people who have a heart attack
report experiencing undue fatigue or lack of energy, increased
irritability and demoralisation before the attack.

They seem to enter a malaise – almost a mild depression. Their vitality declines, they are irritable, listless and lose libido. Many heart disease patients attribute their malaise to a long-standing problem that they have been unable to solve, or to a real or symbolic loss. According to one study, suffering from this collection of symptoms – which doctors called vital exhaustion – increases your risk of suffering your first heart attack tenfold during the next year. While the risk declines over the following years, vital exhaustion still ranked above high blood pressure – but below smoking, age and cholesterol – in the league table of heart disease risk factors.

At least one in six people also suffers severe depression following a heart attack. Another one in four heart attack victims suffers milder symptoms. People who are depressed following a heart attack seem to be between four and eight times more likely to die from heart disease than those without depression.

There seem to be several explanations for the link between depression and heart disease. To start with, stress and depression may make the blood more likely to clot.

Depression also predisposes people to other habits that are harmful to their hearts. They may feel it is not worth bothering with special diets. They may drink or smoke and may not be fully committed to their rehabilitation programme. So patients should make the most of self-help groups and social supports. Social isolation often makes matters worse. Some studies suggest that among those who had experienced a heart attack, the patients who reported feeling depressed or who showed Type B forms of behaviour (see page 25) were more likely to suffer a further heart attack or die. But the higher risk of death or a second heart attack may be less to do with Type B traits and more to do with using withdrawal as a strategy to cope with the stress of a heart attack, so taking part in normal everyday activities may protect you from further heart problems.

Some people find talking to a counsellor or psychotherapist helps. You can also join clubs or societies where you can share your experiences with people of the same age. People suffering from more severe depression may like to consider drug treatment with their doctors. Depression and stress can break your heart.

Hypertension: the silent killer

Hypertension – high blood pressure – is the most common chronic disease. Around one in five people develop hypertension, usually in middle age. By the time you reach your 70th birthday you have a 50:50 chance of having hypertension. Hypertension generally does not cause symptoms and is usually first detected during routine health screens or when you consult your GP about another problem. You should ensure that a doctor or a nurse checks your blood pressure at least once every five years if you are over 35.

If screening detects hypertension, you will probably need treatment. Hypertension dramatically increases your risk of suffering a stroke or heart attack. A 40-year-old with hypertension is 30 times more likely to suffer a stroke than someone with normal blood pressure. Middle-aged men with a diastolic blood pressure (see below) above 90mmHg are at least 1.5 times more likely than someone with normal blood pressure to die from heart disease. Above 100mmHg the risk increases to 2.5 times.

What is blood pressure?

Doctors take two blood pressure measurements, known as the systolic and diastolic. Each heart beat sends a wave of blood into the arteries. The blood pressure produced at the peak of this wave is determined by the amount of the blood expelled and the flexibility of the veins and arteries. Blood vessels tend to be more elastic in younger people, stretching to accommodate the surge in blood. As a result, blood pressure tends to be higher in older people with more rigid vessels.

The pressure when the heart contracts is known as the systolic pressure. The pressure while it is relaxed is called the diastolic. Each is expressed as the pressure in millimetres of mercury (mmHg). A young person may have a systolic blood pressure of 120 and a diastolic of 80 – expressed as 120/80. However, there is no clear cut-off point where blood pressure becomes unacceptably high, and whether a patient has 'hypertension' partly depends on their age. A systolic blood pressure of 145 mmHg in a teenage girl is considered abnormal, but it would be acceptable in her grandmother. As a rule of thumb, doctors aim for a systolic blood pressure below 160mmHg and a diastolic below 90mmHg.

The cause of hypertension

In 90 per cent of cases, the cause of high blood pressure is a mystery. Doctors call this essential hypertension. In the remaining cases, other conditions such as kidney disease lead to hypertension. However, doctors recognise that a number of factors conspire to increase your risk of developing essential hypertension. If your parents had hypertension, your blood pressure is also more likely to be high. Being overweight, unfit or drinking excessive amounts of alcohol tend to drive blood pressure up. Stress may also contribute to your risk of developing hypertension.

During the fight-or-flight response your heart rate increases and blood pressure rises – at least in the short term. Even the stress of having your blood pressure measured by a doctor or nurse can cause it to rise – a problem doctors call 'white coat' hypertension. Around a quarter of people with high blood pressure may have 'white coat' hypertension: outside the surgery, their blood pressure is normal. In some cases 'white coat' hypertension can lead to patients being treated unnecessarily. However, most GPs are now aware of 'white coat' hypertension and the problem declines as patients become used to having their blood pressure measured. So you may have your blood pressure measured on two or three occasions before the GP decides you have hypertension.

Whether long-term stress and anxiety cause chronic hypertension rather than just a short-lived rise in blood pressure is less clear. Some cardiologists believe that sustained high blood pressure – following, for example, prolonged activation of the fight-or-flight response – may thicken artery walls. This may reduce the amount of blood that can flow through the vessel and makes the wall less flexible. Both contribute to hypertension. Furthermore, hypertension tends to be a disease of developed societies. Some scientists speculate that the stress of everyday life in Western societies causes blood pressure to rise. If blood pressure is higher among the population as a whole, then more people will cross the threshold into hypertension. However, it is questionable whether living in a 'primitive' society, surrounded by a hostile environment, disease and predators, is less stressful than commuting every day to a high-pressure office job.

Treating hypertension

If you want to reduce your risk of suffering a stroke or heart attack you need to lower your blood pressure. Treating mild-to-moderate hypertension reduces your risk of suffering a stroke by 40 per cent and a heart attack by 16 per cent, so take any antihypertensives your doctor prescribes. However, hypertension rarely causes symptoms. In contrast, the drugs used to lower blood pressure can cause a range of side-effects including cold hands and feet, fatigue, impotence, rashes and cough, so if you feel anything abnormal talk to your doctor. Doctors can choose from a large number of antihypertensives available and changing the drug may alleviate the side-effect.

You can also change your lifestyle to reduce high blood pressure:

- Lose weight. If you are obese, losing 11lb (5kg) can reduce your systolic blood pressure by 5mmHg.
- Regular exercise lowers blood pressure by around 5mmHg. However, people with hypertension should avoid isometric exercises, such as weight lifting, because drugs used to treat hypertension are ineffective against the rise in blood pressure caused by such exercises. So if you are being treated for high blood pressure try walking, cycling, swimming or other dynamic exercises.
- Reducing your salt intake may reduce systolic blood pressure by around 5mmHg. Avoiding salt can prove difficult, but you can stop using salt at the dinner table and cut back on high salt foods such as crisps, peanuts, canned foods and bacon.
- Limit your alcohol intake. The new government guidelines suggest that men drinking three to four units a day and women who drink two to three units daily do not face a significant health risk. A unit is one glass of wine, one measure of spirits or half a pint of ordinary strength lager.
- Relaxation produces a short-lived reduction in blood pressure. Relaxation's most important benefits are in the long term: an enhanced feeling of control and a more positive outlook. Both blunt the fight-or-flight reflex.
- Learn to modify Type A forms of behaviour (see page 25). Managing anger, hostility and time urgency can lower systolic

blood pressure by 9-12mmHg and diastolic blood pressure by 7-9mmHg.

- Some people benefit from counselling to help them live a more controlled and healthier life.
- Meditation can lower blood pressure among people with hypertension. One recent study found that transcendental meditation* lowered blood pressure as effectively as antihypertensives. However, never stop taking antihypertensives without talking to your GP first.

Arrhythmias and palpitations

The chances are that you have already experienced arrhythmias or palpitations, which are common when we feel stressed, anxious or scared. In certain circumstances – before giving an important presentation at work, for example – you may feel that your heart is beating furiously. This heightened awareness of your heartbeat is called palpitations – although your heart may be beating fast the rhythm is normal. Arrhythmias are disordered heart beats – but often you do not notice that your heart has missed a few beats.

Over 80 per cent of people suffer cardiac arrhythmias at least once daily. Stress undoubtedly makes matters worse – even if you are used to pressure. For example, the cardiac activity of 54 highly experienced pilots was assessed during exercise and in a flight simulator. Five developed arrhythmias during exercise, compared to 34 who developed arrhythmias while in the simulator. However, the arrhythmias were most pronounced while waiting for the results of a medical examination that could deprive them of their pilot's licence.

In extreme cases, stress-induced arrhythmias prove fatal – even if the victim doesn't suffer from heart disease. A 14-year-old girl, for example, suddenly died after being told that her 15-year-old brother dropped dead after an athletics race. In another family, one son died aged 17 after being frightened by his friend. Another son died at 12 years of age while swimming (exercise is physical stress). Another son also died aged 12 years, after being scared by a spider and running to tell his friends.

Similarly, bereaved men tend to drop dead without any sign of disease and men without heart disease are more likely to die suddenly on a Monday. The increased risk of dying before returning to work on Monday morning isn't shared by either cancer patients or patients who have had heart attacks. So these stress-induced deaths cannot be explained by the effects of underlying heart disease. There have even been epidemics of sudden death caused by arrhythmias. In one, young Malaysian and Cambodian immigrants to the US died instantly during the night. The immigrants showed no evidence of heart disease. However, they typically showed poor social integration and more desolation than other immigrants.

Even pleasure can prove fatal. A 20-year-old woman fainted during her wedding ceremony and later died. Another 22-year-old woman died during her first day at medical school. Both died from arrhythmias and neither showed any sign of heart or other disease. In these cases, the stress surrounding a significant life event seems to be the only cause of death.

Nevertheless, palpitations are usually harmless. Keeping calm may reduce their frequency. If relaxation fails, look at your lifestyle. Prescription drugs, alcohol, nicotine and caffeine can all cause palpitations. So review your medication with your doctor, drink less alcohol and caffeine and, of course, stop smoking. More rarely, palpitations are a symptom of a number of diseases – including a thyroid disorder or heart disease. If palpitations persist or become severe, or you experience breathlessness or chest pains during an attack you should consult your GP.

Strokes

Strokes are the third most common cause of death after cancer and heart disease. There are two types of stroke: ischaemic and haemorrhagic. Ischaemic strokes, which account for 85 per cent of strokes, are 'brain attacks' – akin to heart attacks – caused when fatty plaques build up in the blood vessels supplying the brain. If these plaques rupture, the blood clot can starve areas of the brain of oxygen and destroy brain cells. The rarer haemorrhagic stokes are caused when blood vessels burst. Blood leaks into the brain and clots, destroying brain cells. In both cases the damage to the brain is irreparable and causes death or severe disability in two out of three cases.

As with heart attacks you can take several steps to reduce your risk of suffering a stroke:

- Uncontrolled hypertension is the leading cause of stokes, so you need to reduce raised blood pressure with drugs and lifestyle changes (see page 91).
- Quit smoking. Cigarette-smoking increases the risk of stroke threefold.
- Ischaemic strokes result from the same process that causes heart attacks. In other words, following the advice to prevent heart attacks (see page 86) also prevents strokes, so follow a healthy lifestyle and diet.
- Keep your alcohol consumption within the recommended safe limits. Binge drinking increases the risk of a stroke, so spread your drinking out during the week.
- Contact the Stroke Association*.

Stress and the stomach

We have all suffered from the effects of stress on the stomach. Butterflies in your tummy, diarrhoea, feeling you have a lump in your throat, vomiting, nausea and irritable bowel syndrome (IBS) all are gastrointestinal manifestations of stress. Indeed, a stomach ulcer was once assumed to come with the company car, gold card and key to the executive toilet. Doctors even described an 'ulcer personality'. Typical ulcer sufferers were said to be thin, hungry-looking, highly competitive and conscientious. Despite their seemingly self-sufficient personalities, ulcer sufferers, the doctors argued, were 'hungry' for attention, recognition and support. Some psychologists viewed ulcers as a sign of emotional immaturity.

In recent years, this view has come under attack. Overall, there is no convincing evidence that people with certain personalities are more likely to develop ulcers. Doctors are even beginning to question the long-held view that stress causes stomach ulcers. The cause of ulcers may not lie in the mind – but in the microbiology lab.

Stress and stomach ulcers

At least one in ten people develops stomach ulcers at some time. An ulcer is an erosion in the wall of the stomach or duodenum –

the foot-long section of gut immediately below the stomach. Acid in the stomach irritates this erosion, causing a number of symptoms (see box). In a few cases, the erosion reaches the network of blood vessels in the stomach or duodenal wall, which may lead to life-threatening gastrointestinal bleeding.

Ulcer symptoms
* indigestion * abdominal discomfort *gastric pain, especially near the solar plexus and worse at night * nausea * flatulence * feeling bloated or full * heartburn * weight loss * gastrointestinal bleeding

---

The evidence linking stress and ulcers is at best mixed. The link was first noted in 1833 when stress was found to increase blood supply to the stomach and stimulate acid secretion. Around 50 years later, financial ruin was associated with the increased risk of developing an ulcer. Over the years a number of studies suggested that stress and Type A behaviour (see page 25) predisposed people to develop ulcers. In one study, over 80 per cent of people reported that their symptoms emerged after a change in their work, finances or family's health. This compared to only 22 per cent of a similar group of hernia patients. Other studies suggested that people who endure stress lasting more than six months or who strove towards – but did not achieve – a goal were more likely to develop an ulcer. However, other studies have failed to link stress and ulcers. The association is confused by the effects of smoking. Some people smoke to alleviate stress and smoking predisposes people to stomach ulcers.

Stress and dyspepsia

While the jury was out studying the evidence linking stress and ulcers, doctors began questioning another long-held link: the association between stress and dyspepsia – severe indigestion or heartburn caused by excessive acid production. Dyspepsia is one of the most common disorders: around ten per cent of the population suffer heartburn at least once a week and a quarter suffer significant abdominal pain at least six times a year. All this places a heavy burden on the NHS. Dyspepsia accounts for five per cent of GP consultations and up to 30 per cent of hospital gastroenterology clinic appointments. So what lies at the root of dyspepsia?

Some cases follow over-indulgence. In around 20 per cent of people, the dyspepsia is caused by a stomach ulcer. Another half to two-thirds show inflammation in the upper gastrointestinal tract. A few develop dyspepsia as a result of IBS or gallstones. However, in up to a fifth of dyspepsia cases, doctors are unable to find a cause for the symptoms – despite intensive investigation. Many came to believe that these cases of non-ulcer dyspepsia (see box) were caused by the patients' minds rather than their guts.

Non-ulcer dyspepsia symptoms
* upper abdominal pain or discomfort * heartburn * tasting acid in the mouth * vomiting * nausea * difficulty swallowing * lasts for more than four months * no underlying disease * symptoms are unrelated to exercise

---

Their suspicion was supported by studies showing that stress increases acid production and contracts the muscles lining the gastrointestinal tract. Moreover, studies investigating the psychology of non-ulcer dyspepsia patients revealed that a third of people with recurrent or chronic stomach pain were depressed, a fifth suffered from chronic tension and 18 per cent showed signs of 'hysteria'. The studies suggested that people likely to develop dyspepsia tend to be more anxious, neurotic, prone to mood swings and depressed than the rest of the population.

However, a recent study of patients complaining of heartburn, when doctors could not identify any other gastrointestinal disease, disputes this. Heartburn patients were no more likely to suffer anxiety, depression or other psychological disorders than those with a definite disease. Moreover, patients with dyspepsia were no more likely to experience daily hassles – microlevel stressors – than patients with confirmed gastrointestinal disease. While dyspepsia patients tended to be more dependent on other people, it's not clear if this personality trait predisposes people to heartburn or is a consequence of suffering from a chronic disease. Stress may increase the likelihood that patients will consult their GP about the symptoms of dyspepsia that they previously managed themselves.

The role of H pylori

The link between stress, ulcers and dyspepsia was dealt a fatal blow with the discovery of the bacterium *Helicobacter pylori*. Doctors recognised for decades that stomach ulcers tended to run in families. They also noted that stomach ulcers were more common among people living in air-raid shelters or prisoner of war camps during the Second World War, which doctors attributed to the intense stress. However, no-one seriously considered that a bacterium could be responsible for ulcers or dyspepsia. Stomach acid, which evolved in part to sterilise food and drink, makes the stomach one of the most inhospitable parts of the body.

Then in 1983, the Australian microbiologist Robin Warren and the physician Barry Marshall made a discovery that revolutionised gastroenterology. They isolated *H pylori* from the stomach of patients suffering from dyspepsia and ulcers. The bacterium survives by burrowing beneath the thick mucus that protects the stomach wall from attack by acid. However, this burrowing bacterium allows the acid to erode the stomach.

Doctors now know that *H pylori*, which infects about 40 per cent of people living in developed countries, causes at least eight out of ten stomach ulcers and possibly all duodenal ulcers. The rate of infection rises with age although this may reflect *H pylori's* more widespread distribution earlier in the century. Alcohol abuse and non-steroidal anti-inflammatory drugs – widely used to treat arthritis and other inflammatory diseases – cause the remaining ulcers. It seems likely that *H pylori* is also an important cause of non-ulcer dyspepsia.

Drugs for ulcers and dyspepsia

Traditional antacids alleviate symptoms by reducing the acidity of the stomach. More recently, a group of drugs known as the H2-antagonists – such as cimetidine, famotidine, nizatidine and ranitidine – were approved for sale by pharmacists. These reduce acid production in the stomach, which relieves symptoms of dyspepsia. These are safe and effective treatments for dyspepsia. However, consult your GP if your symptoms persist for more than a month.

GPs can prescribe a wider range of anti-ulcer treatments,

including higher doses of H2-antagonists and a group of drugs known as the proton pump inhibitors, that include omeprazole and lansoprazole. These rapidly relieve symptoms and may heal ulcers. They may also alleviate dyspepsia that does not respond to over-the-counter medications.

For years, H2-antagonists and the proton pump inhibitors were the mainstays of ulcer therapy: a two-month course heals around 80 per cent of stomach ulcers. This compares with the 20 or 30 per cent that heal naturally. While patients take the drugs, the ulcer remains healed. However, patients are still infected with *H pylori*. As a result, around two-thirds of ulcer patients relapse within a year of stopping H2-antagonists.

Warren and Marshall's discovery that *H pylori* was responsible for most stomach ulcers transformed treatment. If you develop a stomach ulcer you should ask your GP for a *H pylori* test. If positive, one or two weeks on antibiotics combined with a proton pump inhibitor or ranitidine bismuth citrate will probably eradicate the infection and prevent recurrence. In some cases, you will take the proton pump inhibitor, H2-antagonist or ranitidine bismuth citrate for a further two weeks to completely heal the ulcer.

H pylori plays less of a role among people taking non-steroidal anti-inflammatory drugs (NSAIDs), which include aspirin, ibuprofen, indomethacin and diclofenac. NSAID users are between two and ten times more likely to be admitted to hospital with a bleeding ulcer than non-users. However, NSAIDs are painkillers, which is why arthritis sufferers take them. So patients do not experience the pain that usually alerts the sufferer to the ulcer. If you regularly take a non-steroidal anti-inflammatory you might like to discuss taking another drug – such as an H2-antagonist, a proton pump inhibitor or misoprostol – to protect your stomach. Nevertheless, if you are *H pylori* positive it may still be worth eradicating the infection. The bacteria, rather than the drug, may still cause your ulcer.

Non-drug ulcer treatments

To a certain extent, non-drug ulcer treatments are redundant. If you can eradicate *H pylori* with a two-week course of antibiotics it seems rather pointless trying time-consuming non-drug therapies. Nevertheless, smoking slows ulcer healing and promotes relapse – another good reason, if you needed it, to quit. As caffeine stimulates gastric acid secretion, many doctors and self-help books advise patients with ulcers to cut down on coffee. However, provided you drink caffeine in moderation it probably won't exacerbate your symptoms.

Some studies suggest that relapse rates are lower among people undergoing psychotherapy. However, a recent study of 100 people with ulcers found that a year's psychotherapy did not reduce the ulcer recurrence rate. Indeed, ulcers tended to recur more rapidly among patients receiving psychotherapy unless patients received a proton pump inhibitor or an H2-antagonist. As noted above, some studies suggest chronic stress, goal frustration and physical injury may increase the risk of developing an ulcer, so stress management techniques *may* prevent ulcers, reduce the intensity of the symptoms and lessen patients' dependency on other people. Nevertheless, stress plays a minor role in ulcers. Drugs that eradicate *H pylori* are undoubtedly the treatment of choice.

Non-drug dyspepsia treatments

While it seems likely that *H pylori* causes many cases of dyspepsia, doctors do not yet know whether eradicating the infection improves patients' symptoms. For many non-ulcer dyspepsia patients, reassurance is the first line treatment. Often they feel better after being told that their symptoms do not suggest they are suffering from something more sinister, such as cancer, which is rare among patients aged under 45 years. IBS patients often benefit from hypnotherapy or behavioural therapy and some doctors believe these treatments also alleviate dyspepsia. If your non-ulcer dyspepsia seems to be triggered by stress, you may benefit from relaxation therapy and other stress management techniques.

Irritable bowel syndrome

After dyspepsia, irritable bowel syndrome (IBS) is perhaps the most common gastrointestinal disorder – up to 14 per cent of adults suffer from it. However, relatively few consult their GPs and, despite being so common, IBS – also called spastic colon – is one of the most poorly understood diseases. The cause of IBS has eluded doctors for more than 200 years. Over the years, IBS has been linked to refined low fibre diets, disordered gastrointestinal motility (bowel movements) and a hypersensitivity to having a distended bowel. But stress and other psychological factors undoubtedly play a part.

What is IBS?

IBS sufferers endure painful contractions of their stomach, feeling bloated and changed bowel habits – they may expel 'pellet-like' or 'ribbon-like' stools. IBS patients with diarrhoea often report morning frequency, an urgent need to defecate after meals and a sense of incomplete evacuation. IBS symptoms are fairly non-specific and most people have probably suffered at least some of them at one time or another. So doctors only consider the change to be an IBS 'symptom' if patients experience it for at least three months and if it interferes with normal life. Of course, many people misinterpret bowel actions. Being unable to defecate every morning before breakfast isn't a sign that there is something wrong. Indeed, in healthy people stool frequency ranges from three times daily to three times a week. Many sufferers improve once they recognise this. Only persistent changes in your normal bowel habits are abnormal.

Stool consistency is also important. For example, changing from one to two movements a day does not count as diarrhoea unless the consistency becomes more watery. Likewise, constipation implies both reduced frequency and stools that are difficult to pass. Stools with the consistency of 'rabbit droppings' or 'toothpaste' may be abnormal. Mucus passage with the stool is almost certainly abnormal. Rectal bleeding definitely is.

For example, diarrhoea with blood and mucus is typical of ulcerative colitis. During an acute attack, patients may pass 10 to 20 motions of bloody diarrhoea during the day and night. Patients also tend to feel fatigued, lethargic and, not surprisingly, their appetite declines. Around 10 per cent of ulcerative colitis patients experience persistent symptoms. In others symptoms seem to wax and wane. A few endure a single attack, but in some cases the inflammation attacks other organs, including the eyes, joints and liver.

Ulcerative colitis overlaps with Crohn's disease. Ulcerative colitis tends to affect the colon, while Crohn's disease can develop anywhere from the mouth to the anus, but is most common in the small intestine. While ulcerative colitis is popularly considered to be a stress-related disease, the cause of these so-called inflammatory bowel diseases is unknown. One theory suggests that environmental factors, bacteria or a virus, for example, may trigger inflammation in genetically susceptible people. Stress probably does not cause inflammatory disease – although it undoubtedly makes sufferers feel worse.

IBS symptoms
* abdominal pain, sometimes eased by defecation * changes in bowel habit * dyspepsia * frequent loose stools at the start of pain * feelings of incomplete defecation * weight loss * lump in the throat * mucus with stools * nausea and vomiting * pain often exacerbated after eating * rumbling, gurgling stomach * urgent stools * unpleasant taste in the mouth

---

IBS risk factors

Certain factors increase your risk of developing IBS. For example, studies suggest that anxious, compulsive, over-conscientious, dependent, sensitive, guilty, unassertive and depressed people may be more likely to develop IBS. Nevertheless, not every anxious, compulsive and passive person develops IBS, so non-psychological factors must play a role.

Some IBS patients have hypersensitive bowels that over-react to stress, drugs, eating and wind. When doctors pass a small 'balloon' into the stomach and inflate it, these people report more discomfort than people who do not suffer from IBS. Hypersensitivity to 'gas' or 'bloating' may contribute to some IBS cases. Stress tends to make these patients even more sensitive. Other studies suggest that gastrointestinal motility of IBS patients differs from that among the healthy population. However, none of the findings have been consistent and none adequately explain why patients develop symptoms.

IBS: beyond the gut

In some ways, doctors' focus on the stomach is misplaced. IBS patients often report suffering from a variety of symptoms outside their gut (see box). The list is virtually a catalogue of stress-related illnesses. Indeed, some of the generalised symptoms are more common than many of the bowel complaints. For example, 20 per cent of IBS sufferers lose weight and around half suffer from a lump in the throat, nausea or both. However, over half of IBS sufferers complain of headaches and two-thirds of frequent urination. Over 90 per cent of female IBS sufferers complain of painful periods.

IBS symptoms: beyond the gut
* weakness * fatigue * muscle pains * insomnia * palpitations * nervousness * dizziness * excessive sweating * painful and frequent urination * painful periods * headaches

---

One problem facing doctors trying to assess the role of stress in IBS is that the disease is a stressor in its own right. In a recent study, 30 IBS patients completed diary cards. These revealed that when symptoms increased in severity, patients experienced more stress – measured as microlevel 'hassles' – the following week. The effects of stress may also be delayed: symptoms worsened a few days later. This suggests that patients become caught in a cycle where stress triggers IBS symptoms, which in turn exacerbate stress. Clearly, it is not enough just to treat IBS patients' guts.

Treat more than the gut

IBS patients may learn as children that certain symptoms are a socially acceptable way of dealing with stress. For example, IBS symptoms may help the child avoid responsibilities. They get the added bonus of concern and sympathy from parents and – later – healthcare professionals. A US survey of IBS sufferers found that they tended to receive gifts or were more likely to stay off school when ill as children. These traits persisted in adulthood. Compared to stomach ulcer sufferers, IBS patients view colds and flu more seriously. Indeed, many recognise that they suffer from a psychological disorder, but feel a medical disorder is socially more acceptable. IBS provides an excuse to seek help.

As a result, the first step in treatment is to discover what patients are doing when they experience symptoms. Keep a dairy noting the intensity, location and duration of the symptoms. Also write down what you were doing and thinking about before you suffered the symptoms. This may reveal associations that provide a starting point for therapy. However, in some cases the trigger occurs several days before symptoms emerge. Noting your mental state is as important as recording the physical symptoms. A person who has ignored symptoms for years may suddenly consult their doctor for 'IBS' after a relative is diagnosed as suffering from cancer, loses his or her job or gets divorced.

Next you can try a number of strategies to alleviate the symptoms. However, they do not alleviate the underlying cause and none is universally effective. Indeed, up to 70 per cent of patients taking an inactive (placebo) tablet who believe the pill contains an active ingredient report that their symptoms improve. However, diet and drugs may produce short-term relief while stress management or behavioural therapy begin to act.

- Eating at least 30g of fibre – around six slices of wholemeal bread – a day. This should relieve constipation. Prunes, leeks, onions and garlic may also alleviate constipation.
- Switching to a plain diet, such as simple fish and meat and a few vegetables benefits up to 70 per cent of IBS sufferers. Sticking to the diet can prove more of a problem.
- In a few people, milk and wheat trigger IBS, so if symptoms start after a milky breakfast try a wheat or milk substitute.
- Consider antidepressants or a tranquilliser if there is underlying depression or anxiety.
- Antispasmodic drugs relax the gastrointestinal tract, which may help if you are one of those IBS patients with abnormal gastrointestinal motility.
- Stress management techniques. IBS patients who underwent psychotherapy experienced fewer symptoms and less disability. Psychotherapy also helps patients learn to cope with criticism or disapproval, both of which may trigger IBS. However, it is not known if psychotherapy relieves symptoms more effectively than medical treatments
- Some IBS patients report benefiting from gut-directed autogenic training, marital therapy, biofeedback, hypnotherapy and homeopathy (see chapter six).
- Biofeedback teaches people with chronic constipation to relax their bowels.
- Hypnosis allows patients to modify their gut function. Around

80 per cent of IBS sufferers who undergo hypnosis report improvement in symptoms and well-being and less pain, distension and improved bowel habit. Stress undoubtedly exacerbates IBS. But its most important role may be to prompt people to seek medical help. Perhaps patients should ask themselves: why now?

The British Digestive Foundation* and the IBS Network* can offer advice and support to IBS sufferers.

Psychogenic vomiting

Almost everyone has felt sick with fear. However, in a few people, emotional problems cause recurrent and persistent vomiting. Often sufferers from this syndrome – psychogenic vomiting – are young or middle-aged women, who have endured emotional problems such as bereavement, separation or abuse. However, they usually report suffering from chronic or intermittent bouts of vomiting from childhood. The vomiting usually occurs at mealtimes, although sufferers tend not to suffer nausea. Moreover, they usually make it to the bathroom.

Certain traits may predispose people to psychogenic vomiting. Sufferers tend to have passive, rigid personalities and they avoid confrontations, even when the people around them are hostile. However, despite their frequent attacks of vomiting, they tend not to lose weight, become dehydrated or develop other physical problems. In these patients, vomiting becomes a form of communication – a way to express their anxiety and anger or to escape from stressful situations. Psychogenic vomiting may also allow sufferers to manipulate people around them. Treatment is similar to that of IBS and includes stress management and relaxation.

Migraine

Around one in ten people suffer from migraine. Migraine attacks may last from a few hours to two or three days. Often the attacks are unpredictable. Some patients suffer only one migraine attack a year. Others have two or three attacks a week. However, on average, sufferers experience one attack a month. Most migraine sufferers say that they feel washed out after an attack and it takes a day or two before they feel totally back to normal. For many, stress contributes to their headaches, which can leave sufferers laid up in a dark, quiet room for hours, even days, on end and thoroughly ruins their quality of life.

Migraine sufferers endure an intense, throbbing headache, usually localised over one side of the head. In around 80 to 90 per cent of migraine sufferers, nausea, sometimes vomiting, and a dislike of light and sound accompany the headache. These patients suffer from so-called common migraines. Most of the remainder experience classical migraine – the headache and other symptoms are preceded by a visual 'aura', which includes flashing lights and other visual hallucinations. The aura can last for an hour before the headache starts. In about a third of all migraine sufferers the first symptoms of an attack include euphoria, extreme tiredness, yawning or a craving for sweet foods such as chocolate. These subtle symptoms can be recognised only by keeping a migraine diary.

Migraine triggers

A variety of triggers can cause migraine including stress, alcohol and changed sleeping habits (see box). Many migraine sufferers seem to be hypersensitive to tyramine, an amino acid found in cheese, red wine, beer, chocolate, beef and a number of other common foods and drinks.

> **REBECCA** suffered from migraines – but only at weekends. After keeping a migraine diary, she traced her headaches to the Bordeaux she drank in the wine bar after work on a Friday night, her later bedtimes on Friday and Saturday night, the long lie-ins and the change in stress levels. Like many migraine sufferers, Rebecca suffers migraine when the pressure lifts rather than during the stressful time.

These diverse trigger factors share a common mechanism of action – they cause the blood vessels supplying the brain to swell. This swelling produces the throbbing headache. In classic migraine sufferers, blood vessels in the part of the brain controlling vision temporarily constrict; this produces the visual aura. It is followed by the dilation, which leads to the headache.

Migraine triggers
* alcohol * changes in sleeping pattern * coffee * drugs * exercise
* fatigue * foods e.g. chocolate, citrus fruits and cheese * hunger * low
blood sugar levels e.g. missing a meal * menstruation * stress * travel

---

However, doctors do not understand why certain triggers cause the blood vessels to swell.

In some people, a single factor triggers a migraine. In most, two or three triggers act together. Once the number of trigger factors passes a critical threshold, the patient develops the migraine. We all have a migraine threshold. Given enough trigger factors, anyone can experience a migraine. Moreover, the threshold for a migraine can change: for example, it may fall as women approach the menopause.

Migraine: a woman's lot?

Prepubescent boys and girls are equally likely to suffer from migraines. However, migraine, which usually starts in adolescence or early adulthood, is three times more common among women than men. Around a quarter of women suffer from migraine compared to eight per cent of men. This gender difference led some – predominately male – doctors to regard migraine as a neurotic disease. It also meant that they did not take the condition seriously.

However, migraine is gradually losing its neurotic reputation. Doctors now recognise that women's fluctuating hormone levels are partly responsible for their increased risk of migraine. Women suffering from hormonally triggered migraines do not produce abnormal levels of hormones – rather, they seem to be extremely sensitive to normal hormone levels during the menstrual cycle.

Around 15 per cent of women say that their migraines started in the same year as they began menstruating. Moreover, about 10 per cent of female sufferers experience migraine attacks only during the two or three days around the start of their period. This so-called menstrual migraine is most likely to emerge in a woman's 40s and seems to be triggered by falling oestrogen levels. Another 40 per cent of women attending migraine clinics report that the severity, frequency or duration of their attacks increases around the time of their period.

Three other observations suggest that falling oestrogen levels trigger migraines in sensitive women. First, some women taking oral contraceptives only experience migraines during their 'pill-free' week. Others find the pill reduces the severity of their headaches or changes the type of migraine from common to classic. Migraines aggravated by taking the pill often resolve if you continue to take the pill for three to six months. Alternatively, you may find switching brands alleviates the headache.

Secondly, pregnant women often report that migraines worsen during the first trimester. However, around 70 per cent of female migraine sufferers experience fewer migraines during the last six months of pregnancy. This improvement may reflect more stable hormone levels during the latter stages of pregnancy. Migraines can occur immediately after the birth of the baby when oestrogen levels suddenly fall, but more typically they re-emerge when periods start again.

Finally, declining oestrogen levels may underlie reports of increased frequency of migraine attacks during the menopause. Hormone replacement therapy (HRT) can stabilise oestrogen levels and alleviate the headaches. However, gels and skin patches may be more effective against migraine than tablets. Oestrogen blood levels are more consistent and predictable when the hormone is released from gels and patches than from tablets.

When to visit your doctor

Often there is no need to consult your GP for migraine. Indeed, 70 per cent of migraine sufferers treat their headaches themselves with over-the-counter treatments. However, you should consult your doctor when severe headaches persist, when your headache starts after a blow to the head or when your symptoms are different to normal. Visiting your GP also ensures that you really do suffer from migraine. Even doctors can find it difficult to distinguish migraine and some of the other causes of headaches. Tension, concussion, tumours, haemorrhages, drugs and referred pain can all cause headaches that may mimic migraines.

How to help yourself

You can take a number of steps to alleviate the misery of migraines.

- Look at your lifestyle. Eat regularly, drink plenty of fluids and follow regular sleep patterns. Try not to lie in too long over the weekend.

- Keep a migraine diary: note the date, day, time, symptoms, intensity and duration of the attack. You should also note anything you feel contributed to the attack, such as stress, diet or alcohol consumption. After identifying your trigger factors, split them into those you can control (such as missing a meal; drinking red wine) and those you cannot (your period). Cut out trigger factors one by one.
- If you lead a busy or stressed life, learn relaxation techniques. Exercise is a good way to relax. However, exercise both triggers and alleviates migraine attacks. Regular exercise reduces stress, stabilises blood sugar levels, relieves muscle tension and increases the amount of oxygen getting to your brain. In contrast, erratic exercise often means you push your body to its limits. As a result, blood sugar levels drop dramatically, which can trigger a migraine. Taking glucose tablets before you work out can prevent this.

Treating migraine's misery

To relieve the pain of an acute attack lie down in a dark, quiet room and take simple painkillers, such as soluble aspirin or paracetamol. Many people find anti-sickness medicines settle their stomach. Experiment with the acute migraine remedies available from your pharmacist. For example, Midrid contains paracetamol and isometheptene mucate, which reverses the expansion of blood vessels. Migraleve combines paracetamol, codeine – a painkiller – and buclizine, which alleviates nausea. A number of other treatments are available so talk to your pharmacist. To gain the most benefit, these over-the-counter remedies should be taken as early as possible during the attack. Other migraine drugs are available on prescription, such as sumatriptan, which constricts the swollen blood vessels. Doctors tend to prescribe the expensive drugs only if your migraines are particularly debilitating or you experience more than two attacks a month.

A number of complementary therapies also alleviate the misery of migraines. Overall, preventative techniques each work in around 30 per cent of people, so you should try to tailor the treatment to your migraine.

- Biofeedback can train people to control the diameter of their blood vessels. This allows them to shrink the swollen blood vessels that cause the throbbing headache.

- Homeopathy, hypnosis and cognitive therapy reduce the frequency, intensity and duration of migraine attacks.
- The herb feverfew reduces the frequency and intensity of migraine attacks. Feverfew also seems to relieve some of the other migraine symptoms including vomiting. However, herbalists warn that pregnant women should not take feverfew, as it can cause miscarriage.
- Around 60 per cent of migraine sufferers benefit from acupuncture, usually after six or eight sessions. However, migraine tends to re-emerge after between 12 and 18 months. One or two more acupuncture sessions usually restore the benefits.
- Osteopaths and chiropractors also claim to help migraine sufferers. They argue that some cases of migraine are caused by inflammation and structural problems in the spine. One study of 85 people found that manipulation alleviated migraine. Patients who suffer from migraines and endure stiff, painful necks may have the most to gain from manipulation. However, neither form of manipulation seemed to be more effective than the other.

The British Migraine Association* and the Migraine Trust* offer further advice and support. Patients with migraine can be referred by their GPs to the City of London Migraine Clinic*.

Tension headaches

Patients suffering from tension headaches report feeling a tight band around their heads, pressure behind their eyes and a feeling that their throbbing head is about to burst. The scalp and the neck muscles may feel tender. However, muscle tension probably does not directly cause tension headaches. Nevertheless, a number of factors seem to trigger tension headaches, including heat, noise and concentrated visual effort, such as staring at a computer screen. In some cases, tension headaches can be a physical manifestation of depression.

Treatment usually involves reassuring patients that their symptoms do not mean that they are suffering from a sinister disease, advising them to avoid any trigger factors and suggesting that they take painkillers. Many patients find relaxation, massage, meditation and other stress management techniques reduce the severity and frequency of headaches. Biofeedback seems to help around 60 per cent of tension headache sufferers. If depression contributes to the headache, patients may benefit from a course of antidepressants.

Chronic pain

Pain evolved to keep us out of harm's way. If something hurts enough, you are unlikely to do it again. However, there are two types of pain, each with a distinct biological function. Acute pain is caused by tissue damage. It is a signal that something is wrong and you should get away from the cause of the pain, so when you cut your finger you feel acute pain, which is short-lived. The body's natural opioids quickly dampen the pain to allow you to escape from the immediate threat. Acute pain is often accompanied by increased heart beat and sweating. However, the intensity of pain does not reflect the extent of tissue damage. Attention, anxiety, suggestion, previous experiences and other psychological factors influence the pain sensation.

Chronic pain, in contrast, lasts for at least a month and sufferers do not tend to show raised heart beat and sweating. In a third of sufferers, doctors can find no physical cause for the pain. Despite this, sufferers may feel helpless, depressed and that their lives are out of control. They may withdraw from their social life. Moreover, the quest for effective pain relief often means that patients concentrate on their pain, undermining their quality of life. Patients may limit their activities, even to the point where their disability – rather than the pain – becomes the major problem. Finally, patients may experience prejudice and misunderstanding. You cannot share someone's pain, and chronic pain sufferers are often branded as malingerers. However, even the depression and withdrawal associated with chronic pain may have biological roles to play. Once we have survived the immediate threat, we feel depressed and withdraw. This inactivity allows our bodies to heal.

Treating chronic pain

Obviously analgesics – painkillers – are the mainstay of treatment for chronic pain. These include drugs like aspirin, paracetamol and ibuprofen and opiate analgesics, such as morphine. Although tarnished by the reputation of street heroin abuse, opiate analgesics are highly effective and there seems to be no risk of addiction when used as painkillers. Antidepressants may also help. Antidepressants alleviate the anxiety and depression caused by chronic pain. However, they also have direct painkilling actions that emerge at lower doses than their antidepressant action. In severe cases, patients may undergo neurosurgery – but cutting nerves rarely relieves pain.

Many chronic pain sufferers benefit from psychotherapy, which reduces their distress, disability and drug consumption. Getting the whole family involved is essential. Chronic pain sufferers can make excessive demands on their families. Psychological therapy does not primarily aim to alleviate pain – rather, it aims to help patients cope with their disability. However, as the sensation of pain is intimately intertwined with emotions and anxiety, pain relief often follows successful psychotherapy.

Back pain

Back pain is one of the most common stress-related diseases – which is not surprising if you consider that our poor postures and sedentary lifestyle further weaken one of the weakest parts of the skeleton. You can suffer pain anywhere along your spine. However, the lower back is the most common site of discomfort. If one of the discs of cartilage between the vertebrae bulges – a so-called 'slipped' disc – it can press on the sciatic nerve. This means pain can radiate from the lower back to the buttocks, legs and feet – a problem known as sciatica.

Around one in five people consult their doctor because of low back pain some time during their lives. Around a fifth of these claim their back pain was caused at work, and low back pain does impose a major economic burden, accounting for almost 100 million lost working days a year. However, even this huge economic burden may underestimate the scale of the problem. Surveys suggest that 60 per cent of people experience back pain during any fortnight.

Low back pain tends to be a disease affecting middle-aged, manual workers. Partly this reflects the nature of the job. It is easier to damage your back if you are spreading asphalt than if you are constructing a spreadsheet. However, constant sitting is also a risk factor, along with pregnancy and shift work. Even improving the back's strength, fitness and flexibility does not seem to protect you from low back pain, and the extent of spinal damage does not seem to reflect the severity of the symptoms. X-rays reveal that some people have prominent 'slipped' disks, without experiencing symptoms. This has led doctors to search for other causes of low back pain.

For a while, stress was a prime suspect. Some doctors believed that anxious people had a lower pain threshold, so they were more likely to report suffering low back pain. Moreover, stress often causes muscle tension. Lifting a heavy object triggered low back pain, but the physical trauma acted on a back already weakened by muscle tension.

However, doctors now regard anxiety and depression as the consequences – rather than the causes – of low back pain. Nevertheless, they may influence patients' ability to cope with low back pain. For example, depression can undermine the patient's motivation to get better. Anxiety can also exacerbate pain. So while anxiety, depression and stress probably do not cause low back pain, they can slow your recovery and exacerbate your suffering.

Treating low back pain

Traditionally, patients suffering from low back pain have received painkillers and been told to lie on their back for between two and three weeks. However, lying in bed for as little as a week reduces muscle mass and strength. So this approach further weakens your back and the analgesics mask the pain.

Bed rest is now replaced by physiotherapy, osteopathy, chiropractic and other manipulative techniques. Almost a half of osteopathic consultations are now for low back pain. Osteopaths believe that most cases of back pain are caused by spinal abnormalities. However, back pain may also be caused by other conditions, including arthritis, tumours and osteoporosis (brittle bone disease). Osteopaths admit that they are unable to cure some cases of back pain caused by these other conditions, but they may be able to relieve the pain and stress.

Acupuncture is also effective: some 65 per cent of patients respond after a course of six treatments. However, the improvement may begin to wear off after six to nine months and may need to be repeated. These complementary approaches are helping more low back pain sufferers get back on their feet.

Contact the National Back Pain Association* for further information and advice.

Asthma

Each year more than nine million people suffer from bouts of wheezing, up to three million people suffer asthma and around two million consult their GP. Moreover, asthma seems to be becoming more common. Most asthmatics are now well managed by GPs and practice nurses, but over 100,000 are admitted to hospital each year – double the number in the mid-1970s – and in 1993, 1,877 asthmatics died. Experts believe better management could prevent 80 per cent of asthma deaths.

Better management may mean more than controlling breathlessness, wheezing and other asthmatic symptoms. Psychological and social factors may contribute to almost three-quarters of asthmatic deaths. For example, doctors in East Anglia recently reviewed 24 deaths from asthma and found that 17 patients endured deprived and stress-provoking social circumstances, such as bad housing, homelessness and unemployment. These problems can exacerbate asthma. For example, mould – a common asthma trigger – is widespread in poor housing. The doctors also assessed psychological factors in 20 of the deaths. Twelve showed signs of mental illness, such as deliberate self-harm or alcohol abuse. The survey also suggested that only half the asthmatics received regular medical care. Moreover, around half the patients and relatives failed to seek help when the asthma began to worsen.

Not surprisingly, suffering a near-fatal asthma attack can leave patients and their families experiencing anger, anxiety and considerable stress. Carers may become over-involved and over-protective. Patients may become over-dependent on relatives and medical staff. A survey suggested that almost 60 per cent of people who experience a near-fatal asthma attack show high levels of denial. However, if patients enter denial they may stop taking the drugs that control their asthma. Counselling and a frank discussion with the GP or practice nurse may help reduce the psychological toll exerted by asthma.

Treating asthma

Asthma is caused when a trigger – for example, pollen, exercise or the faeces of the house dust mite – causes the airways to narrow. In most cases this is an allergic reaction. The trigger causes the lining of the airway to become inflamed and swollen, which reduces the airway's diameter and limits the amount of oxygen getting to the lung. Patients may suffocate during severe asthma attacks. While some people go through symptom-free periods – especially if the allergen is seasonal such as pollen – most experience bad patches throughout their lives. This means that almost all asthmatics need to take drugs to control the underlying inflammation and to relieve the symptoms of an acute attack.

Bronchodilators relieve asthma by re-opening airways. However, bronchodilators do not reduce inflammation, so relying on them alone is dangerous and may prove fatal. Unless you suffer from very mild asthma – for example, if you only wheeze during exercise – you probably need to take anti-inflammatories. These include sodium cromoglycate and the inhaled steroids, such as budesonide, fluticasone and beclomethasone, to reduce the risk of a future attack.

Asthma is common, debilitating, stressful and potentially fatal and you should not underestimate its dangers. While stress does not cause asthma, psychological factors seem to exacerbate an already distressing disease and may undermine control. Nevertheless, the effective treatments now available, taking sensible precautions and watching for signs of deteriorating symptoms, mean that most asthmatics can live normal, active lives.

Contact the National Asthma Campaign* for further information and advice.

Eczema

Eczema is one of the most visible, unpleasant and disfiguring diseases. Sufferers endure dry, itchy, inflamed skin that can blister, weep, thicken and crack. Eczema patients' suffering is literally on show and many people regard skin diseases with distaste, which exacerbates the person's stress.

Many eczema patients are children and they often make their condition worse by scratching. Most children suffering from eczema first developed symptoms between the ages of six months and two years, so they are too young to understand their disease and its treatment. They may be unable to sleep, and make constant demands on their parents – which can leave the entire family tired and irritable. Eczema can be an intensely stressful experience for parents, although they can draw some comfort from the long-term outlook. Around half of children with eczema improve by school age. Around 90 per cent of cases resolve during adolescence. However, some eczema patients suffer exacerbations for the rest of their life.

What is eczema?
Eczema can be broadly divided into contact or allergic eczema. Essentially, contact eczema is triggered by an environmental irritant, such as a chemical. Some children develop contact eczema which disappears after changing the bubble bath or the washing powder. Allergic eczema results from a hypersensitive immune system which overreacts to something most people find innocuous, for example the faeces of the house dust mite or animal dander – flakes of skin and fur.

Sufferers often report that stress exacerbates their eczema. Testing this is difficult. Nevertheless, people with allergic eczema tend to be more anxious and neurotic and experience more problems dealing with hostility and anger than the rest of the population. However, this begs a fundamental question: did stress, anxiety and hostility predate the eczema? Or was the psychological distress caused by the prejudice and suffering caused by eczema? Nobody really knows. The relationship between stress and eczema is one of those chicken and egg questions. Nevertheless, reducing stress often helps patients cope with their disease.

Treating eczema
Currently eczema cannot be cured. You can try to avoid trigger

factors, but this can prove difficult, so treatment aims to soothe inflamed skin.

- Adding emollients to the bath removes crusty skin scales and moisturises the skin. You can also apply emollients directly to the areas affected by eczema after a bath. Also, try applying emollients before swimming in a pool – chlorine can worsen eczema. You may have to try several emollients before finding one you or your child prefers.
- Try to bathe daily; pat rather than rub yourself dry.
- Heat exacerbates the itching so keep the skin cool.
- Try soap substitutes.
- Ask your pharmacist for further information.
- Antihistamine tablets may relieve itching. Some antihistamines make you drowsy and so may help you sleep.
- Steroid creams and ointment are highly effective. However, the risk of side-effects means that they are usually applied only to limited areas for a short time.
- Keep nails cut short. This means any inadvertent scratching is less likely to damage the skin (damaged skin is more likely to become infected). Children may prefer wearing mittens.
- Many people are allergic to the faeces of the house dust mite, which lives in warm, damp places and feeds on shed skin cells – beds are their ideal habitat. Dusting, vacuuming, covering mattresses and pillows with plastic sheets available from chemists, and keeping the sufferer's room cool and well ventilated can help. Putting soft toys in the freezer for six hours every week can reduce the number of house dust mites using teddy as a home.
- Fur and flakes of skin shed by household pets are another common eczema trigger, so make sure you or your child wash after stroking the animal, and keep pets off bedding.
- Sleep on cotton bedclothes.
- Minimise stress. Try some of the techniques outlined in the directory (chapter six). Whether or not stress exacerbates eczema, relaxation reduces scratching and alleviates anxiety.

If eczema does not respond to the treatments outlined above, GPs may refer the patient to a dermatologist, who can instigate more aggressive therapies. The National Eczema Society* offers further advice and support.

Food and nutritional supplements

In severe cases, even hospital therapies may fail to alleviate eczema. Moreover, many people worry about the side-effects of drugs. As a result, many eczema sufferers try complementary therapies. Some of these seem to work. Around 15 per cent of children with eczema benefit from evening primrose oil, which seems to alleviate inflammation. However, they need to take evening primrose oil supplements for around three months before the maximum benefits emerge.

Chinese and western herbalism may both alleviate eczema. The recent success of traditional Chinese herbalism where conventional medicines had failed has been well publicised. For example, in one study, half the children treated with a herbal tea obtained at least a 50 per cent reduction in symptoms. Chinese herbs seem to be especially effective against itching. However, some doctors have questioned the safety of Chinese herbal medicine and it certainly has not been tested as rigorously as most Western medicines. Western herbalists use marigold tea to alleviate itching, blisters and flaking skin. Marigold ointment, available from some health food shops, may also soothe the skin.

The role of food triggers in eczema is more controversial. Keeping an accurate diary of the frequency and severity of your symptoms and diet for a month or six weeks may indicate if food exacerbates your eczema. Milk, dairy products, wheat, tomatoes and citrus fruits are the most common eczema triggers. You can then see if excluding a suspected trigger from your diet alleviates symptoms. However, following exclusion diets can cause considerable stress – for the patient as well as the chef. Moreover, most exclusion diets need to be designed by experts: excluding dairy products and eggs, for example, can cause nutritional problems.

Some people find that a number of other therapies – such as acupuncture, hypnosis and homeopathy – alleviate their eczema. However, patients using homeopathy may experience a transitory exacerbation of their symptoms. Your homeopath will probably advise you to temporarily stop taking the remedy if the worsening lasts for more than a few days.

Counselling, psychotherapy, group and cognitive therapies help sufferers cope with eczema. Behavioural treatment and autogenic therapy may help patients break the cycle of itching prompting scratching, which damages the skin and leads to more irritation, scratching and damage. Even simple relaxation can help reduce the anxiety and stress caused by eczema. (See chapter six for more on all these treatments.)

Bed-wetting

Bed-wetting is one of the most common stress signals among children. A few cases are caused by urinary tract infections, bladder disorders or diabetes. However, most children who wet their beds do so in response to emotional or psychological stress.

Most children gain control of their bladders as toddlers. Three-quarters of children are dry overnight by the age of three-and-a-half years. By the age of five, 80 to 90 per cent are dry. However, the birth of a new baby may result in older siblings bed-wetting – an example of regression. In many children, bed-wetting (or enuresis) is a short-lived problem. Half of nocturnal enuresis sufferers grow out of their problem within four years. However, one or two per cent of young adults still wet their beds.

Nocturnal enuresis tends to cause the child considerable distress – which they may be unable to express – and undermines their self-confidence and self-esteem. Sometimes, especially if bed-wetting is infrequent, reassurance and understanding will do the trick. However, 15 per cent of sufferers wet the bed virtually every night, 35 per cent more than once a week, and half more than once a month. Apart from being unpleasant and causing considerable stress for sufferers and their families, bed-wetting bumps up the laundry costs.

Alarms that sound when the child wets the bed may help to retrain the bladder. Using alarms, around 70 per cent of older children are completely dry within 16 weeks. However, between 10 and 40 per cent relapse within two years. You could also try star charts and other incentives. In more difficult cases, doctors can prescribe drugs, but children almost invariably relapse when they stop taking them. Nevertheless, drugs can also help keep children dry in potentially embarrassing situations – going on holiday or to camp, for example. The Enuresis Advice and Information Centre* offers an information pack and helpline.

CHAPTER 5

STRESS AND MENTAL ILLNESS

ONE IN FOUR people seek help for mental problems some time during their lives. Each year, 12 million people consult their GP because they are suffering from mental symptoms. Seven million people suffer from a serious mental disorder, such as severe depression, phobia or schizophrenia. However, despite mental illness being more common than cancer, GPs fail to recognise mental disorders in 40 per cent of the mentally ill who come through the surgery door. Many more suffer in silence and never consult a doctor.

This chapter focuses on the two most common stress-related mental disorders – depression and anxiety. Together, they make up around 80 per cent of GPs' mental health workload. However, the two diseases overlap considerably. Between 60 and 90 per cent of patients with serious depression also suffer significant levels of anxiety, which may mask underlying depression. Not surprisingly, suffering from anxiety and depression tends to make both diseases worse. Depression tends to be more prolonged and less likely to respond to treatment if the patient also suffers from anxiety.

Depression

PAUL had everything going for him – or so it seemed. He was a systems analyst with a leading merchant bank. His wife, a secondary school geography teacher, had just given birth to their first child. They lived in an 'executive' development in Surrey. But beneath the surface Paul's well-controlled life was falling apart.

Paul's immediate superior was the boss from hell: excessively critical, unfairly demanding and taking credit for Paul's innovations. Paul, faced with the added responsibility of the new baby, felt he could not jeopardise his job by standing his ground. The family income fell substantially after his wife left her teaching job and the financial problems were mounting. Paul began drinking heavily: two or three cans of special strength lager on the train home each night, followed by several whiskies during the evening. He also kept a bottle of vodka in his desk drawer to spike his coffee after particularly bad sessions with his boss. Fortunately, he didn't need to drive – he lived within staggering distance of the station.

Not surprisingly, Paul's work began to suffer – which handed his boss more ammunition. The drinking began to drain his depleted bank account. The arguments with his wife, who was suffering a bout of post-natal depression, got more intense. Paul struggled on, determined not to give in. He tried talking to his father whose advice was to 'pull himself together', followed by a long lecture about how much harder it was when he was young.

However, Paul was feeling worse by the day. He would wake at 3am and not be able to get back to sleep. He suffered constant headaches, muscle tension and vague aches and pains. Eventually, Paul consulted his GP. The GP saw through Paul's excuse of fatigue and prescribed antidepressants. But the antidepressants made Paul feel terrible. His mouth was always dry, he gained weight and was constipated. To make matters worse, the tablets undermined what remained of his concentration and interacted with alcohol. So instead of stopping the alcohol he stopped the antidepressants.

Then a month into his breakdown, Paul was given a formal warning about the quality of his work. The bank was being 'restructured' and Paul was an easy target to fire without having to pay redundancy. Paul's mind ran riot. He would lose his home. His child would be taken into care. His wife would leave him. Paul couldn't see how unjustified his thoughts had become. He became obsessed with the thought that he had failed – not just himself, but his wife and his child. He would be the first member of his family to be on the dole. He thought of the humiliation and the comments behind his back from his neighbours. They would be better off without him. In any case, he'd had enough. Paul did not return home from work that night.

Three nights later, the police pulled Paul's body from the Thames.

Paul isn't alone. Between two and three million people in the UK suffer depression. Despite their suffering, despite their increased risk of suicide, despite the effective treatments now available, at least 370,000 people with moderate-to-severe depression may currently be untreated. Some are treated for vague symptoms and complaints, such as irritable bowel syndrome or persistent headaches, without their GPs ever getting to the root of their patients' suffering. However, at least 25 per cent of people with marked depression never consult their GP. Of those that do, GPs fail to recognise depression in about half – probably because many patients don't directly consult their GP about depression.

In some cases, people suffering from depression may not realise that they are ill. Depression can creep up on patients. Others regard depression as an appropriate reaction to a life event such as unemployment or bereavement. Others hope the symptoms will go away, fear the stigma that still, wrongly, surrounds mental illness or fear becoming addicted (though in fact antidepressants are non-addictive). Others believe that they are weak, lazy or feeble and that they must not give in. They struggle on living a life of abject despair. So sometimes it is up to the relatives to persuade the patient to seek treatment.

What is depression?

Major depression is far more than the 'blues'. Unless you've suffered severe – also called major – depression, it is hard to appreciate sufferers' mental torment. Depression undermines a patient's quality of life more than many other chronic diseases including arthritis, hypertension, diabetes and back pain. Only heart disease has a bigger impact.

Depression is a crushing feeling of being unable to cope with life that produces a number of symptoms (see box). In some

---

Symptoms of depression
* loss of interest and enjoyment in life * feeling useless, inadequate, bad and helpless *lack of drive and motivation * avoiding meeting people * agitation or restlessness * irritability * change in appetite or weight * feeling worse at certain times of the day * insomnia or excessive sleepiness * suicidal thoughts * fatigue * loss of sexual interest * few displays of affection * loss of self-confidence

---

cases, the intense mental torment drives patients to suicide. About 15 per cent of people suffering from recurrent episodes of major depression ultimately kill themselves and 20 to 40 per cent of patients with depression show suicidal behaviour.

The cause of these symptoms is a mystery. Depressed patients show abnormalities in their brain chemistry (see below). But often the cause of these chemical changes cannot be pinned down. Some estimates suggest that 80 per cent of depression arises in response to a stressful life event and some psychiatrists regard depression as an 'out-of-control' stress response. Certainly, depression may be a reaction to physical illness, bereavement, stress or overwork. However, there are other causes.

For example, women are more likely to develop depression than men. Around 12 per cent of men and a quarter of women suffer from major depression at some time in their lives. Partly this difference reflects women's fluctuating hormones. Depression is common during the menopause and after child-birth. However, these 'biological' depressions do not account for all the extra cases among women and social factors may also be important. Men may be less likely to admit their feelings to them-selves – let alone a doctor. They may bottle up their emotions, or express their distress as bouts of aggression or drinking.

Even the seasons can play a part. People with seasonal affective disorder (SAD) experience mild-to-moderate depression during the autumn and winter. They may sleep more, crave carbohy-drates, lack energy, feel fatigued and suffer headaches during the winter. At least these sufferers get some respite: the symptoms tend to resolve in the spring and summer and improve with light therapy. The Seasonal Affective Disorder Association[*] helps patients with this type of depression.

Treating depression

Don't underestimate depression. Remember the symptoms are so crippling that 15 per cent of sufferers commit suicide. However, depression can be effectively treated. Drugs, psychotherapy and meditation all alleviate mild depression. Choose the approach you're most comfortable with, although drugs may alleviate the symptoms more rapidly.

Drugs are by far the most effective treatment for moderate and severe depression. Between 60 and 85 per cent of patients report an improvement in their symptoms after taking antidepressants. Modern antidepressants are so effective that only one in 100 people with depression is admitted to a mental hospital. In the rare cases where drugs fail, doctors still have a few options. Electroconvulsive therapy, which has something of a tarnished image, can alleviate depression. Another option is to combine the antidepressant with lithium, a drug more commonly used to manage manic depression.

Long-term treatment

Once you are over the acute symptoms, you'll probably need long-term treatment. Most psychiatrists believe that patients should continue to take antidepressants for four to six months after recovering from a bout of depression. However, while drugs remain the mainstay of treatment you can take a few simple steps that may take the edge off your symptoms and reduce the risk of a relapse. Some of these might be enough to resolve mild depression – although be careful not to underestimate the severity of your symptoms.

- Try to develop social supports. Friends and a sympathetic family make handling difficult situations easier.
- Talk to someone. Work through your pain. Cry. Simply telling someone how terrible you feel can help. You could consider counselling or psychotherapy, which may help you understand the source of your stress and depression and offer a new perspective on your problems. However, both require a degree of commitment that is difficult when your motivation and energy are at a low ebb.
- Depression can result from marital difficulties or bereavement. Relate*, Compassionate Friends*, Cruse* and other self-help groups can help with specific problems. Remember the Samaritans* are always at the end of a phone.
- Learn about depression: the Royal College of Psychiatrists* publishes information leaflets on depression and runs the Defeat Depression* campaign. Self-help groups such as the Depression Alliance* and MIND* also offer advice and support.

- Don't just sit there brooding. While motivating yourself can be difficult, try to walk around the shops or through the country, do some housework or gardening. This will keep you fit and help you sleep. Exercise also distracts you from your worries and helps lift your mood. Sitting brooding makes you feel worse.

- Early morning waking is one of the hallmarks of depression. Typically, patients wake around 4am and cannot get back to sleep. However, other sleep disorders are also common. If you cannot sleep, follow the tips on good sleep hygiene (page 170).

- Eat a healthy diet. People with depression often do not feel like eating – or they eat only chocolates or junk food. However, a poor diet makes you feel even worse. Not eating enough exacerbates fatigue, for example. There may also be a biological motive underlying carbohydrate craving. People suffering from depression may find eating frequent, high carbohydrate meals lifts their depression. Studies show that high carbohydrate foods boost levels of serotonin in the brain. However, some proteins can interfere with carbohydrate's effects. So you are better off eating pasta, rice and bread than cakes and chocolate, which contain small amounts of protein.

- You can't drown depression in alcohol. Rather, depression feeds on alcohol. Alcoholics are almost twice as likely as non-alcoholics to suffer depression. If you're depressed and drink, remember that alcohol is more likely to trigger depression than vice versa. Depression rarely leads to alcohol abuse. Only around 5 per cent of depressed patients become alcoholics. Despite this, even moderate drinking can be dangerous for people with depression: alcohol interacts with certain antidepressants increasing your likelihood of developing side effects. *If you suffer from depression, don't drink.*

- Remember that thousands of people have recovered from depression. Indeed, you can emerge better able to cope with life than before. You may gain a new perspective, and depression can act as a spur to change your life. For some people, depression improves the rest of their lives.

How antidepressants work

Understanding how antidepressants work means making a brief diversion into pharmacology, the science that studies the biological effects of drugs. The nerves carry messages to and from the brain.

These messages are transmitted along nerves as electrical impulses. When an electrical impulse reaches the end of a nerve it triggers the release of chemical messengers, known as neurotransmitters. These diffuse across a small gap to another nerve where they bind to specialised proteins – called receptors – on the nerve's surface. This binding is specific, rather like a key fitting into a lock. The binding switches on a complicated chemical cascade in the nerve cell, which biologists are only beginning to understand, and the message continues its journey around the nervous system.

There are more than 50 neurotransmitters. Some neurotransmitters, like acetylcholine, increase the nerve's activity. Other neurotransmitters, such as gamma-aminobutyric acid (GABA), inhibit the nerve's activity. The balance between these rival neurotransmitters determines whether the electrical impulse is passed along to the next nerve.

Many drugs work by binding to the receptors, thereby changing the balance of nervous activity. Some drugs, known as antagonists, bind to the receptor without stimulating it. This blocks the natural neurotransmitter from binding to the receptor. In contrast, agonists bind to and stimulate the receptor. In other words, agonists mimic the action of the natural transmitter.

So to return to depression. One major group of neurotransmitters, known as the monoamines, contains adrenaline, noradrenaline, dopamine and serotonin. Low brain levels of monoamines, experts believe, may underlie depression. This insight came after investigations into two drugs, reserpine and amphetamine, in the late 1950s. Reserpine, derived from an Indian herb, was used to treat hypertension. However, up to 15 per cent of people treated with reserpine developed severe depression. Pharmacologists noted that reserpine depleted monoamine stores in the brain.

Around the same time, pharmacologists were investigating amphetamine's mode of action. Amphetamine is a popular drug of abuse because it boosts users' energy and makes them feel euphoric. Researchers discovered that amphetamine increases the brain's sensitivity to monoamines. These observations made monoamines the prime suspect as the chemical culprit underlying depression. Since then monoamine neurotransmitters – especially serotonin – have been implicated in other disorders, including obsessive-compulsive disease, panic disorder, alcoholism and obesity.

Antidepressants normalise monoamine levels. The actions of monoamines are curtailed in part by being taken back up into the nerve ending. One group of antidepressants – the tricyclic antidepressants – act by blocking reuptake of serotonin and noradrenaline. Another group, the selective serotonin reuptake inhibitors (SSRI), block only the reuptake of serotonin. The monoamines' actions are also curtailed by an enzyme called monoamine oxidase. The monoamine oxidase inhibitors increase levels of the neurotransmitter by inhibiting this enzyme. All these mechanisms ultimately restore levels of monoamines in the patient's brain. A number of less commonly used drugs re-establish this balance in a number of other ways.

However, restoring the brain's chemical balance takes time, so patients have to take antidepressants for up to four weeks before their depressed mood begins to lift; some symptoms such as anxiety, insomnia and tension may improve more rapidly. There is little to choose between the antidepressants for efficacy – all resolve the symptoms. The real differences emerge when you look at their side effects.

Tricyclic antidepressants

Tricyclic antidepressants – for example, dothiepin, amitriptyline, imipramine and desipramine – have been available for over 40 years. They remain the most widely used group of antidepressants, mainly because they are cheap. However, tricyclic antidepressants cause a large number of side effects. Between 27 and 60 per cent of patients taking tricyclic antidepressants discontinue treatment, largely as a result of these side effects.

In certain circumstances, the side effects are dangerous. Tricyclic antidepressants can cause blurred vision, disorientation, drowsiness, lethargy and sedation, and reduce hand-eye co-ordination. These side effects conspire to undermine a patient's driving ability. An analysis of nearly 500 road accidents revealed patients taking tricyclic antidepressants were more than twice as likely to be involved in an accident than other drivers. Among patients taking higher doses of tricyclic antidepressants the risk increased sixfold. Indeed, tricyclic antidepressants may impair driving ability more than the legal limit of alcohol.

The side effects of tricyclic antidepressants are dose-related: the higher the dose the more likely the patient is to develop them. As a result, many GPs prescribe a low dose to limit side effects. However, for between 75 and 80 per cent of patients taking tricyclic antidepressants, the dose is too low to be effective. Whether patients stop taking antidepressants or whether the GP prescribes an ineffective dose, the outcome is the same: the depression remains untreated.

Monoamine Oxidase Inhibitors

Monoamine Oxidase Inhibitors (MAOIs) block the action of the enzyme that breaks down monoamine neurotransmitters. There are two types of monoamine oxidase (MAO). MAO-A tends to break down serotonin and noradrenaline. MAO-B tends to metabolise dopamine and certain dietary monoamines, such as the amino acid tyramine, found in cheese, Marmite, beer, pickled herring, soy sauce and a number of other foods and drinks. However, there is a certain overlap between the two enzymes.

The first generation of MAOIs were non-selective: they blocked both MAO-A and B. But if you inhibit MAO-B, dietary tyramine is not broken down, and excess levels of tyramine can trigger a potentially dangerous rise in blood pressure. So patients taking the early MAOIs have to avoid certain foods.

The second generation of MAOIs are more selective for MAO-A. However, their selectivity is not absolute. Patients who consume large amounts of monoamines could still suffer the rise in blood pressure. Furthermore, conventional MAOIs bind permanently with MAO, so to overcome their action your body has to synthesise the new enzyme. As a result the effects of conventional MAOIs take several days to wear off after you stop taking the drug.

Moclobemide is the first of a new class of drugs – known as RIMAs (Reversible Inhibitors of Monoamine Oxidase A) – that selectively and reversibly block MAO-A. This means that MAO-B can metabolise tyramine and patients don't have to avoid monoamine-rich foods. Moreover, moclobemide's effects wear off more rapidly than those of conventional MAOIs.

SSRIs and the problem of Prozac

Prozac, the leading selective serotonin reuptake inhibitor (SSRI), is probably the best known antidepressant. Fluoxetine – Prozac's active ingredient – is a member of a group of related antidepressants that also includes citalopram, nefazodone, venlafaxine, sertraline, fluvoxamine and paroxetine. All act by blocking the reuptake of serotonin back into the nerve terminal.

The SSRIs have several advantages over conventional MAOIs and tricyclics. For example, because the SSRIs do not inhibit MAO, patients do not have to restrict their diets. As SSRIs are more selective they cause fewer and less serious side effects than the tricyclics. For example, SSRIs are non-sedating, don't cause dry mouth and blurred vision, do not promote weight gain and do not interact with alcohol to the same extent as tricyclics. And because the SSRIs do not inhibit MAO, patients do not have to restrict their diets. However, the SSRIs do cause side effects, most commonly impotence in men and an inability to experience an orgasm in women, as well as nausea, diarrhoea and headaches. Most of these usually wear off quickly, although the effect on sexual performance may be more persistent. SSRIs are also relatively safe in overdose, which is important for drugs used by people prone to suicide.

Despite its efficacy and relatively benign side effect profile, Prozac has been dogged by other concerns. For example, in one study six patients reported increased suicidal thoughts during the first few weeks of treatment. This lead to a re-examination of the link between Prozac and suicidal tendencies. Overall, the number of patients who reported experiencing suicidal thoughts was lower among Prozac users (1.2 per cent) than those receiving tricyclics (3.6 per cent) or inactive placebo (2.6 per cent). Other reports suggest that Prozac may promote aggressive behaviour – even turn previously mild-mannered people into manic killers. While these claims gained much media coverage, no firm link between Prozac and increased violence has been proved.

But there are other problems. Over the years, Prozac and the other SSRIs emerged as effective treatments for a wide range of mental disorders including obsessive-compulsive disorder, social phobia and obesity. However, some people claim that Prozac has the power to transform their personalities – even if they have no diagnosed mental illness. They claim it makes them feel more confident, less emotionally impoverished and less melancholy.

These more extreme claims have yet to be proven; the evidence is largely anecdotal. The danger is that the hype surrounding Prozac diverts attention from its undoubted safety and efficacy in a number of debilitating and serious mental illnesses.

Electro-convulsive therapy

Electro-convulsive therapy (ECT) seems to shock depression into submission – but it also seems to run counter to common sense. We protect ourselves from electric shocks during the rest of our lives. ECT's already tarnished reputation was further tainted by movies such as *One flew over the cuckoo's nest*.

Despite its image, ECT is an effective and generally safe treatment that works more rapidly than antidepressant drugs, so ECT may be used if patients seem suicidal, retarded to the point of self-neglect, especially distressed or are not responding to antidepressants. Patients are given a light anaesthetic and a drug that relaxes muscles. An electrical current is then passed through their brain for a split-second. For reasons scientists don't understand, this often alleviates even severe, psychotic depression. One suggestion is that ECT increases serotonin levels.

Patients feel that they have gone to sleep. Most receive between six and 12 treatments, twice a week. Patients commonly report memory loss for events just before the ECT or patchy memory loss during the following two or three weeks. Many patients also feel nauseous, confused, restless or experience headaches. Nevertheless, ECT may be safer than using antidepressants in patients suffering from severe depression.

Suicide

Suicide – or a suicide attempt – is the ultimate condemnation of our care of the mentally ill and may be the tragic outcome of severe stress. Despite the millions of pounds spent on treatment, despite the best efforts of doctors, despite the care of the family, every two hours one person – over 4,000 people a year – tells society that life isn't worth living. Another 200,000 people attempt to take their own lives – equivalent to one person every three minutes. Suicides are as common as deaths on the road. Recent figures suggest that overall suicide rates may be falling. However, among young men aged between 15 and 24 years – an increasingly embattled group in society because of the recession and threats to their traditional roles – suicide rates have risen by at least a third over the last 15 years. The rate among women of the same age has remained roughly constant. Two-thirds of suicides are now in people aged under 49.

Depression, anxiety, personal tragedy and alcohol abuse all increase the risk of suicide. Women are four times more likely to attempt suicide than men. However, men are more likely to succeed. Women opt for overdose in around half of suicide attempts, hanging in about 29 per cent, and breathing car exhaust fumes in 13 per cent. Men use exhaust fumes and hanging about equally (37 and 36 per cent respectively). Among men overdoses account for just 18 per cent of suicide attempts.

Parasuicide – deliberate self-harm without intending to die – is often a cry for help. However, it's a cry that often goes unheeded. Even some health professionals feel that parasuicide detracts from 'real' medical problems – even heart attacks or strokes caused by deliberate acts such as smoking. Health professionals may make these snap judgements without appreciating the distress leading to the parasuicide. Moreover, while suicide is no longer criminal, it conflicts with many moral and religious codes. Some people still regard suicide attempts as an unforgivable sin. These attitudes hinder attempts to help some of society's most vulnerable and distressed members.

Helping the vulnerable

People living with or caring for depressed patients need to watch for the signs of suicide and, where necessary, encourage sufferers to get help before it's too late. Ironically, recovering from depression temporarily increases suicide risk. When depressed patients are at their lowest ebb, many lack the energy and motivation to kill themselves. However, antidepressants often increase energy before they lift mood. As a result, patients are more likely to kill themselves as their energy levels begin to rise. There are a number of other risk factors to watch for that may signal someone is contemplating suicide (see box).

Suicide risks and signals
* people who have deliberately hurt themselves in the past * people who threaten suicide * the unemployed * people working in certain occupations, such as doctors, farmers, vets * people living alone, divorced or separated * people suffering from physical illness * drug addicts and alcoholics * depression * insomnia * weight change — usually a loss * general loss of interest * lethargy * hypochondria

---

Anxiety disorders

JANE, who lives with her husband and two young children, came from an anxious family. As a young child, Jane had to make phone calls for her mother, who was too scared to use the phone. Jane's father was intensely shy and passive. He never left the house unless he had no choice. Her parental grandmother was a chronic agoraphobic who did not leave her house for 36 years. Jane grew up a timid wallflower, unable to stand up to her over-demanding boss.

Then, one summer day, the tube stopped between stations. It was the rush hour and Jane was crushed on all sides. She was hot, claustrophobic and intensely anxious. Jane began to feel sweaty and breathless, made all the worse by the stifling lack of air in the tube. She had been delayed getting her children off to school and was running 15 minutes late. The fact she always got to work half an hour before the official starting time didn't enter her mental equation. Her heart began pounding and Jane began to worry that she might be having a heart attack. She felt terrified of breaking down in front of everyone and began to feel disorientated and faint. Her vision began to swim. Suddenly the train started moving again. Jane left the tube at the next station and walked the rest of the way to the office.

Jane's feelings of anxiety are familiar to everyone – especially during times of great stress. Many of us experience the occasional panic attack. However, anxiety disorders cover a spectrum of suffering, from generalised vague anxiety and panic attacks, to the rituals of obsessive-compulsive disorders and the tragic legacy of post-traumatic stress disorder. Overall, 2.8 million people suffer from anxiety disorders, which can cripple them with terror.

Anxiety can even prove fatal. Premature death rates among people with panic disorder are three times higher than among the general population.

Types of anxiety

Many people are prone to bouts of generalised anxiety – an unshakeable feeling that something terrible is going to happen. Sufferers can't put their finger on the cause of their anxiety and stress. Nevertheless, people with generalised anxiety show certain characteristics. They worry habitually, feel apprehensive, are constantly vigilant, always seem on edge, have difficulty concentrating, are easily startled.

There are several other types of anxiety:

- Panic attacks are periods when the patient experiences debilitating, overwhelming and intense 'fear'. However, unlike generalised anxiety, the feeling subsides within a few minutes.
- Phobia is a fear linked to something specific – heights, spiders or speaking in public, for example. The fear is out of all proportion to the stimulus.
- Obsessive-compulsive disorder. Patients with obsessions endure persistent, disturbing thoughts that they try to resist. This causes intense anxiety. Other patients experience severe stress if they don't perform their compulsions (see page 139).
- Post-traumatic stress emerges following an intensely stressful, usually life-threatening, event that falls outside the normal range of human experience.

Clearly, anxiety causes considerable stress. Sufferers become sensitised to stress: events that would hardly bother a healthy person can have an enormous impact on the anxious. However, stress also contributes to your risk of developing these anxiety-spectrum disorders. Anxia*, the Phobic Society* and Triumph over Phobia* provide advice and support to people suffering from anxiety disorders, and their families.

Mimicking anxiety

A number of conditions mimic anxiety. For example, high levels of caffeine – usually between 10 and 15 cups of brewed coffee daily – can produce symptoms that mimic anxiety. One patient complained of severe anxiety that did not respond to tranquillisers. Doctors were stumped until they discovered he drank 50 cups of coffee a day. But some people may develop anxiety following just five cups of coffee. Excessive alcohol, certain thyroid diseases and low blood sugar can also mimic anxiety. Moreover, some people experience panic attacks when they stop taking certain drugs, including barbiturates, benzodiazepines and amphetamines.

Anxiety symptoms

Anxious people experience a range of symptoms (see box). Many result from an over-stimulation of the autonomic nervous system, which controls the fight-or-flight reflex. Others are somatic symptoms – patients convert their anxiety into physical symptoms, including headaches, bowel disturbances and muscle tension. Around a half of people with generalised anxiety disorder suffer from mainly somatic symptoms, usually in their gut or chest.

Anxiety symptoms
* Patients may feel that they are about to go crazy or lose control * feelings of unreality – which strengthens the feeling of going mad * feeling they are dying or having a heart attack * avoidance behaviour: anxious people go out of their way to avoid situations or people that trigger the symptoms * feeling on edge and keyed up, easily startled, irritable * restlessness * difficulty concentrating * fatigue and insomnia * breathlessness or feeling smothered * pins and needles in the fingers and toes *dizziness, feeling unsteady, faintness * chest pains or palpitations * hot flushes or blushing * chills, sweating, cold, clammy hands * dry mouth * shaking, twitching or trembling uncontrollably * muscle tension, aches and pains * nausea * an urge to urinate or defecate * trouble swallowing * feeling there is a lump in the throat

---

Panic attacks

Panic attacks – bouts of intense, debilitating, oppressive fear – are very common. A recent estimate suggests that over 3 per cent of people suffer from panic disorder (essentially regular attacks) and 8.5 per cent from limited symptoms at least once during their lives.

Panic attack sufferers tend to experience few symptoms.

Generalised anxiety patients often run a gamut of less intense anxiety symptoms. During a panic attack, sufferers may feel dizzy, faint or feel they are dying; others may feel breathless and convinced they are having a heart attack. Typically, patients first suffer panic attacks during their late 20s, although social phobia (opposite) emerges at a younger age. However, the roots of panic disorder may go back into childhood. For example, children who experience separation anxiety – being denied, perhaps thorough death or divorce, the support and love of a parent – are more likely to develop panic attacks in later life.

Panic attacks start suddenly and reach a peak within ten minutes – although in rare cases panic attacks last for several hours. Once the panic has passed, patients feel weak and exhausted. Panic attacks are distressing rather than dangerous. Some patients suffer attacks for only a few weeks or months. In others, the attacks recur. Some suffer for years on end, especially if the panic attacks are triggered by agoraphobia.

Panic attacks often develop in response to a certain situation, such as agoraphobia or social phobia, for example. However, panic attacks may strike without warning. Nevertheless, sufferers may begin to associate certain events with suffering a panic attack and will go out of their way to avoid these triggers. For example, some people find travelling in underground trains intensely stressful and develop panic attacks. As a result, they either take slower over-ground transport or avoid working in areas where they need to travel by underground. Nevertheless, the situation does not invariably cause a panic attack, in contrast to a phobia. Cognitive therapy, psychotherapies and drugs can all alleviate the suffering caused by panic disorders.

Phobias

Phobias are fears out of all proportion to their cause. Many of us are scared by snakes, blood, bees, heights, flying or speaking in public, but we overcome these fears. People with phobias experience a fear so intense, so debilitating, that it affects the way they lead their lives. Agoraphobics may be unable to leave the house. Social phobics may avoid social gatherings. Arachnophobia sufferers may be terrified by a tiny house spider. Ironically, sufferers often recognise that their fears are unrealistic or excessive, but they are often unable to do anything about it.

Agoraphobia

Agoraphobia, which tends to develop in a patient's 20s or 30s, is a fear of being in places where escape might be difficult or embarrassing or where help might be unavailable if the person experiences a panic attack. As a result, people with agoraphobia commonly fear being alone outside the house, in a crowd or travelling by public transport. People with agoraphobia – women, usually – find these situations intensely stressful and they experience a panic attack. This can leave sufferers terrified of going outside the house in case they experience another attack. Other sufferers fear that the symptoms will incapacitate them – even if they have never experienced a panic attack.

Behavioural therapy improves symptoms in only around 60 per cent of agoraphobia patients and only around a quarter recover completely. The outlook is even bleaker for patients suffering from chronic stress. In a recent study, 43 per cent of agoraphobics reported experiencing severe or moderate chronic stressors, such as marital or financial problems or conflicts with parents or in-laws. Marital problems were the most common stressor, reported by 15 per cent of those interviewed. The agoraphobics with chronic stress experienced worse symptoms and were less likely to recover than those under less pressure.

Social phobia

Everyone gets nervous before an important meeting, performing on stage or giving a presentation. It is abnormal *not* to feel tense, and the fight-or-flight reflex ensures that we give our best performance. Most of us learn to handle the stress surrounding these difficult social situations. However, social phobia sufferers go out of their way to avoid social gatherings. These people may be so nervous beforehand that they drink before meeting their friends down the pub or at a party. Social phobics are around 19 times more likely to abuse alcohol and drugs than more sociable people. Around one in five alcoholics are also social phobics.

Around two per cent of men and three per cent of women – one million people in the UK – suffer from severe social phobia. Another seven per cent of the population shows a trait towards social phobia. They do everything they can to avoid anxiety-pro-voking situations.

While social phobia is one of the most common phobias, it remains under-diagnosed and under-treated. Only two per cent of people suffering from severe social phobia are recognised and treated. Many people – even the sufferers themselves – dismiss their symptoms as shyness. However, social phobia is more than being intensely shy. In surveys, some 40 per cent of the general population regard themselves as 'shy'. But 40 per cent of the pop-ulation aren't debilitated by shyness. In contrast, social phobia cripples a person's life.

Social phobia triggers
Nobody really knows why certain people develop social phobia. It tends to emerge in adolescence; some psychologists believe that teenagers with social phobia are stuck at the normal stage of shy-ness and fear of strangers that children go through between the ages of three and seven years. Indeed, when sufferers look back, the signs of social phobia were often there for several years. In childhood, social phobics are typically regarded as 'shy' and 'introverted'. They tend to sit at the back of the class and don't raise their hand to answer the teacher's questions. When the teacher quizzes them they panic and can't answer, so they gain the reputation of being 'slow' and their education suffers. Later in life around half of social phobia sufferers cannot enter into long-term relationships. A few social phobics turn into recluses or even develop agoraphobia: social phobia sufferers are 45 times more likely to develop agoraphobia some time during their lives than the healthy population.

There are two main types of social phobia: general and perfor-mance (see box). People suffering from general social phobia worry about possibly being the centre of attention. They feel that

---

Typical fears in social phobia
General: * being introduced to strangers * meeting people in author-ity * eating or drinking in public * participating in small groups * entering a party group * being teased
Performance: * speaking in public * writing in front of others * acting or playing a musical instrument in public * giving a report to a group * expressing disagreement

---

everyone is scrutinising their every action, so they may worry about eating, drinking or undressing in public. Others endure considerable stress at work because they can't stand their ground with an over-demanding boss. Indeed, they may settle for a lower position than they are capable of simply to avoid situations that trigger their symptoms.

People with performance – also called specific – social phobias are naturally the centre of attention. Sales representatives, actors, teachers and musicians can suffer specific social phobia. They socialise normally, but 'go to pieces' when they have to perform in front of other people. They may become anxious, stammer or dry up completely. Even experienced public speakers may develop performance social phobia. In severe cases, sufferers with general social phobia are unable even to ask a question, or tremble so violently they cannot write cheques.

Symptoms of social phobia

Whatever the trigger, people with social phobia develop typical stress-related symptoms (see diagram). These can be extremely unpleasant and social phobics live in dread of experiencing the symptoms. They tend to worry about an anxiety-provoking event – sometimes for weeks before. Many lie awake at night worrying about the event. However, lack of sleep undermines their performance and exacerbates stress and anxiety. This constant tension means that many people with social phobia are unable to relax – sometimes for years on end – and traps sufferers in a cycle of fearing fear.

The anxiety and stress surrounding social phobia doesn't end when the person has stopped speaking or returns home from the social event. People with social phobia often perform a mental post-mortem. They re-run the event in their minds and wish that things had been different. Social phobics want clear signals about their performance. However, social interactions are rarely unambiguous, so when they re-run the event in their heads, social phobics tend to assume the worse and believe that their social performance was a failure, when, in reality, it was normal. So perhaps it's not surprising that this behaviour leaves people with social phobia feeling stressed, anxious and depressed. Many people with social phobia turn to drink and drugs to mask their anxiety and to

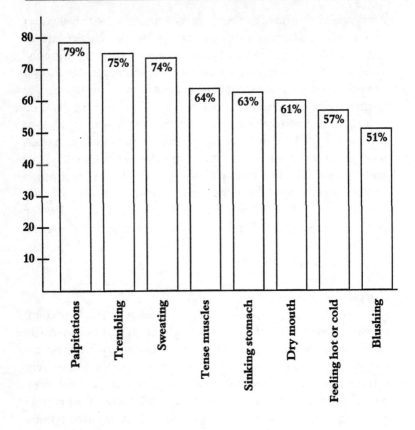

Number of social phobia sufferers reporting stress-related symptoms

provide them with the 'Dutch courage' to socialise. However, social phobia can be treated with drugs or behavioural therapies.

Simple phobia

Patients with simple phobias experience intense panic when confronted with a specific object or event – such as animals, closed spaces (claustrophobia) or heights (acrophobia). People suffering from arachnophobia may feel panicky, sweaty and breathless when they see a spider. Their anxiety increases the closer they get to the spider and is more intense the larger the spider. Simple phobia sufferers also experience anxiety when they anticipate facing their fear. An acrophobic may suffer anticipatory anxiety when entering a tall building – even though his or her feet are firmly planted on the ground floor. Simple phobias rarely dramatically impair patients' lives, although claustrophobia may be more debilitating and stressful if, for example, patients can't enter a tube train. Ironically, sufferers usually recognise that their fear is excessive.

The age when the symptoms first emerge depends, partly, on the phobia. Animal phobias usually emerge in childhood. Blood-injury phobias usually begin in adolescence or early adulthood. Acrophobia and phobias of driving, closed spaces and air travel start in patients' 30s. Most simple phobias that emerge in childhood disappear without treatment. Those that persist or first emerge in adults tend to require intensive treatment.

Obsessive-compulsive disorder

Around one per cent of the population suffers from obsessive-compulsive disorder. Many more suffer from mild obsessions or compulsions – repeatedly checking that the gas is turned off or that the front door is locked before going to bed. Others have an obsessive-compulsive personality – perfectionist, stubborn, indecisive, devoted to work and emotionally flat – that may be an advantage in certain jobs requiring, for example, an intense attention to detail. While many medical textbooks lump obsessive-compulsive disorder with the anxiety states, many psychiatrists regard them as different diseases.

What is obsessive-compulsive disorder?

Obsessions are persistent ideas, thoughts, impulses or images that a person recognises as senseless. A mother may feel an urge to kill her child. A vicar may repeatedly experience perverted thoughts. A businesswoman may fear becoming infected through shaking her clients' hands. Not surprisingly, these thoughts cause considerable stress and anxiety.

Compulsions are repetitive actions performed to alleviate the stress generated by an obsession. Examples are repeated hand-washing, counting, checking and touching. The sufferer derives no pleasure from these unrealistic and time-consuming actions. Even if you are scrupulous about avoiding infection, there is no need to wash your hands 50 times a day.

At first, patients feel compelled to behave in a certain way and – as they recognise their behaviour is unreasonable – try to resist. However, resisting the compulsions causes intense and increasing stress. Yielding releases tension. After repeated failures to counter the compulsion the sufferer may give in and no longer resist the compulsion. However, they try to avoid situations likely to trigger the obsession. A housewife obsessed about dirt may avoid public toilets. The businesswoman obsessed about contamination may avoid shaking hands.

Obsessive-compulsive disorder usually begins in adolescence or early adulthood and symptoms tend to wax and wane throughout the patient's life. However, obsessive-compulsive disorder may also emerge during pregnancy. Some women find pregnancy stressful and this may maintain, trigger and exacerbate obsessive-compulsive disorder.

Like other anxiety diseases, obsessive-compulsive disorder is usually treated by combining drugs and behavioural therapies. However, only around a quarter of people with obsessive-compulsive disorder attend for treatment. Many more probably suffer in silence.

Post-traumatic stress disorder

The idea that intense stress can leave sufferers traumatised for long periods, if not for life, first emerged during the horrors of the First World War. Soldiers returned suffering from a number of 'hysterical' symptoms that doctors attributed to the pressure of exploding shells – so-called 'shell shock'. However, during the Second World War doctors recognised that shell shock had its roots in the mind rather than the body. They renamed the syndrome 'combat neurosis' or 'combat fatigue'. Doctors now describe the tragic psychological legacy of intense stress as post-traumatic stress disorder.

Post-traumatic stress disorder follows an intensely stressful, often life-threatening, 'trigger' event that falls outside the range of normal human experience, such as being involved in a man-made or natural disaster, being raped or seeing a serious accident. In contrast to other anxiety disorders, the fear experienced by post-traumatic stress sufferers is not out of proportion to its cause.

Anyone would find a major disaster, a serious earthquake or a war stressful.

However, following the event some survivors develop intense fear, terror and helplessness. They either repeatedly run through the event in their minds or avoid anything that reminds them of the tragedy. Others become apathetic and 'numb' to life generally, agitated or dependent on other people. Most can't sleep properly. A study of Vietnam veterans with combat-related post-traumatic stress disorder found they experienced threatening dreams, thrashed around during the night and woke in panic. Following some stressors, such as some cases of childhood sexual abuse, these symptoms may not emerge until several years later.

Currently, doctors cannot offer patients a drug that alleviates post-traumatic stress disorder. They may prescribe benzodiazepines or antidepressants if the patient also suffers anxiety, depression or insomnia. However, most patients have to undergo psychotherapy or exposure therapy to face the fear underlying post-traumatic stress disorder.

Take control of your anxiety

Many people endure the torment of intense anxiety for years, but it's never too late to take control of your anxiety. You may need professional help from either your GP, a counsellor or a psychiatrist.

Initially, doctors aim to provide support, reassurance and counselling. They may also prescribe a short course – perhaps a week or fortnight – of benzodiazepines if you suffer from very severe anxiety or panic attacks. By alleviating symptoms, patients are in the 'right frame of mind' to embark on a course of non-drug treatment. So don't regard behavioural therapies as an alternative to drugs: they work hand-in-hand. Drugs alleviate symptoms in the short term, while psychological therapies control anxiety in the longer term and so reduce the risk of relapse.

Non-drug treatments for anxiety

Counselling often alleviates anxiety after only a few sessions. Counsellors define the problem and encourage 'problem solving'

– similar to that outlined in chapter two – to tackle the source of stress. Counselling may be backed by self-help materials, such as those provided by Anxia*, the Royal College of Psychiatrists*, the Phobic Society*, Triumph over Phobia* and Lifeskills*. The aim is to break the cycle of stress that fuels anxiety. So patients are taught relaxation, stress management or meditation. Moreover, some of the behavioural techniques used to overcome phobias can be intensely stressful. Relaxation and stress management techniques help patients remain calm during treatment.

Several other non-drug treatments may also alleviate anxiety. Few studies have compared the effectiveness of these techniques with either other drugs or an inactive placebo. Nevertheless, cognitive therapy seems to be especially effective. However, the biggest problem may be obtaining treatment on the NHS. Clinical psychologists are something of a rare breed.

- *Cognitive therapy* replaces a destructive thought pattern with a more realistic and positive approach. By reinterpreting anxiety-provoking thoughts and events, cognitive therapists change patients' behaviour. Patients undergoing cognitive therapy for social phobia may watch a video of themselves. This gives patients an insight into how they appear – rather than how they think they appear. For example, people with social phobia often believe that they sweat heavily. When they watch the video it is clear that they don't. However, patients need to see this for themselves, rather than relying on someone else telling them.

- During *exposure therapy* patients learn to control their anxiety while they confront their fears. For example, people suffering from arachnophobia try to relax as a spider crawls over their hand. During each session the exposure gradually becomes more intense and frightening. In the first session, agoraphobics may walk down the road. During the next session they walk to the local supermarket, then take a bus ride, and so on. Similar techniques are used to gradually desensitise patients with post-traumatic stress disorder to the trigger event.

- In '*flooding*' the patient learns relaxation techniques and then is suddenly exposed to an intense form of the anxiety-provoking event. The patient tries to relax and waits for the anxiety to abate. So someone scared of crowds goes shopping in a crowded shopping centre.

- *Aversion therapy*: clients are punished if they perform a certain act. Combined with positive approaches, this can break unpleasant habits. Smokers, for example, may sit in a room surrounded by cigarette advertisements. Each time they light a cigarette they receive an electric shock.
- *Meditation* alleviates acute anxiety and panic and reduces sensitivity to stress. It enhances patients' feelings of control and allows them to confront stress-provoking situations more effectively. This maintains the improvement among people undergoing therapy for generalised anxiety disorder, panic disorder and agoraphobia.
- *Social skills training* can help you feel relaxed and confident in company by learning simple social skills, such as how to start a conversation. Social skills training usually means role-playing in front of a video camera.
- *Psychotherapy* reaches into a patient's psyche to examine and dispel repressed feelings. This may undermine the beliefs that sustain the phobia.

Drugs for anxiety

While non-drug treatments often alleviate anxiety and phobias, it may be several months before the full benefits emerge. In the meantime, patients want to lift their burden of fear quickly. Drugs alleviate anxiety and panic more rapidly than non-drug treatments. With drugs, anxiety and panic tend to subside within four to eight weeks, and around 50 to 60 per cent of patients improve after taking them. However, between 30 and 90 per cent of patients with panic disorder relapse within a year of discontinuing their drugs.

After ensuring the patient has stabilised – which takes between four and six months – the dose is gradually reduced. However, side effects can be a problem. Anxious patients are often over sensitive to side effects. Deciding which treatment to use depends on the balance of risk and benefits.

- Benzodiazepines may take the edge off a panic attack. However, side effects – including memory loss, impaired concentration and interactions with alcohol – are common.

Moreover, benzodiazepines are addictive and can cause rebound reactions: when patients stop taking them the symptoms recur with added intensity.

● Beta-blockers may alleviate mild performance-related stress, such as 'nerves' before giving a public presentation. They slow rapid heart beat, are non-addictive and can stop shaking. However, beta-blockers can cause tiredness and nightmares.

● Antidepressants – several groups of antidepressants are available, each of which has advantages and disadvantages. The selective serotonin reuptake inhibitors often relieve obsessive-compulsive disorder and panic attacks; Moclobemide and the monoamine oxidase inhibitors may alleviate social phobia.

Benzodiazepine withdrawal

You can become addicted to legal, prescription drugs as easily as their illegal counterparts. Kicking the habit can be just as hard.

Benzodiazepines, for example, are widely prescribed to alleviate insomnia, anxiety, panic attacks and a number of other stress-related mental disorders. However, when some patients stop taking benzodiazepines they develop a 'withdrawal' syndrome (see box).

Symptoms of benzodiazepine withdrawal
* agitation and restlessness * anxiety and tension * confusion
* depression * difficulty concentrating * dizziness * faintness * fatigue
and lethargy * feeling strange * increased acuity for smell, sound and
touch * insomnia * nausea * numbness and tingling * poor appetite
* poor co-ordination * sweating * trembling * upset stomach * vomiting
* weakness

More seriously, about one or two per cent of long-term high-dose benzodiazepine users develop symptoms that resemble alcoholic delirium tremens (see page 151). In rare cases this proves fatal. Benzodiazepines can also cross the placenta, so babies born to mothers who use benzodiazepines during the last stages of pregnancy can develop withdrawal symptoms that last for between a few hours and several days.

Benzodiazepine withdrawal isn't a problem isolated to a few people with addictive personalities. The risk largely depends on the length of treatment. Withdrawal symptoms are rare among people taking benzodiazepines for less than four months. After six months, between five and ten per cent experience withdrawal symptoms. After two years the number of users who experience withdrawal symptoms increases to around half. After eight years, almost all users are likely to experience withdrawal.

Nevertheless, people with a history of anxiety are also more likely to suffer withdrawal symptoms. Depression can also make withdrawal more difficult. Moreover, most of the UK's 250,000 long-term benzodiazepine users are middle-aged women with chronic anxiety who are grappling with other problems.

How to stop taking benzodiazepines

You can minimise your risk of developing the withdrawal syndrome. First, remember that benzodiazepines do not treat the cause of your problems. Up to 65 per cent of people taking benzodiazepines for anxiety and 95 per cent of those using them for panic disorders relapse. So tackle the cause of your stress and anxiety (see chapter two). Then, with your doctor's help, gradually reduce your benzodiazepine dose. Some people reduce their dose by a quarter each week without symptoms emerging. Others need to taper the dose more slowly. Any withdrawal symptoms will usually resolve within a fortnight and you can continue tapering the dose. A gradual reduction in dose – over four to six weeks – reduces the number of withdrawal symptoms you're likely to experience and increases your chance of being able to stay off benzodiazepines.

The Tranquilliser Advice and Support Project* offers advice to people trying to stop taking benzodiazepines.

Other psychological diseases

Almost any of the 300 or so mental disorders listed in psychiatry textbooks can either cause stress or be exacerbated by it. Fortunately, these disorders are much rarer than anxiety or depression. For example, manic depression and schizophrenia each affect approximately one per cent of the population. However, they cause considerable stress for the patient and their families.

Manic depression

Some people experience periods when they are intensely depressed and periods when they seem elated and over-excited. During the latter phase, patients may formulate grandiose plans that they are simply unable to carry out. Their judgement fails – so they may become involved in dubious business deals or even crimes. They tend to talk fast, drink heavily, get into fights or become promiscuous. Many then crash into depression.

When these mood swings begin interfering with work or social life or when they endanger the patient's life, doctors describe the condition as manic or bi-polar depression. They prescribe lithium, which reduces the severity and frequency of the mood swings. In mild cases they may use the anti-psychotics used to treat schizophrenia.

Unfortunately, lithium causes a number of side effects including nausea, vomiting, diarrhoea and tremor. Patients undergo regular blood monitoring to ensure blood levels of the drug stay within safe limits. The Manic Depression Fellowship* offers a network of self-help groups for sufferers and their families.

Schizophrenia

Schizophrenia is surrounded by myths and misconceptions. To many people, 'schizophrenics' are homeless vagrants with Jekyll and Hyde personalities, ready to explode into violence at the slightest provocation. In the past, schizophrenics were swept under the carpet of the local asylum. However, community care brought schizophrenia back into the public eye, especially following well-publicised violent assaults by recently released mental patients.

But this picture is false. Around one per cent of the population develop schizophrenia sometime during their lives – a deterioration in personality that translates into a number of debilitating symptoms (see box). Rather than having 'split' minds, the split is

---

The symptoms of schizophrenia
* delusions * lack of emotion * hallucinations * social withdrawal
* bizarre behaviour * poor concentration * thought disorders * apathy

---

between internal thoughts and external reality. For example, some schizophrenics believe their actions are controlled by a radio-transmitter implanted in their brains by aliens.

Some patients suffer a single schizophrenic episode and then recover. However, in around 80 per cent of patients the first episode – usually in late adolescence or early adulthood – marks the beginning of the erosion of the patient's personality. As a result, most patients take drugs known as anti-psychotics or neuroleptics for life. These cause a number of debilitating side effects ranging from fatigue to movement disorders reminiscent of Parkinson's disease. Around ten per cent of patients suffer a breakdown – when they experience hallucinations, for example – each year. The rest of the time they seem emotionally flat and apathetic.

Members of some ethnic minorities are more likely to develop psychotic reactions, including schizophrenia, than Caucasians. For example, rates of schizophrenia among young West Indians are between 12 and 18 times higher than among the general population. Partly, this may reflect the stress of living as part of an ethnic minority. Partly, ethnic minorities may be more likely to be branded schizophrenic. However, genetic factors may also play a part.

A first-degree relative of a schizophrenic – a son or daughter, for example – has a 10 per cent chance of developing schizophrenia. However, the risk of a child developing schizophrenia if both parents suffer rises to 40 per cent. But is this nature or nurture? Could the increased chance of a sufferer's child developing the disease reflect the damage wrought by the stress of growing up in a schizophrenic household?

To answer this, psychiatrists compared the number of identical and non-identical twins who developed schizophrenia. If the risk of developing the disease is totally genetically determined, and environment plays no part, identical twins are equally likely to develop schizophrenia. If a disease is caused by environmental factors alone, the identical twin of a sufferer is no more likely to suffer it than the non-identical twins. Several studies show that the risk of an identical twin developing the disease if the other suffers from schizophrenia is around 40 and 50 per cent. Among non-identical twins the risk falls to around 10 per cent. So both genetics and environment play a role.

Viral infections, complications at birth and physical alterations to the architecture of the brain may predispose to schizophrenia – at least in some patients. Stress also contributes. Stressful life events tend to cluster before a schizophrenia breakdown. An excessively critical hostile family that pressurises the patient, the breakdown of a relationship or losing a job may also provoke a relapse. However, epidemics of schizophrenia don't follow wars and other major catastrophes. In other words, stress is unlikely to cause schizophrenia.

Contact SANE*, the National Schizophrenia Fellowship*, the Royal College of Psychiatrists* and MIND* for further information. The African-Caribbean Mental Health Association* offers advice specifically for black people.

Alcohol and nicotine

Social drugs can prove as hard to kick of addiction as illegal drugs. After undergoing a rehabilitation programme, between 50 and 80 per cent of heroin addicts show more than a 50 per cent reduction in their addictive behaviours and associated problems, such as employment, medical and family difficulties. The success rate for cocaine addiction is between 50 and 60 per cent. However, the success rate for alcohol abuse is 40 to 70 per cent and nicotine 20 to 40 per cent. In other words, it is often harder to quit smoking than to stop taking heroin.

Problem drinking

In any bar on any night, you'll see people attempting to drown their stress in alcohol. For most of them a couple of pints isn't going to do any harm. Indeed, light drinking may be good for your health. But the key word is light. Drinking doesn't drown your problems. Stress feeds on alcohol. So how much can you drink without putting your physical or mental health at risk? How do you know if you're over the limit? And how can you defeat problem drinking?

How much can you drink?
Just before Christmas 1995, the Government raised the 'safe' alcohol limit to 28 units a week for men and 21 units for women. A

unit is half a pint of normal strength beer, a glass of wine or a pub measure of spirits. This doesn't mean you can 'spend' your entire weekly allowance each Friday night down the pub. Indeed, the guidelines suggest that you should keep to a daily rather than weekly limit. Men who drink three to four units a day and women who drink two to three units daily do not face a 'significant health risk'. Consistently drinking over these limits does carry an increased risk of damaging your health. However, these are only guidelines. Individuals' tolerance for alcohol varies widely.

Binge drinking is dangerous – it increases your risk of suffering a stroke, for example. Regular drinking is even more hazardous as your body doesn't get the time to recover. You don't even have to get regularly drunk to suffer some of alcohol's harmful effects.

Have you got an alcohol problem?

Alcoholism conjures up an image of a homeless degenerate swilling super-strength lager. However, alcoholism also strikes successful executives, actors and housewives. In 1990, 28 per cent of men and 11 per cent of women drank more than the then recommended weekly limits of 21 and 14 units respectively. Of these, around five per cent of men and two per cent of women had serious alcohol-related problems. Moreover, one in five seemingly healthy men show biochemical evidence of alcohol abuse. Many people who abuse alcohol hide or deny their problem even to themselves.

So how do you determine if you – or a loved one – has an alcohol problem? Doctors recognise certain key features of alcohol dependence. The more of these features that apply to you, the more likely you are to have an alcohol problem.

Do you recognise these signs?

- Compulsion – an irresistible urge to drink. Drinking alcohol is the most important thing in your life.
- Withdrawal symptoms (see below).
- A regular drinking pattern. Most people vary their drinking pattern. Alcoholics drink regularly to stave off withdrawal symptoms.
- Tolerance. As you drink more, you metabolise alcohol more efficiently and your tolerance increases. Alcoholics are often

unaffected by amounts of alcohol that would leave a moderate drinker thoroughly drunk.
● Returning to your old pattern of alcohol consumption after abstaining for a while.

Withdrawal symptoms can be a major problem for people trying to reduce their drinking. Between 6 and 24 hours after the end of a drinking session, alcohol levels fall and withdrawal symptoms emerge, including tremor ('the shakes'), insomnia, agitation and fits. Symptoms usually peak within 24 and 48 hours of the last drink.

Delirium tremens, the most serious withdrawal symptom, develops between one and five days after the alcoholic stops drinking alcohol. Around five per cent of heavy drinkers develop delirium tremens: they shake violently and appear disorientated and agitated. Their heart beat and respiration rate rises. They may experience epileptic fits and hallucinate. Seeing 'pink elephants' is something of a joke, but the hallucinations brought on by delirium tremens can be terrifying. One alcoholic saw spiders the size of dinner plates crawling over the wall and floor of his bedroom. Another felt maggots burrowing under her skin. Untreated delirium tremens kills around one in five alcoholics. However, modern management means that less than five per cent of patients being treated for delirium tremens die.

The dangers of withdrawal mean alcoholics likely to develop delirium tremens are managed in detoxification units. However, increasing numbers of mild-to-moderate withdrawal symptoms are managed at home with the support of a nurse. This avoids the stigma of needing to go into a detoxification unit.

Many people with a drink problem fall short of being full-blown alcoholics. Nevertheless, you may still have an alcohol problem if you get drunk every Friday night after work. It may help you unwind after a stressful week at work, but it damages your health. You could have a drink problem if:

● you feel you should cut down on your drinking
● you feel guilty about drinking
● people annoy you when they criticise your drinking.

You could also try not to drink for a fortnight. You might be surprised how difficult this is.

Drinking to alleviate stress • Developing a regular drinking pattern • Unable

to limit drinking • Can't avoid getting drunk • Spending a considerable

time drinking • Missing meals • Memory lapses • Agitated with-

out a drink • Organise day around drinking • Trembling

the morning after • Mornings spent retching and

vomiting • Sweating excessively at night •

Withdrawal fits • Morning drinking •

Reduced tolerance • Hallu-

cinations • Delirium

tremens

The downward spiral of alcohol abuse

The downward spiral of alcohol abuse

Alcoholism can catch you in a downward spiral. Say you're under stress at work or at home. So you begin to stop off at the pub and drink three pints a night to unwind or give you the Dutch courage to go home. At this level, you're considered a heavy social drinker. When your alcohol consumption increases to around eight units a day you may begin to experience medical, legal, social and employment problems. Around half of people drinking eight units a day return to controlled drinking or stop altogether. However, around a quarter of people drinking at this level develop chronic alcoholism. They may need detoxification and can end up socially isolated, unemployed – or dead.

What causes excessive drinking?

Many people drink to drown their sorrows. Certainly, many problems increase the risk of excessive alcohol consumption (see box). However, heavy drinking also causes these problems and exacerbates stress, anxiety and depression. Alcohol abuse traps the drinker in a cycle of increasing stress. Jack's story is a sobering reminder.

JACK was a salesman for an engineering company facing widespread rationalisation after a hostile takeover. Since joining the firm ten years ago, Jack had become a backbone of the company. However, he was still recovering from the breakdown of his 14-year marriage six months before. The risk of redundancy left Jack feeling increasingly stressed out, worried and anxious. He started drinking heavily in the pub after work and in hotel bars during sales trips.

Jack then started bringing his drinking home with him. He felt his judgement slip and, once a legend for his punctuality, he started missing appointments and taking more time off sick to nurse his increasingly frequent hangovers. Jack's sales figures began to slip. When the rationalisation reached the sales force, Jack was one of the first to be made redundant.

Jack probably wouldn't have been singled out if he hadn't started drinking heavily. However, alcohol abuse often undermines performance at work. A reputation as a 'drinker' is not good for your employment prospects – even among professions traditionally likely to abuse alcohol such as sales reps, doctors, journalists, publicans and seamen. Neither is a poor sickness record. Alcohol abusers take around two-and-a-half times as many days off work as their colleagues.

Problems linked to alcohol abuse
* stress social and other phobias * anxiety * depression * employment problems * financial problems * marital problems * boredom * loneliness * child abuse * family problems * alcoholism in the family

---

Why can't some people control their drinking?

Why is one person able to control their drinking, while another under the same amount of stress gets drunk every night? Not everyone who loses a spouse or a job descends into alcoholism. Personality seems to play a part.

Psychologists divide alcoholics into two broad groups. Type 1 alcoholism affects both men and women and begins in adulthood. These people are psychologically dependent on alcohol but they feel guilty about their drinking and live in fear of losing control. Type 1 alcoholism often develops in the wake of a stressful life event – marital problems, unemployment or bereavement. Type 1 alcoholics tend to worry, are shy, fear uncertainty and are pessimistic. They want to avoid novelty and harming themselves and tend to have reflective, rigid and stoic personalities. Type 1 alcoholics feel the need for rewards, form warm social attachments and are dependent and sentimental. Parents of Type 1 alcoholics also tend to suffer from this type of alcoholism.

Type 2 alcoholics show the opposite tendencies. Type 2 alcoholics are typically men and drinking starts in adolescence. These alcoholics tend to be aggressive and violent. Often they are arrested during drinking bouts. Fathers of Type 2 alcoholics tended to abuse alcohol themselves from an early age and showed criminal behaviour.

There also seems to be a difference in the brains of alcoholics that predisposes them to alcohol abuse. Alcoholics may be more sensitised to endorphins – the chemicals in your brain that make you feel euphoric. These 'feel good' chemicals also encourage addictions. Alcohol triggers endorphin release which makes

ood, reinforcing their need to drink and increasing
veloping alcoholism.

rt of the jigsaw lies in your genes. Alcoholism
runs in families. But is this genetic? Or do children
learn to drink from their alcoholic parents? Or both? Studies comparing the children of alcoholics adopted by non-alcoholics with children of non-alcoholics raised in a similar environment provides part of the answer. If your genetic profile influences your chance of becoming an alcoholic, adopted children of alcoholics should be more likely to develop alcohol problems as adults than the children of non-alcoholics. This is just what researchers discovered. Overall, children of alcoholics adopted by non-alcoholics are two-and-a-half times more likely to develop alcoholism.

Other studies confirm that your alcohol tolerance is, partly at least, genetically determined. When young men with a family history of alcoholism drink alcohol, they report less intoxication, sway less and show different hormonal response and brain activity to those without a family history.

The risks of excessive drinking

Heavy drinking carries a number of risks – not least a blinding hangover the following morning. The worst hangovers follow drinks, such as brandy and bourbon, that contain high levels of additional substances, known as congeners. However, drinking's long-term damage to health depends on the alcohol content. So you damage your health whether you drink vodka, beer or wine to excess. Overall, heavy drinkers are two to three times more likely to die prematurely than non-drinkers of the same age and sex. Around one in five men admitted to hospital is there because of alcohol-related problems. In casualty units this increases to 40 per cent. So alcohol may increase your stress levels – not only by undermining your work and marriage – but by ruining your health. Over the years, doctors have linked alcohol to an increased risk of developing a large number of diseases.

Cancer

Alcohol contributes to between two and four per cent of all cases of cancer. The mouth and throat are especially vulnerable. Excessive, long-term drinking causes about 75 per cent of cancers of the oesophagus and nearly half those of the mouth, throat and voice box. More controversially, alcohol consumption has been linked to liver, breast and colorectal cancer.

Even moderate drinking may increase your risk of developing certain cancers. For example, in one study breast cancer was 50 per cent more likely to develop in women who consumed between three to nine drinks a week than in women drinking fewer than three. Another study suggests that one or more drinks daily may slightly increase your chance of contracting bowel cancer.

Despite these sobering figures, there is no firm evidence that alcohol directly causes cancer. However, alcohol may enhance the effects of cancer-producing chemicals in tobacco and food. For example, the risk of developing mouth, tracheal and oesophageal cancers is 35 times higher among drinkers who also smoke compared to those who abstain from either vice. Nevertheless, doctors find it difficult to untangle the relative importance of diet and alcohol. Heavy drinkers often eat poorly. Their poor nutritional status is further undermined by alcohol-related damage to the stomach lining, which reduces the amount of nutrients absorbed from food. So alcoholics may lack essential vitamins and minerals including the free radical scavengers such as vitamins A, C and E. Low levels of free radical scavengers may increase your risk of developing cancer.

Liver disease
Between ten and 20 per cent of people who drink heavily develop liver cirrhosis. Alcohol kills liver cells. This forms scar tissue that chokes the liver's blood supply. As a result, patients develop the symptoms of cirrhosis including jaundice, fever, enlarged spleen, confusion and drowsiness. Before the 1970s, doctors believed alcoholics' poor diets caused cirrhosis. However, most doctors now agree that alcohol directly causes cirrhosis – even if alcoholics eat adequate diets. A further ten to 35 per cent of heavy drinkers develop hepatitis.

Brain damage
We all know that alcohol affects the brain. That's often the whole point of drinking! Alcohol relaxes, reduces inhibitions and acts as a social lubricant. However, chronic drinking can cause memory

loss, seizures and absent-mindedness. It also undermines concentration and co-ordination. In severe cases, alcohol-induced brain damage can mimic Alzheimer's disease. Drinkers who develop Korsakoff's syndrome are unable to remember recent events or learn new information.

The link between alcohol and depression is complex. Moderate drinkers are less likely to suffer depression than either abstainers or alcoholics – which may reflect alcohol's relaxant properties. Alcoholics are almost twice as likely as non-alcoholics to suffer depression. Only around five per cent of depressed patients become alcoholics. However, up to 30 per cent of alcoholics develop depression. Similarly, people with social phobia (page 135) are more likely to drink heavily.

Heart disease

The government's recent revision of the safe drinking guidelines was partly based on studies showing that 'light to moderate' drinking reduces the risk of heart disease. Drinking one to two units of alcohol a day reduces the risk of heart disease in men over 40 years of age and in post-menopausal women by between 20 and 40 per cent. However, once alcohol consumption exceeds the recommended level the risk of developing heart disease begins to increase. Excessive drinking exacerbates high blood pressure and damages heart muscle.

This U shaped relationship between alcohol consumption and heart disease is difficult to explain. Certainly, people who stay within the recommended limits may be more likely to exercise, eat healthy diets and look after other aspects of their health. Moreover, some red wines contain high levels of chemicals known as flavonoids, which may mop up potentially harmful free radicals and, of course, a few drinks help you relax. Whatever the explanation, it seems that in this case, a little of what you fancy does your heart good.

Strokes

Doctors first noted the link between heavy drinking and strokes in 1725. Then in the 1970s and 1980s a number of studies suggested that heavy drinking – even occasionally getting drunk – increased your chance of suffering an ischaemic stroke. These account for 85 per cent of stokes, and are caused, like heart attacks, by atherosclerosis – a hardening of the arteries. Moderate drinking also doubles or trebles the risk of suffering the less common haemorrhagic stoke – where the blood vessel bursts and blood leaks into the brain.

However, there is some evidence that the relationship between stroke and alcohol consumption is also U shaped. One study reported that deaths from stokes decreased by 40 per cent among people with hypertension who drank less than 21 units a week compared to abstainers. But other studies suggest that this only applies to Caucasians – and possibly not to other ethnic groups. Again the message seems to be: drink in moderation.

Digestive system

Alcohol damages the lining of the gastrointestinal tract. This can lead to stomach ulcers (page 94) and reduces the amount of vitamins and minerals absorbed by the body. For example, alcoholics may absorb lower amounts of vitamins A, E and D. Vitamin A deficiency impairs night vision and may increase the risk of certain cancers. A lack of vitamin D may cause softening of the bones, which predisposes to osteoporosis. Alcoholics commonly develop folate deficiency, which may predispose to anaemia.

Impotence

Brewers' droop is probably the best known form of alcohol-induced impotence. Fortunately, it's short lived. However, while it lasts, brewers' droop can cause considerable anxiety, embarrassment and stress. Chronic alcohol abuse can cause the testes to waste away, and may lead to nerve damage, which may be irreversible. Both can lead to impotence. Among women, chronic alcohol abuse can impair the menstrual cycle and speed the onset of the menopause.

Osteoporosis

As women's bone loss declines rapidly after the menopause, heavy drinkers are more likely to develop osteoporosis – brittle bone disease – which leaves them vulnerable to life-threatening fractures. Several factors increase heavy drinkers' risk of developing osteoporosis, including poor vitamin D absorption and hormonal changes. Alcohol also seems to poison cells known as osteoblasts that lay down new bone. Heavy drinkers' poor diet exacerbates the decline and they are more likely to fall than the general population increasing their risk of fractures. However, bone formation returns to normal within a fortnight of stopping drinking – even among chronic alcoholics.

How to cut down

If you are worried about your drinking, you may be able to reduce your alcohol consumption by following a few simple rules:

- set yourself a limit – and stick to it
- quench your thirst with non-alcoholic drinks
- alternate alcoholic and non-alcoholic drinks
- dilute your drink with a mixer
- drink low alcohol wine and beer
- have drink-free days each week
- you may have to avoid your usual haunts and drinking partners on 'dry' days
- find a hobby or exercise that doesn't involve going down the pub
- drink slowly – you eliminate one unit of alcohol an hour
- don't drink on an empty stomach – food slows the rate at which you absorb alcohol into the blood
- keep a drink diary for a month recording how much and where you drank, the number of drink-free days and the amount of money you spent on alcohol – the latter can be very sobering!

Stopping drinking – or even cutting down – can be unpleasant. Your body gets used to a certain amount of alcohol circulating in the blood. Some people find that taking vitamin supplements including folic acid, the B complex and vitamins A, C and E helps stave off some of the most unpleasant feelings. Alcohol upsets your body's glucose balance, so during the first few weeks of withdrawal, add a spoonful of sugar to your tea. Low blood sugar levels may underlie some of the craving for a drink, so try eating chocolate instead. You can worry about losing weight later. After three months or so you should be over the worst of the craving.

Once you have begun to reduce your alcohol consumption, you need to deal with some of the problems that led you there. Relaxation and other stress management techniques outlined in chapter six should help. In scientific studies, transcendental meditation (page 208) produced abstinence rates of between 51 and 89 per cent over 18 months. This was up to eight times more effective than other techniques, including relaxation and education.

How to get help

If you still cannot cut down your drinking, you may need professional help. In some cases this may mean consulting a doctor. Some diseases – such as social phobia and anxiety – increase the risk of developing alcoholism. Indeed, people with social phobia often drink to give them the Dutch courage to go down the pub. Doctors can prescribe antidepressants to help people suffering from depression or social phobia to break the cycle of alcohol abuse. More recent studies suggest that some antidepressants may reduce alcohol consumption even among non-depressed alcoholics. Alcoholics sometimes receive disulfiram. When they drink alcohol, the interaction with disulfiram leads to vomiting and flushing. The unpleasant experience becomes associated with drinking alcohol and – in theory at least – the alcoholic stops drinking. US studies suggest that disulfiram may reduce the number of days patients drink alcohol. However, alcoholics receiving disulfiram are no more likely to abstain after a year than those who don't receive the drug.

If you, a friend or partner has a drink problem, voluntary organisations such as Alcoholics Anonymous* may be more approachable and more sympathetic than the local GP. Alcoholics Anonymous and other self-help groups aim to fill the void when someone stops drinking. Moreover, if the stress gets too much, the recovering alcoholic has someone to turn to for advice and support. Al-Anon* and Alcohol Concern* can help the family cope with drink and educate about ways to help.

But even with the help of these support groups stopping drinking is very difficult – especially if the person has abused alcohol for several years. Between 40 and 50 per cent of alcoholics are either totally abstinent or drinking significantly less after joining a group. However, as alcoholics who are able to control their drinking cannot be identified in advance, most groups suggest complete abstinence. Recovery from alcoholism follows several steps:

- alleviating withdrawal symptoms – benzodiazepines often help. This should only be used in the short term – otherwise alcoholics may become hooked on benzodiazepines
- abstinence
- reducing craving
- dealing with associated problems, including stress management; individual, group and family psychotherapy; overcoming vocational problems.

In the future, doctors may be able to prescribe drugs to help abstinence. Studies of the anxiolytic buspirone and naltrexone, which blocks the action of the natural opioids, have shown promising results. In the meantime, Alcoholics Anonymous* and similar groups remain an alcoholic's best route to recovery.

Stress and smoking

Smoking and stress are intimately linked. The so-called sedative smokers smoke to calm down. Other smokers – stimulant smokers – use cigarettes like cups of coffee to increase their arousal and to enhance their performance. Smoking moves people up and down the n-shaped arousal performance curve (see opposite).

Everyone knows smoking is bad for them. Unlike alcohol, there is no safe daily number of cigarettes. Nevertheless, around 28 per cent of adults still smoke. In a classic example of denial, smokers don't believe that they will have to endure smoking-induced heart disease, respiratory problems and cancer. The reality is somewhat different.

Smoking causes almost one third of cancers. If every smoker stopped tomorrow, the number of lung cancers would fall by more than 80 per cent. Smoking also increases your likelihood of developing cancer of the mouth, throat, oesophagus, pancreas, bladder, kidney, cervix and stomach. If that is not enough to put you off, smoking increases your risk of developing heart disease, circulatory problems and non-cancerous lung diseases such as emphysema and bronchitis. Moreover, smokers increasingly find themselves social lepers, banished outside or to a polluted room at

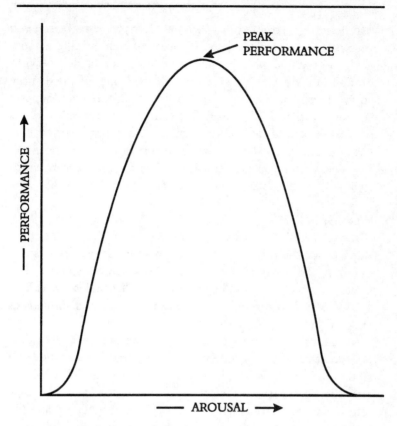

The relationship between performance and arousal

work. Smoke-free zones in restaurants and cinemas and smoke-less flights and trains are increasingly common.

In smokers' defence it is incredibly difficult to quit especially if you smoke under stress or because you suffer from depression, anxiety or alcoholism. Family problems, stressful occupations and financial difficulties increase the likelihood of smoking and the number of cigarettes smoked, and make it much more difficult to quit. Around 60 per cent of smokers report suffering from depression at some time. People suffering from anxiety disorders are twice as likely to smoke than less anxious people. Alcoholics are almost five times more likely to smoke than the general population. Stress can also lead people who have managed to give up for a while to start again.

The intimate link between stress and smoking means that you

may have to sort out some of your other problems before you become able to stop smoking. It's hard enough quitting without having to contend with the burden of depression or alcohol withdrawal, but it's worth making the effort. Much of the damage you've already done to your lungs is irreversible, but you can prevent any further decline. Stopping smoking dramatically reduces the likelihood of developing cancer. Moreover, many of the changes that predispose you to heart disease return to normal a few weeks after you stop smoking. This means that it is worth trying to quit no matter how old you are.

A passive killer

If staying healthy – or alive – isn't a good enough reason to quit, think about the harm you're doing to your partner, friends and children. You would not allow a toddler to smoke. The Children's Act banned selling cigarettes to the under-16s as long ago as 1908. But parents still endanger the health of millions of children through passive smoking.

Mounting evidence suggests that passive smoking is more than just unpleasant. It's also dangerous. Consider the findings of a study of over 10,000 children aged between 9 and 12. Children raised in homes where the parents smoked more than five cigarettes a day were more than twice as likely to cough, produce sputum and wheeze (a sign of asthma) than those living in non-smoking households.

Experts suggest that in the US, passive smoking claims 2,000 lives a year. Passive smoking may increase your likelihood of developing heart disease, brain tumours and eczema. It also increases the risk of developing lung cancer by up to 30 per cent. Furthermore, differences in the chemical composition of inhaled and environmental smoke means that passive smokers may, ironically, inhale higher levels of some carcinogens (chemicals that cause cancer) than smokers. If you don't quit for yourself quit for your family.

How to quit

As with many life changes, the first step is to want to quit. Many women stop smoking when they become pregnant. Pregnancy can also provide fathers-to-be with the motivation they need.

It's also important to be realistic and recognise how hard it is to quit – only 40 per cent of smokers succeed. Often they take several attempts. Even nicotine patches sold in pharmacists help you quit only if you really want to, but provided you are well motivated, nicotine patches roughly double your chances of quitting.

It is also important to remain positive – even if you have a setback. The problem is that nicotine withdrawal can cause depression during the first few days and weeks. You are especially likely to develop depression if you have suffered from it in the past. Three-quarters of smokers who report a history of depression suffer a recurrence after they stop smoking. Moreover, around 30 per cent of people who haven't experienced bouts of depression in the past report low mood during the first week after giving up. However, you can take a number of steps to make quitting smoking less stressful:

- Try to identify your smoking triggers. Do you smoke when you're tense? When you're bored? Only after meals? Are you a social smoker? Keep a diary and note when, where and how you feel when you light up. Once you've identified your smoking triggers you may be able to avoid them.
- Don't cut down. Give up. There isn't a safe level of regular smoking. In any case, nicotine is so addictive that few heavy smokers are able to cut down to a few cigarettes a day for any time. Each puff of each cigarette reinforces your addiction.
- Switching to low-tar cigarettes is better than nothing, but you'll be healthier still giving up. However, many people who switch to low nicotine cigarettes end up smoking more.
- Get other health problems treated, such as depression and anxiety.
- If you smoke to relieve anxiety or stress, try other ways to relax. Sedative smokers are especially likely to benefit from relaxation. Often smokers feel irritable for a while after they give up so ask for your family's support and understanding. If they know you've quit smoking they might be more willing to forgive a grouchy mood.
- Tell people you've stopped. Ask them to help by not smoking in front of you.
- Choose a date to stop – such as New Year's Day, National No Smoking Day or your birthday.

- Sit in no-smoking areas in restaurants.
- Resist the urge to smoke by chewing vegetables, sugar-free chewing gum, and so on.
- Spend at least some of the money you save on yourself, such as a holiday.
- Quitline* and Action on Smoking and Health* offer advice, information and support.

Overcoming alcohol abuse and quitting smoking is difficult and can be a source of considerable stress for patients and their families, but most feel it's worth the effort.

Dizziness, vertigo and tinnitus

Dizziness, vertigo and tinnitus are common stress-related symptoms. During panic attacks many sufferers feel on the edge of passing out. Under stress, some people feel their head is swimming or that the room is spinning. Others hear the unpleasant, persistent and intrusive ringing or hissing in their ears known as tinnitus.

Dizziness and vertigo

The link between stress, dizziness and vertigo – the feeling that the room is spinning – was first studied scientifically in the 1940s. Stress emerged as the leading cause of dizziness and vertigo, which can lead to the person passing out. Around 78 per cent of anxious patients and 56 per cent of people with post-traumatic stress disorder complain of faintness or dizziness.

Stress provokes three reactions that increase your likelihood of feeling dizzy or even fainting:

- A short-lived fall in blood pressure in situations that provoke fear or anxiety but from which escape is impossible or impracticable. For example, some people faint before a blood sample is taken. Men are more likely to experience this transitory fall in blood pressure than women.
- Hyperventilation – rapid, shallow breathing – increases levels of carbon dioxide in your blood. This reduces the amount of oxygen getting to your brain and so you feel light-headed.

- 'Hysterical faint' – this is the rather cliché'd image of a highly strung young woman who passes out at the slightest – usually sexual – provocation.

Tinnitus: the silent noise

Up to 45 per cent of adults experience tinnitus at one time or another – which causes stress out of all proportion to its volume. One per cent of people suffer from chronic tinnitus. Stress is intimately linked to tinnitus. A survey among members of a tinnitus self-help group revealed that 70 per cent reported emotional difficulties. The louder the tinnitus the greater the patients' anxiety and depression – although whether the emotional difficulties predated the tinnitus is unclear. The cause of chronic tinnitus is usually a mystery.

The incessant noise means tinnitus sufferers often find relaxation impossible and experience difficulty falling asleep. In the still of the night, even mild tinnitus can seem deafening. As a result, tinnitus undermines sufferers' concentration and leaves them tired and irritable – a combination that conspires to cause considerable stress.

So tinnitus shows the typical pattern of a stress-related disease. Stress may contribute, at least partly, to some cases. But tinnitus undoubtedly exacerbates stress, emotional distress and fatigue. Sufferers frequently feel depressed, anxious, irritable, hopeless and helpless. Anxious people running on their fight-or-flight reflex tend to show heightened perceptual acuity, so they hear their tinnitus all the more acutely.

Clearly, tinnitus sufferers have an additional motivation to lead stress-free lives. Some studies suggest that biofeedback reduces the severity of tinnitus, although results using biofeedback are mixed. Another approach involves cognitive therapy. One study compared the impact on tinnitus of cognitive therapy, yoga and patience keeping a record of their symptoms. Both cognitive therapy and yoga improved tinnitus compared to monitoring symptoms, but cognitive therapy was more effective than yoga. Patients treated with cognitive therapy were more likely to feel in control of their tinnitus and were better able to ignore the noise than those trying yoga.

But the authors admit that the study has an important limitation. Patients were randomly assigned to the three groups. In other words, they couldn't choose between cognitive therapy and yoga. While yoga can produce a profound state of relaxation and encourage a positive mind-body relationship, to gain the most benefit practitioners need a degree of sympathy for its philosophy, which is firmly rooted in Asian traditions. So randomly assigning patients may mean some subjects did not have empathy for yoga and 'went through the motions' rather than make the necessary commitment. In contrast, cognitive therapy reflects Western attitudes. Many tinnitus sufferers may feel more comfortable with a scientific and medical philosophy.

When to see your doctor

Dizziness, vertigo and tinnitus are often stress-related, but they can also signal more sinister diseases, including brain tumours, inner ear problems or multiple sclerosis. Moreover, a number of drugs – including antihypertensives, antihistamines and antidiabetic drugs – can cause dizziness, vertigo or both. So if symptoms persist, especially after you've tried some stress-relieving exercises (see chapter six) consult your doctor. You should also see your GP if you suffer blackouts or a seizure. But it is important to keep the risks in perspective. Doctors can find no evidence of a physical disease in up to 80 per cent of people who experience vertigo or dizziness.

Contact the British Tinnitus Association* or the Royal National Institute for Deaf People* for further information.

Insomnia and fatigue

Insomnia and chronic fatigue are two of the most common and most distressing stress-related symptoms. Forty per cent of insomnia cases seen by GPs are caused by stress, anxiety and depression. As many as half of all patients consulting their GP complain of feeling tired all the time. However, the suffering caused by insomnia doesn't go away when you wake in the morning. Insomnia often leads to daytime tiredness, irritation, anxiety and depression. In response GPs write 215 million prescriptions for sleeping pills a year. So how can you can you give your energy a boost?

Beating fatigue

Coffee is the most widely used way to give yourself a lift. According to legend, an Ethiopian holy man discovered coffee when he noticed that goats eating the bush's berries frisked all night. Yemeni farmers cultivated coffee in the ninth century and it was introduced to the west about 700 years later. But coffee was not welcomed with open arms. Seventeenth-century Parisians were warned that coffee shortened life. Germans in the eighteenth century could be caned for drinking coffee and King Frederick II of Prussia tried to get his subjects to switch from coffee to beer for the good of their health.

Caffeine is valued for its effects on the mind. Doses of caffeine between 85 and 200mg reduce drowsiness and fatigue and improve alertness and productivity. A cup of brewed coffee contains around 100 to 200mg, a cup of instant coffee 60-80mg and a cup of tea 40 to 100mg. The more tea and coffee you drink the greater the improvement. However, too much caffeine – over about 600mg per day – can cause headaches, irritability, tremor, palpitations and nervousness. Regular drinkers become tolerant to caffeine's effects – so you may need to brew stronger coffee to get the same effect – and caffeine's effects are short-lived. Nevertheless, caffeine remains the most popular way to boost flagging energy levels.

Eat to beat fatigue

Your cells use glucose to fuel their activities, so skipping breakfast, gobbling a chocolate bar at coffee time, grabbing a sandwich on the run between meetings and flushing it down with cola isn't the best way to beat fatigue. The sugar in chocolate and soft drinks is called sucrose. Unlike the complex carbohydrates in pasta, potatoes and whole grains, sucrose is rapidly absorbed and broken down into glucose. The body absorbs and metabolises complex carbohydrates more slowly and so the supply of glucose is more constant.

In other words, sugary drinks or chocolate provide an instant boost – but it is quickly burned off. After reaching a 'peak', blood sugar levels plummet. These fluctuating blood sugar levels promote fatigue. If you want to give yourself a longer-lasting energy boost, take a tip from athletes who eat vegetables, whole grains and fruits before a race. Ideally, carbohydrates should form 60-70 per cent of your diet, protein 10-20 per cent and fat 20-30 per cent – but keep animal (saturated) fat below 10 per cent.

Vitamin and mineral supplements

Vitamin and mineral supplements are another popular way of giving yourself a lift. Our diets are often the first casualties of stress. Many people therefore feel that taking a supplement boosts their energy levels. For example, B vitamins, ginseng and co-enzyme Q10 can combat stress-related fatigue. There is some evidence that the advocates of vitamins may be right especially about ginseng and co-enzyme Q10. Moreover, low levels of iron can lead to anaemia, especially in women, which leaves you tired and worn out. However, tablets don't replace a healthy diet.

Sleep and insomnia

Getting enough rest is one of the best ways to beat fatigue. Everyone suffers from insomnia at one time or another, and jet lag, nerves, bereavement and general stress can lead to a few sleepless nights. But at any one time one person in five suffers from chronic insomnia and for between 10 and 15 per cent of the population insomnia becomes an entrenched problem. Some people suffer from insomnia for 10 or 20 years – sometimes longer.

Insomnia leaves sufferers worn out, irritable and stressed. It can also prove dangerous. A sleepless night reduces alertness, concentration and ability to cope with stress. Insomniacs also take more sick leave. But for some occupations – pilots, taxi and lorry drivers and doctors, for example – poor concentration or falling asleep during the day may threaten the lives of themselves and others. A quarter of motorway crashes may be caused by sleepiness and 80 per cent of these crashes involve fatalities.

What is sleep?

Considering that we spend a third of our lives asleep we know remarkably little about it. Nobody knows why sleep evolved. Some specialists believe sleep helps us recuperate. Other researchers see sleep as 'mental downtime' allowing us to process the day's input of sensations, information and experiences. Still others suggest sleep evolved to keep us out of danger at night. But there is no doubt that sleep is more complex than unconsciousness punctuated by dreams.

Recordings of the brain's electrical activity reveal that sleep consists of five main stages. One stage, Rapid Eye Movement (REM) sleep, is associated with dreaming and may contribute to learning, memory, mood and sexuality. REM sleep usually accounts for around a quarter of normal sleep. Slow wave sleep occurs during two of the four non-REM stages we go through each night and may assist rest and recuperation. In normal adults, there are five non-REM/REM cycles, organised into a pattern known as the sleep architecture.

How much sleep is normal?

Most of us sleep for around seven or eight hours a night, but the amount of sleep we actually need varies widely. Some people get away with five or six hours, while others need ten. The amount of sleep we need changes with age. Babies sleep for up to 16 hours a day; teenagers need about 10 hours; young adults need eight hours; and the middle-aged and elderly less than seven hours. As we get older, the biological clock controlling the sleep-wake cycle begins to wind down. As a result, many elderly patients nap during the day, so they sleep less at night and complain of insomnia. Sleep quality is more important that quantity: you're getting enough if you don't feel sleepy, tired, lethargic and apathetic during the day.

What is insomnia?

Strictly speaking, insomnia is a total inability to sleep. However, all insomniacs sleep. Time drags during the night and insomniacs often overestimate the amount of time they spend awake. For example, insomniacs who say they took 90 minutes to fall asleep may be awake for less than half an hour. Most of us fall asleep within 20 minutes. Insomniacs often claim that they get less than four hours' sleep a night. In reality, it's closer to six. Insomnia is highly subjective and attitudes about how much sleep is normal colour patients' expectations.

Doctors recognise three broad types of insomnia.

- initial insomnia: patients experience difficulties falling asleep
- sleep maintenance insomnia: patients wake frequently during the night
- terminal insomnia: patients wake early in the morning and cannot fall asleep again – terminal insomnia is a hallmark of depression.

Stress, anxiety, depression, chronic pain and a variety of other diseases can cause any of the three types of insomnia, but they may also result from conditioned insomnia. If you sleep terribly at home, but well on business trips, or if you doze off in front of the TV but then can't sleep in bed, you could be suffering from conditioned insomnia. In other words, you have come to associate your bed and bedroom with not sleeping. When you enter the bedroom you become more alert, which makes it harder to sleep.

How to get a good night's sleep

The first step is to treat any underlying condition that could contribute to insomnia. For example, the chronic pain of arthritis can leave patients unable to sleep. People suffering from tinnitus often find falling asleep difficult. Depression can cause a range of sleep disturbances, and sleep apnoea, where sleepers snore more and more loudly, then jerk awake, leaves sufferers – and their partners – tired, stressed and irritable. Most people with sleep apnoea have no recollection of waking many times in the night – they complain of feeling excessively tired during the day without reason. They are usually male and with a collar size of at least 17. A number of treatments are now available for sleep apnoea – which affects around four per cent of middle-aged men and two per cent of middle-aged women. The British Snoring and Sleep Apnoea Association* offers advice about sleep apnoea, snoring and sleep disturbances.

Once you are undergoing treatment for any physical problems, try following these good sleep hygiene tips. The box on page 172 contains some specific suggestions to beat jet lag.

- Go to bed at the same time each night and set your alarm for the same time each morning – including weekends. This re-establishes a normal sleep pattern.

- Try not to take your troubles to bed with you. Stress keeps you awake. Brooding on your problems makes them seem worse, exacerbates stress, keeps you awake and, as you're tired in the morning, less able to deal with your difficulties.
- Don't worry about anything you've forgotten to do. Get up. Note what you have to do and then forget it until the morning.
- If you're going to have an argument or a heavy discussion, don't have it just before you go to bed. Emotional upsets can lead to a disturbed night.
- Avoid naps during the day.
- Avoid stimulants such as nicotine and caffeine for a couple of hours before bed. Remember that tea, coffee, cocoa, cola and some medications contain caffeine.
- Try hot milk: milky drinks help some people sleep. However, too much fluid in the evening can mean regular nocturnal trips to the bathroom.
- Avoid alcohol at bedtime. Many insomniacs believe that an alcoholic nightcap helps them sleep. In fact, alcohol has the opposite effect. A nightcap may help you fall asleep and sleep more deeply during the first third of the night, but as blood alcohol levels fall sleep becomes lighter, more fragmented and drinkers tend to wake repeatedly during the latter half of the night – partly because they repeatedly visit the bathroom. Furthermore, alcohol increases the volume and amount of snoring and exacerbates sleep apnoea, which can leave your partner unable to sleep.
- Try eating a light meal in the early evening rather than a curry an hour before bedtime. Heavily spiced meals often disrupt sleep. Some people find, however, that a light snack before bed staves off hunger pangs that keep them awake.
- Regular exercise during the day helps you sleep but exercising just before you go to bed can make insomnia worse.
- A hot bath helps relax tense muscles.
- Learn relaxation and correct breathing techniques – these can alleviate anxiety and stress and relax tense muscles.
- Use the bed for sleep and sex only. Don't work or watch TV in bed.
- Make the bed as comfortable as possible. Sleep on a comfort-

able mattress, with enough bed clothes.
- Make sure the bedroom isn't too hot, too cold or too bright.
- Try to limit sudden noise. You can sleep against a considerable amount of background noise – provided the volume is constant. Some people find white noise – the random sounds produced by a fan, for example – aids sleep.
- If you still can't sleep – don't lie there worrying about your insomnia: there's nothing worse for keeping you awake. Get up and read or watch TV until you feel tired. Then go back to bed.

Good sleep hygiene often helps overcome insomnia without the need for sleeping pills. However, even after sticking to the rules a 'hard core' of insomniacs remain unable to get a good night's rest. If you find yourself in this situation, consider taking a short course of sleeping tablets. Alternatively, take the sleeping tablets intermittently as you need them. This will help re-establish a normal sleep pattern, while the sleep hygiene begins to work.

Beating jet lag
* avoid stimulants during the flight, including coffee, tea and cola
* avoid alcohol during the flight – alcohol promotes dehydration * try to keep going; sleep as little as possible until the night after landing or until the local bedtime * a sleeping tablet, such as zopiclone and zolpidem, helps establish a local sleep pattern * consider taking 2 mg of melatonin before going to bed

---

A brief history of sleeping pills

We've been searching for ways to get a good night's sleep for millennia. Our ancestors tried bloodletting, elaborate ceremonies to local gods and concoctions made from snakes and geese as insomnia remedies. The Ancient Egyptians drank wine and probably used opium in sleeping potions. Insomniacs continued to use opium well into the nineteenth century. Western herbalists still use a number of plants, including hops, skullcap and valerian, to treat insomnia. Some undoubtedly work – but the same criticism can be applied to many herbal remedies as to sleeping pills: they don't tackle the cause of the insomnia.

Victorian England overcame insomnia with bromide, paraldehyde, laudanum and chloral hydrate. Only chloral hydrate is still used today, as a sleeping potion for children. The early years of this century saw the launch of the first barbiturates, which certainly helped insomniacs sleep. But at a price. Barbiturates are highly addictive, interact with alcohol and other drugs, and are lethal in overdose.

Then in the 1960s the benzodiazepines were launched. The first benzodiazepines, including chlordiazepoxide (Librium) and diazepam (Valium), were tranquillisers. The first benzodiazepine specifically for insomnia was nitrazepam (Mogadon) launched in 1965. Benzodiazepines are much safer than barbiturates and, at the time, doctors believed they were non-addictive. They quickly became the nation's favourite sleeping pills.

Despite their popularity, sleeping pills have a limited impact – a 15-minute reduction in the time people take to fall asleep and perhaps 30 or 40 minutes longer asleep. Furthermore, over the years, doctors recognised that benzodiazepines had important disadvantages. For example, they can cause rebound insomnia. In other words, when long-term benzodiazepine users stop taking the tablets the insomnia returns: sometimes worse than ever.

Benzodiazepines are also highly addictive. Their effects on sleep begin to decline in as little as three weeks. Some patients take higher doses to get the same effect, but most remain on the same – possibly ineffective – dose indefinitely. This cycle of reduced effect leading to increasing dose can lead to addiction.

Furthermore, many benzodiazepines are long-acting. With some, such as nitrazepam, the blood concentration in the morning is high enough to produce a hangover and impair daytime performance. Benzodiazepines can, for example, impair driving ability. Less commonly, benzodiazepines can cause amnesia, especially of short-term memory.

So is there ever a role for sleeping tablets? Newer sleeping pills, such as zopiclone and zolpidem, are prescribed for only 10-14 days at a time and do not cause rebound insomnia. By relieving the burden of insomnia, these short courses give you time to deal with your underlying stress and give the sleep hygiene techniques a chance to work.

Chronic fatigue syndrome

Chronic fatigue syndrome is one of the most controversial diseases to emerge in recent years. Also known as 'myalgic encephalomyelitis' (ME) and 'yuppie flu', it typically strikes young, female professionals with hectic, stressful lives. Once they contract chronic fatigue syndrome they begin to endure a crippling, severe, persistent fatigue that lasts at least six months and that dramatically reduces their ability to live their hectic lives.

Despite intensive research, the cause of chronic fatigue syndrome remains a mystery. Viral infections, allergy, dietary intolerance and poisoning have all been suggested. Around one third to three-quarters of people with chronic fatigue syndrome also suffer from other psychological diseases, particularly depression, anxiety and panic disorder, which they may be reluctant to acknowledge. However, it is unclear whether psychological problems cause or follow chronic fatigue syndrome. Whatever the cause, chronic fatigue syndrome can be a devastating, frustrating and stressful disease.

Doctors believe that patients with chronic fatigue syndrome are trapped in a cycle of despair. An initial trigger, possibly but not always viral, leads to chronic, untreated post-viral depression or a cycle of fatigue, pain and disability – especially if patients do not give themselves enough time to recover from the infection. This fatigue becomes self-sustaining and disables the patient. A number of factors trigger and maintain chronic fatigue syndrome including depression and insufficient rest while recuperating from illness.

Some chronic fatigue syndrome sufferers believe that trying to do too much too soon causes irreparable harm, so they lead a house-bound or even bed-bound life. This reduces exercise tolerance and means that sufferers are even less able to live normally. Other sufferers intersperse intense exercise with prolonged rest – the so-called 'boom and bust' pattern. Frustration, boredom, personal expectations and social pressures can lead to patients adopting a boom and bust lifestyle.

Treating a disease without a cause

Treating a disease without a cause is frustrating for patients and their doctors. Around 50 per cent of CFS patients benefit from antidepressants. The best hope seems to be cognitive therapy to break the cycle of disability exacerbating fatigue. In one study 70 per cent of patients improved after three months' treatment.

Cognitive behavioural therapy takes a four step approach:

- Patients keep a diary recording the type and severity of their symptoms, an hour-by-hour assessment of their activities and rest periods. This forms the basis of the programme. During treatment, the diary allows sufferers to assess progress.
- Patients follow a regular pattern of activity and rest, regardless of symptoms. For example, instead of doing all the housework during a single day when they feel more energetic, they may split the tasks over a week.
- Patients gradually increase the duration, range and number of activities. However, rest and activity are spread evenly throughout the day, rather than following a boom and bust pattern. Moreover, the tasks are those that patients want to perform, such as meeting friends, gardening or cooking.
- The therapist identifies and modifies beliefs, fears and anxieties that maintain the illness. For example, sufferers may believe that 'chronic fatigue syndrome is an untreatable, persistent and irreversible condition'. But this view simply fuels fatigue.

Many chronic fatigue syndrome sufferers find help in the complementary therapies – although no treatment, conventional or alternative, works for everyone. Some people benefit from vitamin supplements, herbalism, yoga, acupuncture and naturopathy. However, overcoming chronic fatigue syndrome requires patience and perseverance. It is often deeply entrenched and there are no overnight cures.

Contact the ME Association* for further advice and information.

CHAPTER 6

THE ANTI-STRESS DIRECTORY

THE PRECEDING chapters have examined the causes of stress, explored the link between stress and physical and psychological illness, and suggested ways you can look at your life to tackle your problem. However, change exerts an emotional toll. This chapter looks at some of the ways you can bolster your stress defences.

In many cases, there is little scientific evidence that these techniques work. However, people undoubtedly benefit. Cynics claim that this merely reflects the power of suggestion. But doctors are beginning to view alternative medicine in a more favourable light. According to a recent survey, almost half of all GPs support using complementary therapies, especially acupuncture and homeopathy. The survey revealed that almost 40 per cent of GPs now offer some complementary medicine to patients.

This directory briefly summarises some techniques. Regard the search as something of a voyage of discovery. You may need to try a few approaches before finding the one that's right for you. However, the experimentation will provide you with new insights into your life. So read through the directory until you find two or three approaches for which you feel an affinity – then find out more. Most of the therapies have organisations where you can receive further information, and there are books which you should be able to obtain through your local book shop or library. The Institute for Complementary Medicine*, the Council for Complementary and Alternative Medicine* and the British Complementary Medicine Association* are umbrella organisations for complementary and alternative therapies.

In some ways, waiting until stress develops means you have left it too late. Many of the techniques listed in the directory can act as first-aid for stress, but the majority are at their most effective when used to prevent stress arising in the first place.

Acupuncture

Acupuncture, one of the oldest treatments for stress, remains one of the most widely used. Archaeologists have uncovered stone needles dating from 10,000 BC and the first acupuncture texts were written over 2,000 years ago. Now over three million practitioners use acupuncture worldwide. Most of these are in Asia, although acupuncture is increasingly used by Western doctors and complementary practitioners.

Acupuncture's roots lie deep in Eastern philosophy. Over the last 25 years acupuncture has been increasingly accepted by Western doctors, although there are differences between Western and Eastern approaches. The Chinese believe that every organ, every process and every action contains chi – also transliterated as ki or qi. The chi flows along 12 meridians or 'channels' running through the body linking internal organs. Diseases arise when stress, anxiety, fear, grief, infections or trauma disturb the flow of chi. Acupuncture aims to balance the flow of chi along these meridians and so prevent and treat illness, while reinforcing your stress defences.

As chi flows along meridians, acupuncture needles inserted into one part of your body influence organs some distance away. For instance, inserting a needle into the nose influences the lungs. Likewise, needling the foot alleviates severe headaches. The acupuncturist may also examine your tongue or pulse, but this reveals, Chinese doctors believe, far more about your health than just your heart rate. Pulse and tongue diagnosis is backed by questions about your lifestyle, medical history, diet, sleep patterns and emotions, which allow the practitioner to develop a picture of you and your problem.

The view from the West

Western medical acupuncturists look for sensitive trigger points. These trigger points are known as Ashi in traditional Chinese medicine, where they are associated with fixed points on the

177

meridians. When pressed, trigger points cause a sensation in another part of the body, usually pain. Injury, strain, stress, damp, cold, infection and muscle tension can set off trigger points. For example, when stressed we tense our muscles. Over time, muscle tension leads to trigger points, which in turn may establish other trigger points.

Medical acupuncturists insert a needle into these trigger points. For example, needling an arthritis patient's trigger points can alleviate pain. This reduces the stress associated with arthritis and, as pain often causes insomnia, helps the patient get a good night's rest.

Traditionally, needles are left in place for around 20 or 30 minutes. However, some Western physicians use needling times of about five minutes with, they claim, similar results.

While the needle is in place, and for a while after the session, many people report feeling relaxed. However, the underlying problem begins to improve after around five sessions – although pain can respond more quickly. Around 60 per cent of migraine sufferers benefit from acupuncture after between six and eight sessions. However, the effect may begin to wear off after between 12 and 18 months, although some people benefit for longer.

Trigger points can also be warmed using moxa, a herb that burns without producing an intense heat. Moxa – the common mugwort – is applied directly to the skin or to the end of the acupuncture needle. In other cases, the needle is stimulated using an electric current. Practitioners may also manipulate the needle to stimulate the points. Alternatively, especially in children or people with a fear of needles, the practitioner may use acupressure, where points on the meridians are stimulated using finger pressure.

Conventional doctors regard acupuncture as safe and effective but only for reversible conditions, such as pain. According to conventional medical theory, acupuncture works by stimulating the release of natural opioid pain killers. In contrast, traditional practitioners believe that acupuncture helps a wide range of conditions including anxiety, allergies, migraine, high blood pressure and menstrual problems by re-balancing the physical, spiritual and emotional aspects of a person's character. This stimulates the body's innate healing abilities. The arguments between conventional doctors and traditional acupuncturists now focus on what conditions acupuncture treats rather than whether or not it works.

The British Acupuncture Council*, which governs acupuncture in the UK, can supply a list of qualified practitioners in your area. Many GPs also now offer acupuncture – usually only for pain relief. Whoever treats you, make sure they use sterile needles.

Alexander technique

The end of the nineteenth century was a golden age for manipulation. Chiropractic and osteopathy were being developed and, around the same time, the Australian actor F. Matthias Alexander began experiencing serious voice problems, which doctors failed to alleviate. However, Alexander noticed that when he began to speak he pulled his head back and inhaled. By changing the way he held his head and neck he found that he could improve his breathing. That observation lead to the Alexander technique, which practitioners claim relieves many stress-related problems throughout the body.

For example, a bored computer clerk slumped over her keyboard isn't going to do much for her lower back pain. Similarly, stress can lead to bad posture, which in turn may cause headaches, so if you habitually adopt postures for which the body isn't designed, Alexander argued, your muscles and nerves aren't going to work correctly. If your nerves don't work properly, neither do the organs they serve. Alexander practitioners re-educate you about the correct postures. This restores the body's normal functions.

During an Alexander session, you perform exercises to restore your bodily control, alleviate the strain and relax. You will also learn to watch for and correct poor posture. Eventually, this becomes second nature. However, you cannot teach yourself the Alexander technique: practitioners can take 30 or more sessions to re-educate your body.

Alexander Technique International*, Alexander Teaching Network* and the Society of Teachers of Alexander Technique* all hold lists of approved teachers.

Aromatherapy

Aromatherapy uses aromatic essential oils distilled from plants, leaves, petals, barks and roots to promote mental, physical and emotional health. Plants produce essential oils to encourage pollination, prevent invasion by bacteria and fungi, and to attract insects. Aromatherapists claim that essential oils also alleviate stress-related diseases, anxiety and tension. A growing body of scientific evidence supports aromatherapists' claims.

A brief history of aromatherapy

The 400 essential oils in widespread use have a rich heritage. Priests anointed their followers with oil. Lovers have long used essential oils as aphrodisiacs. Nowadays we spend millions on perfumes and after-shaves to make ourselves feel good.

Essential oils also have a long medical history. The Ancient Egyptians used aromatic oils to treat skin diseases. Later medieval physicians believed that essential oils protected people from the plague. Aromatherapists suggest that essential oils have proved their worth over the years in thousands of people treated for chronic illnesses. However, aromatherapy is more than a quaint folk remedy. In the 1930s, French chemists used essential oils as antibacterials and to treat skin cancers, ulcers and gangrene. More recently, coronary care wards and hospices caring for critically ill cancer patients have begun to use essential oils not to cure, but to relieve anxiety, tension and stress.

In one study, patients with advanced cancers were massaged using an essential oil or the carrier (base oil) alone. The patients massaged using the aromatherapy oils showed fewer physical symptoms and reported less anxiety, tension and pain. While aromatherapy does not cure cancer it seems to reduce patients' suffering. Midwives are also trying aromatherapy to help in childbirth.

How aromatherapy works

Aromatherapists use essential oils to alleviate tension, restlessness, anxiety and other stress-related symptoms. During stress you tend to take shallow breaths. Aromatherapy can make you breathe more deeply – which relieves stress. Try sprinkling lavender oil on a handkerchief and taking a few deep breaths. It is difficult – if not impossible – to remain physically and mentally tense if you breathe deeply. Some people find sprinkling essential oils on their pillows at night helps them sleep. Essential oils blended with almond oil or other fats can be massaged into tense muscles. You can also add a few drops of essential oils into your bath, but you need to soak for at least a quarter of an hour. Using essential oils, aromatherapists suggest, can reduce stress, lift mood and keep your outlook positive (see the box).

Aromatherapy in stress
* Basil: for fatigue, anxiety, depression
* Camomile: for anger
* Frankincense: uplifting, aids concentration
* Jasmine: for anxiety, depression; a general tonic
* Lavender: for muscle tension, headaches, insomnia
* Lemon grass: for headaches
* Neroli (bitter orange): sedative; for depression, palpitations, pre-menstrual tension, insomnia
* Peppermint: for headaches, indigestion, nausea
* Rose: for depression, headaches, mental fatigue, pre-menstrual tension
*Ylang-ylang: for anxiety, depression, insomnia

Scientists do not fully understand how essential oils work. Part of the problem is that the essential oils are complex cocktails of active ingredients. No one is sure which ingredient, or which combination, underlies their benefits.

Nevertheless, there are two main theories explaining aromatherapy's benefits. Our sense of smell is very sensitive – some 10,000 times more sensitive than taste, for example. Babies bond to their mothers, in part, through smell, and pheromones – scents secreted to attract a mate – may contribute to sexual attraction. Some researchers believe that essential oils work by stimulating the brain's pleasure centres. They suggest that the fragrance of essential oils stimulates the olfactory – smell – centre, which lies close to the brain's limbic centre. The limbic centre is the region of the brain governing emotions, including love, sexual desire, excitement and pleasure, so stimulating the limbic system counters stress and produces pleasurable sensations.

Other scientists suggest that essential oils act in a way similar to some medicines. A fatty membrane surrounds each cell in our bodies. Floating in the membrane – rather like icebergs in the sea – are protein channels which allow calcium, chloride and other ions to flow in and out of the cell. For example, muscular contraction follows an influx of calcium into muscle cells. Some drugs – including calcium antagonists used to treat high blood pressure and angina – act by blocking the flow of calcium into muscles in the heart and blood vessels. The muscles relax, which lowers blood pressure and relieves the pain of angina. The ion flow also releases chemicals that cause inflammation and promote nerve signals.

Some researchers believe that essential oils influence the flow of ions into and out of cells. Essential oils penetrate rapidly through skin, nose, mouth, throat and gut. Once in the body, the oils may enter the fatty membrane surrounding each cell. Essential oils that inhibit the flow of calcium would, therefore, alleviate muscle contraction and ease stress-induced muscle tension. Of course, aromatherapy's benefits could be a combination of both actions.

Whatever the explanation, there is no doubt that thousands of people find aromatherapy alleviates stress and helps them relax. However, aromatherapy isn't totally free from side-effects. For example, bergamot and lemon can make the skin more sensitive to ultraviolet light – in other words, you sunburn more easily; and pregnant women should avoid certain essential oils, such as parsley and camphor, which can trigger miscarriages. However, some women find pregnancy a stressful experience and mothers-to-be – and perhaps their partners – may benefit from using oils under the supervision of a qualified aromatherapist.

Buying essential oils

The rapidly growing interest in aromatherapy means that 'aromatherapy oils' are turning up in health shops, chemists and supermarkets. However, the quality varies dramatically between suppliers. Environmental factors, such as soil, climate and the season, can alter the subtle balance of active chemicals in the essential oil.

Rosemary oil, for instance, can help relieve stress-induced muscle tension. Rosemary contains two main active ingredients: eucalyptol and alpha-pinene. But these have opposite effects on muscles. Eucalyptol alleviates muscle spasm, while alpha-pinene induces spasm. Contradictory effects are common in chemicals isolated plants, a phenomenon known as balancing. However, depending on when and where the rosemary is harvested the essential oil's muscle relaxing potency varies. Other 'aromatherapy' oils contain dilute essential oil or cheaper and less effective herbs, the end product resulting in a pleasant smelling oil with about as much therapeutic value as a bubble bath.

Finding a therapist

Aromatherapy is rapidly becoming one of the most popular complementary therapies and you can use essential oils to bolster your stress defences. However, treating more serious stress-related problems may mean consulting a registered aromatherapist. The International Federation of Aromatherapists* and the Aromatherapy Organisations Council* can supply lists of approved practitioners.

Assertiveness training

Feeling in control is one of the strongest stress defences. Nurturing this feeling means being assertive when you need to be. If this doesn't come naturally, assertiveness training helps you stand up for your rights without infringing anyone else's. Perhaps most importantly assertiveness training teaches you to be able to say 'no' without feeling guilty. Always saying yes to every request inevitably causes stress – through lack of time if nothing else.

During assertiveness training you may act out situations where you need to be assertive – an unreasonable, last-minute request from your boss to work late that conflicts with other plans, for example. The trainer then comments on your performance, including your voice and body language. Many adult education centres run assertiveness training. Contact your local library or local adult education centre for details.

Autogenic training

Try to will your saliva to flow. You probably can't. Now imagine your favourite meal. Your saliva probably pours out. Visualisation and autogenic training rely on the same principle to retrain your body and 'down-regulate' the stress response.

Autogenic training comes from humble origins. Towards the end of the last century, a French chemist, Emile Coué, became interested in placebos. He attributed their effectiveness to auto-suggestion. In other words, patients benefited because they willed themselves well. Coué decided to cut out the placebo and directly tap the power of the mind. Coué asked his patients to repeat the saying 'every day, in every way, I'm getting better and better' several times a day as a general health tonic. The phrase could vary depending on your complaint. 'Every day, I'm feeling more and more relaxed,' for example.

Couéism became a worldwide craze. By the First World War, Coué was training 40,000 people a year. People chanted in the bath, on trains and over breakfast. However, the medical establishment viewed Couéism as a simplistic joke during the 1930s. Like all crazes, Couéism gradually faded away.

However, around the same time as Couéism was in decline, the German physician Johannes Schultz took autosuggestion one step further. Schultz trained patients to alter their blood flow so that by reciting to themselves 'my hands are warm' they became warm. His technique, autogenic training, allows practitioners to exert some control over their autonomic nervous systems. As the autonomic nervous system drives the fight-or-flight reflex, autogenic training can be used to reduce stress, fatigue and tension.

Autogenic training is most effective when taught by approved trainers, but you can try autogenic training at home. You need to relax completely. So lie or sit comfortably in a quiet, dark room. Close your eyes. Then, as in progressive muscle relaxation, you focus your attention on one part of your body at a time. For example, you could say 'My left leg is warm'. Repeat this a few times and then move to another part of your body. Alternatively, repeat: 'My breathing is calm and regular,' until you relax.

Autogenic training is harder than it sounds. Ideally, you should practise twice daily for twenty minutes. Contact the British Association for Autogenic Training* for details of approved practitioners.

Visualisation

Once you have mastered the basic autogenic training you can 'implant' suggestions by visualising them in as much detail as possible. So, if your golf handicap is a source of frustration, try to visualise every stroke on the course. Visualise the ball missing the bunker you always hit. Visualise making the putt you always miss.

You can use visualisation to counter stress. Some people build a place of their own in their minds. They may walk along a favourite river bank surrounded by the early morning mist. They may sit by a cool mountain lake surrounded by the scent of pine trees or lie on a quiet, hot tropical beach. At times of stress, they can close their eyes and take a mental vacation in their favourite spot.

However, visualisation helps you make a more direct assault on stress. Say, for example, that you're feeling stressed because you plan to ask your boss for a rise. You can use visualisation to imagine that your meeting is successful. Visualising success increases the likelihood of it becoming reality – a fact well known, and widely used, by sportsmen.

Bach flower remedies

Bach flower remedies fuse herbalism and homeopathy into a system that, its advocates claim, tackles the stress-related mental disorders underlying physical illness. The system's founder, Dr Edward Bach, believed that the efficacy of the remedies lay in more than their herbal constituents or homeopathic potency: the plant, and in turn the remedy, also draws on a spiritual power that 'cleanses mind and body.'

Dr Bach practised for over 20 years as a Harley Street consultant, bacteriologist and homeopath. While working in the Royal London Homeopathic Hospital, he realised that patients who required the same homeopathic preparation did not necessarily experience the same symptoms. However, he believed that they suffered from the same underlying mental and emotional problems. As a result, he successfully based his homeopathic treatment on patients' mental and emotional states rather than their physical symptoms.

Bach understood his patients' distress – he suffered from acute attacks of every negative emotion. During these bouts of mental torment, he would wander around country lanes and fields until he felt drawn to a flower, tree or bush that restored his serenity. Bach believed that he could 'sense' a plant's therapeutic properties – in much the same way that intuition guides traditional healers. Based on his intuition, Bach developed 38 remedies – each for a different mood, emotion or personality (see box).

Within each category, the remedies tackle specific problems. For example, Bach's disciples use hornbeam to overcome the

---

Bach flower remedies
* Fear, apprehension, anxiety, terror: e.g. mimulus, aspen or rock rose
* Uncertainty, indecision: e.g. scleranthus or cerato
* Hopelessness, despondency, dejection: e.g. gorse, gentian or sweet chestnut
* Over-concern for others' welfare: e.g. red chestnut or chicory
* Hatred and envy, intolerance, impatience: e.g. holly, beech or impatiens
* Lack of confidence, 'putting on a brave face': e.g. larch or agrimony
* Day-dreaming, bemused, apathetic: e.g. clematis or wild rose
* Dominating, autocratic, rigid, tense, hyperactive: e.g. vine, rock water or vervain

---

'Monday morning blues' and procrastination. Olive helps fatigue. Walnut, they claim, smooths the adjustment to new circumstances, including puberty, menopause and divorce. Wild oat helps you determine your path in life. However, Bach is most famous for the rescue remedy – a concoction containing cherry plum, clematis, impatiens, rock rose and star of Bethlehem. Bach developed the rescue remedy as an emergency composite to comfort and reassure people who received bad news or who sank into a 'numbed, bemused state of mind'. Many people take the rescue remedy to help themselves cope with everyday stressors, such as taking exams and going to the dentist.

Bach flower remedies do not treat physical illness, but Bach's followers believe that, by overcoming negative emotions, his flower remedies gently restore the balance between mind, body and spirit. This produces a state of mind that allows the body's innate healing powers to take over. The Bach centre's curators claim that these remedies have been used successfully by more than a million people worldwide, including medical practitioners and homeopaths. However, unlike homeopathy, no scientific studies have been performed to confirm their claims.

Using Bach flower remedies
Bach prepared his remedies using homeopathic principles. The 'mother tinctures' are still prepared by the Dr Edward Bach Centre* in Oxfordshire, using the methods passed down by Dr

Bach to two of his personal assistants and their chosen successors. The mother tinctures are then diluted into concentrates, which you can buy in dark glass bottles fitted with a dropper from chemists and health shops. You add two drops of the remedy to a cup of water, which you sip at intervals. Alternatively, put the two drops in a 30ml bottle of spring water and place four drops on your tongue four times daily. The rescue remedy can also be applied to the skin as a liquid and cream. Even animals and plants are said to benefit from the rescue remedy.

As with homeopathy, Bach flower remedies are said to be most effective when tailored to your personality, outlook, worries, and so on, so while you can treat yourself, some people may benefit from the insights provided by trained Bach counsellors, who can be contacted through the Dr Edward Bach Centre*. There are now some 300 registered Bach counsellors drawn from a cross-section of homeopaths, GPs, nurses, chiropractors and reflexologists.

Biofeedback

Biofeedback allows you to exert some control over autonomic nervous system activity, which, unlike the voluntary nervous system, is not normally under conscious control. A biofeedback machine may make a sound or flash a light that varies according to the level of activity in your autonomic nervous system. By listening to the clicks or watching the display, practitioners train themselves to regulate the signals. This allows them to exert some control over their autonomic functions.

Some biofeedback machines respond to heart beat, blood pressure, respiration rate and muscle tension. Others, for example those used to aid general relaxation, respond to skin changes. As you become more stressed or aroused, you tend to sweat more. As a result, your skin conducts electricity more easily. The machine converts these changes in conductance into a noise that increases in pitch as you became more aroused. More sophisticated biofeedback machines respond to brain wave patterns that seem to relate to mental states – relaxation, for example.

Biofeedback, introduced in the late 1960s, alleviates a variety of stress-related disorders including migraine, insomnia, high blood pressure and chronic pain – in some patients at least. Using biofeedback, one client reduced her blood pressure sufficiently to allow her to stop taking antihypertensives. (But never reduce your dose of any drug without talking to your doctor first.) Biofeedback has even helped hyperactive children and those with reading difficulties.

A group of tension headache sufferers learnt to control muscle tension in the forehead by using biofeedback. The machine 'clicked' more rapidly as muscle tension increased. When the subjects relaxed, the frequency of the clicks slowed. By learning to slow the 'click rate', the sufferers reduced muscle tension. The results were compared with sufferers who did not undergo biofeedback training and others who received false feedback. Compared with the other groups, biofeedback subjects experienced less muscle tension, fatigue and insomnia, suffered fewer headaches, used fewer drugs and reported a general improvement in well-being. However, there is no proof that biofeedback offers any advantages over the other relaxation techniques.

Moreover, biofeedback is not universally effective. It can take perseverance and persistence to learn correctly and patients' response varies. People with type A personalities (see chapter one) may be more suited to biofeedback than other relaxation techniques. They seem to respond best when their achievements are on show – which probably says as much about their personalities as it does about biofeedback. Nevertheless, biofeedback is undoubtedly effective in some people. However, biofeedback is not widely available beyond research centres and you may have to buy your own machine. Aleph One* supplies biofeedback machines commercially.

Chiropractic

Chiropractic was developed by Daniel David Palmer in 1895. Over the intervening century, chiropractic became one of the most widely used complementary therapies. Chiropractic has much in common with osteopathy. Practitioners in both disciplines believe that spinal misalignment underlies many diseases.

The spine acts as a conduit for nerves to and from the brain and body. Spinal misalignment may pinch nerves and blood vessels and so affect the organs they serve. So depending on the site, a misalignment may affect the heart, liver, lungs, gastrointestinal tract or kidneys. Correcting the abnormality allows the body to heal itself. As a result, osteopaths and chiropractors claim to alleviate migraine, asthma, constipation, period pains, heart disease and digestive disorders. So while many people consult a chiropractor to treat a back problem they may find treatment relieves other stress-related disorders, such as irritable bowel syndrome.

Chiropractic and osteopathy differ mainly in the type of manipulation the practitioners employ. Traditionally, chiropractors use short, sharp thrusts and pulling directly to the spine. Osteopaths (see page 217) tend to use leverage. For example, nine out of ten patients consulting a chiropractor undergo spinal adjustment. The remaining 10 per cent undergo mobilisation, stretching, and so on. Osteopaths use mobilisation, stretching and wiggling joints to about the same extent as spinal manipulation. However, these differences mean that chiropractic and osteopathy complement each other. If one fails try the other.

Chiropractors strive to uncover the cause of the spinal misalignment by examining posture, occupation, weight and so on. This may include taking an X-ray – despite the majority of chiropractic consultations being for musculoskeletal and joints problems rather than fractures. If the examination uncovers a 'medical' condition – such as heart disease, an infection or lung disease – the patient is referred to a conventional doctor. Chiropractors may also suggest changes in diet and personal hygiene. They may, for example, advise the patient on the correct posture and changing the way they sit, sleep and walk. The British Association for Applied Chiropractic*, McTimoney Chiropractic Association* and the British Chiropractic Association* can provide the names of approved chiropractors.

Colour therapy

We react emotionally to colour, which is why the ancient Egyptians and Greeks painted their temples in bright colours. For instance, a red light universally means stop or – as it's the colour of blood – danger.

Modern colour therapy uses our emotional responses to colour to treat stress-related ailments. Therapists use colour, shapes and rhythm to treat emotional, psychological and physical problems. They believe, for example, that bright colours enhance self-confidence and spontaneity. Pale colours suggest immaturity. Dark colours are negative.

Colour's psychological effects are enhanced with certain shapes and rhythms – blue is associated with the sphere for instance. The combination of colours, shapes and movement produces a physical response, such as relaxation or stimulation. Therapists suggest surrounding yourself with this combination, in the colours of your walls, lights and fabrics. Coloured images can also be used as a focus for meditation.

There is no doubt that colour schemes can make a room seem warm and inviting or cold and unattractive. We all choose clothes of colours that reflect our personality. However, there is little evidence that colour therapy can effectively treat stress-related illness – other than the anecdotal reports of people who have benefited.

Contact the Universal Colour Healers Research Foundation* for more information.

Counselling

Counselling's popularity has grown rapidly in recent years. Around a third of GP practices – mainly in the south-east – employ a practice counsellor and thousands more counsellors practise privately. Advocates of counselling claim that GPs offering a full range of counselling services are able to reduce the number of people referred to out-patient psychiatric units by 80 or 90 per cent. Its critics counter that studies have not yet proven counselling to be any more effective than drugs or even a placebo. Nevertheless, many people seem to need someone to talk to. The Samaritans* receive almost four million calls a year – one every nine seconds. Moreover, calls to the Samaritans have increased by almost 30 per cent during the last decade.

Whether you will benefit from counselling seems to depend on the severity of your problem and whether you've identified the cause (see chapter two). Counselling tends to be most successful when patients suffer from a defined problem, possibly because some counsellors offer a refreshing new perspective on your problems. Some mild stress-related ailments improve after the cause of the symptoms and the prospects for recovery have been explained, and the person has been prompted to deal with any pressing problems. As many as half the patients consulting their GP for stress-related disorders recover after this simple counselling. Another 20 to 30 per cent improve. The remainder require drugs or more intensive therapy.

More severe symptoms may respond less well to counselling than to drugs. Some people suffering from severe anxiety or depression benefit from learning assertive coping strategies to solve their problems and this approach may reduce the risk of relapse. However, counselling may not reduce the need for drugs especially among clients suffering from major depression. Indeed, counselling sometimes uncovers psychological problems requiring drugs. If you experience more severe symptoms, it is probably best to regard counselling as complementary to drugs rather than as an alternative.

Nevertheless, there is a humanitarian argument supporting counselling as it provides advice and support and enhances clients' self-confidence. Moreover, around 80 per cent of depressions are 'reactive' – they were triggered by stressful life events such as bereavement. Reactive depressions do not differ in their symptoms, the dangers or the response to treatment from those that cannot be associated with a specific event, and identifying a possible cause does not alter the choice of treatment. Nevertheless, if you can identify a cause counselling may help you come to terms with the source of your distress.

Finding a counsellor

There are around 11,000 counsellors practising in the UK, so although the choice can be daunting, you will probably be able to find someone that you can talk to easily. Remember that the relationship between counsellor and client can be intimate; trust is essential as you will be airing your fears, hopes and anxieties.

Currently, counselling is not controlled by a statutory register so word of mouth and the suggestion of a healthcare professional may help your choice. Your GP may employ a practice counsellor, or refer you to a local counsellor. However, you should still make sure you are happy with your choice. Alternatively, the British Association of Counselling* can put you in touch with counsellors in your area. Next, interview the counsellor. Most counsellors hold an initial consultation to ask about your problems and background. You can use the consultation to ensure that you are happy exposing your mental self to this person.

You can also undergo counselling for specific problems, such as anger management, bereavement, disabilities and PMT. Alternatively, support groups – such as British Association for Sexual and Marital Therapy*, Compassionate Friends*, Cruse* (bereavement), Cry-sis* (sleepless crying babies) and Relate* tackle specific problems. Some offer 'befriending' to complement counselling.

Exercise

You know that exercise is good for your health. Estimates vary, but remaining physically fit reduces the risk of premature death by around 40 per cent. You know you look and feel better. Jogging for as little as two hours a week – about 10 to 15km – reduces anger, alleviates depression and enhances feelings of calmness and vigour. You know that exercise helps you feel in control and reduces stress. Regular exercise even helps problem drinkers control their habit, reducing alcohol consumption by up to 60 per cent.

So why are we a nation of couch potatoes? Essentially, because we cannot be bothered. We may not reap the health benefits of exercise for several years. It is hard to be motivated by the prospect of good health in 20 years if it means getting up an hour earlier on a damp February morning. So how can you make exercise part of your life?

Exercise for fun

Exercise is supposed to reduce your stress, not make it worse. Exercise, despite what it often felt like at school, can be fun. First, if you are in any doubt about your health consult your GP. Then it's trial and error. With a bit of imagination, everyone can find an exercise they enjoy. It may be performing step aerobics to loud dance music; or you may prefer taking the dog for a long walk; or yoga. Your local library holds lists of local sports clubs – you will probably be surprised at the choice.

If your mobility is already restricted, with arthritis, for example, try swimming and aqua-aerobics. Your local swimming-pool probably runs classes. You could also ask your GP to refer you to a physiotherapist who will devise an individual exercise programme. After a few training sessions you will be able to exercise at home.

Do it with a friend

Many people gain most by exercising outside the house. Stationary bikes, rowing and skiing machines keep you fit; getting out of the house – especially if you are looking after children or caring for an ill relative – is a stress-buster. Your body may not care whether you work out on a ski machine or in the fresh air, but your mind might.

The social side of exercise in a group helps beat stress in its own right. And, of course, it's harder to quit if a friend is waiting for you at the gym. Exercising with a friend also offers some practical benefits, for example helping you assess if you are pushing yourself too hard. The idea of 'no pain no gain' is a myth. If you're too out of breath to hold a conversation, you're overdoing it. Alternatively, monitor your pulse. You should exercise at a maximum pulse rate of 220 minus your age multiplied by 0.75. So the maximum pulse rate for a 40-year-old is 220 minus 40 equals 180; multiplying this by 0.75 gives 135. In other words, a 40-year-old's pulse rate should not exceed 135 beats per minute during exercise.

Have you got the time?

Not having the time to exercise is another common excuse. But be honest: is lack of time really your problem, or is it just easier to slump in front of the TV than work out? Most of us can find the time if we try (see chapter two). If you feel too tired at night, try getting up 45 minutes earlier. Many swimming-pools and gyms run lunch-time sessions. You could ask your partner to cook a meal while you go to aerobics.

When planning your schedule, remember that just three 20-minute sessions of moderate exercise a week keeps you fit. Even allowing for showering and changing, that's around 45 minutes each time you work out. There are 168 hours in the week. You need to devote just two-and-a-quarter to stay fit.

Family therapy

Family tensions commonly cause stress, emotional disturbances and psychological problems. Family therapists examine the root of these conflicts to resolve problems by changing family interactions.

So sessions usually involve parents and children and, if appropriate, in-laws and extended family members.

The therapist may need to see how the family interacts naturally. This may mean visiting the family home or videoing therapy sessions. Playing the video to the family allows the therapist to explain where problems arise. Alternatively, other therapists may view sessions through one-way mirrors to provide additional insights. Many family therapists take a break during therapy to review progress. Referrals may be through the GP or social services. Alternatively contact the Institute for Family Therapy*.

Food and nutritional therapy

Nutritional therapists build on healthy eating to treat disease and protect against stress. Food, they argue, provides the raw material of life, so poor nutritional status undermines our ability to function optimally. Nutritional therapists believe that several factors contribute to poor nutritional status including:

- food or environmental allergies or intolerance – therapists may ask their clients to follow an exclusion diet to identify problem foods
- nutritional deficiencies resulting from poor diet, reduced absorption or special needs
- excessive intakes and poor elimination of heavy metals and other toxins.

Nutritional therapists use diet, herbs and supplements to correct the problems – although most avoid mega-dosing vitamins. This approach works for many people: in a recent survey, most people suffering from a variety of stress-related diseases benefited from nutritional therapy within two or three months.

Contact the Society for the Promotion of Nutritional Therapy* for a local practitioner.

Group therapy

Many psychotherapists use group therapy. Partly this reflects the lack of psychotherapists and the expense of individual treatment. However, group therapy may offer benefits over individual sessions. Group therapy involves six to nine people with similar problems or people with socialisation problems, so the client does not feel isolated. Alcoholics Anonymous*, for example, uses group sessions to develop social supports that help participants keep off the bottle. The therapist balances the group so everyone participates. However, each group inevitably develops a unique style reflecting the personalities in the group. The therapist watches the interaction between members and guides therapy.

Encounter groups

Encounter groups encourage people to cast aside the masks they wear in public through activities, games and conversations. This, encounter group leaders claim, allows us to develop in a more honest and open direction. However, encounter groups can be a very visceral experience as you face naked emotion, anger and hostility. For some people, this encourages self-awareness and self-expression, but encounter groups may exacerbate stress. In one study, a third of participants improved, a third reported no change and a third felt worse. People with low self-esteem, who find facing criticism difficult, may be especially likely to suffer harm from encounter groups.

Many 'new age' psychotherapies that aim to expand consciousness are essentially encounter groups. Gestalt therapy, for example, explores clients' past lives to help them understand the present. Clients are encouraged to act out feelings – to swear, scream and kick. This allows the person to understand, confront and control his or her feelings. A number of these 'self-improvement' groups and courses are advertised in the 'alternative' health press. Participants often report feeling better. Whether you will benefit seems to depend on your personality.

Herbalism

It doesn't matter whether you live in the tropical or concrete jungle, you are still likely to suffer from stress-related headaches, depression and anxiety, so cultures the world over have developed their own home-grown stress treatments. Worldwide, some four billion people rely on plants as their main source of medicines. Meanwhile, herbalism is growing in popularity in the UK as a treatment for a range of stress-related problems.

No one seriously disputes the efficacy of herbalism. After all, many conventional medicines – from aspirin to potent new cancer treatments – have their roots in chemicals derived from plants. But some doctors dispute the safety of herbalism. They point out that some herbs contain potent, even toxic, chemicals. After all, heroin, cocaine and cannabis are derived from plants. Some may interact with conventional medicines prescribed by your doctor. So if you suffer from a serious illness, are taking conventional drugs or are unsure about what you are doing, consult a qualified herbalist. You should also always consult a professional if you are pregnant or want to use herbs to treat a child. As with most drugs, it is probably prudent to avoid taking herbs during pregnancy. The National Institute of Medical Herbalists[*] can help you find a local practitioner.

Herbs as drugs

Having said that, you can use herbs to treat a number of stress-related problems (see box). Herbalism takes two approaches to treating disease. The first is pharmacological: you take sufficient quantities of the herb to produce a drug-like effect. For example, a tablespoonful of valerian can overcome stress-induced insomnia. Herbs are generally less addictive and produce fewer side effects than their conventional counterparts. However, using

---

Herbs for stress symptoms
* Basil: general tonic, digestive problems
* Camomile: insomnia, tension, dyspepsia, nervous bowel, tension headaches
* Feverfew: migraine
* Ginseng: general tonic against stress
* Hops: insomnia, tension, stomach contractions
* Lemon balm: anxiety, tension, dyspepsia
* Passionflower: stomach contractions, restlessness, irritability, insomnia
* Rosemary: depression, nervous tension, migraine, stomach irritation, dyspepsia
* Skullcap: insomnia, nervousness, anxiety, irritability, nervous exhaustion
* Valerian: stress, anxiety, insomnia, nervous tension, emotional problems

---

herbs as drugs increases the risk of developing side effects. In around five per cent of people, valerian produces paradoxical effects – users become tense, anxious and agitated. Moreover, neither herbs nor drugs tackle the cause of your stress. Neither mends the broken marriage that underlies your insomnia, for example.

A gentle approach to stress

In the West, adherents of herbalism tend to visit a herbalist when they are ill. In contrast, the Chinese use herbs to keep the body healthy. The second approach uses herbs as tonics. For example, taking a smaller quantity of valerian produces a much milder effect that supports your natural sleep cycle.

Ginseng is the best-known example of this gentle approach to tackling stress. Millions of people across Asia take ginseng to help them cope with the difficulties of daily life. Chinese soldiers use ginseng to counter the stress of battle. Indeed, ginseng's reputation as an aphrodisiac may rest on its ability to help you adapt to stress. In other words, it keeps you at the peak of the n-shaped arousal performance curve (see page 161). Ginseng also alleviates fatigue. Russian scientists tested mice's exercise tolerance when made to swim in cold water or climb a rope. The mice taking ginseng were able to exercise for almost twice as long as those who did not take the herb. Similar results have been seen in trials involving nurses, soldiers and athletes. Ginseng seems to improve mental and physical performance, mood and well-being. No wonder some old roots cost up to £5,000 each!

How to take herbs

Herbs are taken in several ways:

- Pre-packaged: herbal treatments for insomnia and stress are sold pre-packaged from many health food shops, supermarkets and pharmacists. Ginseng capsules are available both alone and formulated with multi-vitamins.
- Infusions: place the herbs in a vacuum flask and add boiling water. Seal the flask and leave for 15 to 30 minutes. Then strain and drink. Herbal teas, including ginseng, are also widely available. Some of these – the ones with exotic names – are fantasy

teas and offer an alternative to caffeine-laden coffee and tea. Other commonly available herbal teas help you sleep or relax.

- Inhalation: some herbs, such as rosemary and lavender, are rich in volatile oils. A handful of herbs can be added to a bowl of steaming water and the vapours inhaled (see aromatherapy).
- Decoction: herbalists use decoction to prepare bark and woody samples. The herb is boiled in water until the total volume reduces by a third. The remaining fluid is collected and strained.
- Tincture: the herb is steeped in a mixture of water and alcohol. This allows the preparation to be stored for several months.

Herbalism also relieves stress in other ways. Try planting a herb garden. Apart from the herbs' medicinal properties and culinary uses, many people find that working in the open air is an excellent stress-buster.

Is herbalism safe?

Herbalism's critics point out that some herbs can cause liver damage, which occasionally proves fatal. They argue that few herbs undergo the same rigorous long-term safety testing as drugs. Herbalists counter that they draw on a rich heritage. Herbalists know which herbs are dangerous – and which are safe – and they treat all herbs with respect.

For example, comfrey contains a chemical that scientists linked with liver damage in animals; the government now bans some comfrey preparations. But the scientists injected the purified chemical. Herbalists argue that you would have to eat about 5,500 leaves to reach the levels injected into animals. If the same rules applied to food, the government would also have to ban potatoes and peanuts: both contain potentially harmful chemicals. Furthermore, paracetamol – not to mention alcohol – may cause liver damage, but is freely available.

Herbalism's critics also point out that herbal medicines can become contaminated – some Asian herbal medicines may contain poisonous heavy metals, for example. Environmental factors such as soil, climate and the season can also alter the subtle balance of active chemicals in herbs – known as the essential oil. Similar problems can arise with aromatherapy oils. However, reputable commercial manufacturers employ stringent quality control measures to minimise the risk.

In moderation, herbalism seems to be a safe and effective treatment for a variety of stress-related disorders, especially if you consult a qualified herbalist. The bottom line seems to be that too much of anything can do harm. Just because it's natural doesn't mean it's safe.

Exotic herbalism

Kampo, traditional Japanese herbal medicine, is growing in popularity in the West. However, don't try kampo if you want a quick fix for stress. Usually symptoms show a slow, steady, mild improvement.

Kampo practitioners make diagnoses using patients' sho: the pattern of psychological and bodily symptoms. Based on this they prescribe traditional herbal concoctions. Traditionally, practitioners use Kami-Kihito, which combines 14 herbs, including liquorice and ginger, for anxiety, depression, irritation and insomnia. They use another formulation of nine plants, Yokukan-sann-ka-chinnpi-hannge, to treat irritable, explosive patients and may also alleviate insomnia.

Recently doctors from Tokyo tested various Kampo medicines in 55 depressed patients, many of whom also suffered anxiety. Yokukan-sann-ka-chinnpi-hannge produced a moderate improvement in 15 per cent and a mild improvement in another 70 per cent. Kami-Kihito produced a mild improvement in 57 per cent of patients.

Traditional Chinese medicine is also growing in popularity. Chinese herbalists believe that illness is caused by a disruption in the flow of chi, which differs in everyone, so Chinese herbalists tailor the mix of herbs to the patient. Chinese medicine has had some remarkable successes – most notably in chronic eczema that did not respond to other treatments.

Success stories such as these have led scientists to assess traditional herbal remedies as treatments for common diseases. They hope that these traditional herbal medicines might lead to a new source of more effective and less toxic drugs. For example, Hindu doctors traditionally used rauwolfia to treat insomnia and insanity, but it wasn't until 1954 that Western doctors admitted it helped psychotic patients. Indian scientists are now searching their herbal heritage for new drugs. One herb, alstonia, was recently discovered to contain natural antidepressants. These exotic herbs are undoubtedly an untapped source for new drugs – not just for stress but for all diseases.

Homeopathy

Homeopathy is recognised by an Act of Parliament, and you have a right to be treated using homeopathy on the NHS. Millions of people swear by homeopathy's benefits against stress and everything from infections to depression. But homeopathy attracted controversy almost as soon as it was discovered, and some scientists treat its claims with scorn – despite a growing number of studies suggesting that it works. Homeopathy's problem is that it challenges the foundations of Western medicine.

Homeopathy's challenge to convention

By 1811, the German physician Dr Samuel Hahnemann was disillusioned. He had trained as a doctor but his treatments often did more harm than good. Hahnemann believed that the symptoms of a disease reflected the body's efforts to overcome illness. This belief directly opposed the views of conventional doctors who believed that illnesses caused the symptoms.

This difference in opinion is reflected in the aims of treatment. Homeopathy aims to work with the body by treating 'like with like'. For example, the bark of the cinchona tree alleviates malaria's symptoms, but when healthy people took the bark they developed symptoms similar to malaria. Hahnemann found that a number of other chemicals seemed to share this property: in healthy people they caused symptoms similar to those they treated. This idea that 'like treats like' forms the basis of homeopathy. In contrast, conventional doctors aim to suppress symptoms even though this can be counterproductive. For example, doctors advise that patients take aspirin for mild fever – but in fact a raised temperature enhances the immune system's ability to fight infection.

To avoid side-effects, Hahnemann diluted the substances in water and alcohol, which he mixed by vigorous shaking. Remarkably, he found that the more dilute the substance became, the more potent the agent's therapeutic action. Hahnemann called his method of diluting chemicals 'potentisation' and the serial dilutions 'potencies'. The dilutions allow homeopaths to prescribe safely poisons such as arsenic, morphine and cocaine. Moreover, potentisation transforms sand, salt and charcoal into potent remedies for the right person, suffering from the 'right' disease.

Potentisation contributes to some doctors' claim that homeopathy is inherently implausible. The formulations are so dilute that the patient is unlikely to receive a single molecule of the 'active' ingredient. Moreover, the claim that a treatment could become more potent as the dilution increases goes against some fundamental principles of medical science. Pharmacologists – scientists who study the effects of drugs on the body – suggest that biologically active substances follow a 'dose-response' relationship. Below a certain dose, the drug produces no effect. Past this threshold, the response increases with increased dose until it reaches a plateau. Further increasing the dose has no further effect. Homeopathy turns the dose-response relationship on its head. What makes the idea of homeopathy even more unpalatable for pharmacologists is that no one can adequately explain how it works.

Is homeopathy effective?

Homeopaths counter that the idea of like treating like isn't as strange as it sounds. Vaccines work on much the same principle: doctors inject a small amount of either the whole, inactivated virus or a critical part of its protein coat. This triggers the same immune reaction as exposure to the live and virulent microorganism without causing serious symptoms, so when you next encounter the organism your immune system is primed to tackle the infection rapidly. Hyperactive children can be treated with Ritalin (methylphenidate) and amphetamine – both are powerful stimulants. Digitalis, used for heart failure, produces similar symptoms in overdose as those it treats.

Critics argue that homeopathy's reported benefits could be a placebo effect. The power of the placebo is well recognised. Patients in trials of new medicines usually take either the drug or a tablet that looks and tastes identical – except it lacks the active ingredient. Neither the patient nor the doctor knows if the treatment is active. Nevertheless, many patients respond to placebos. Among people suffering from irritable bowel syndrome, for example, over 70 per cent report feeling better after taking a placebo.

Moreover, homeopaths are holistic practitioners. Instead of enquiring about only symptoms, they ask about medical history, lifestyle, family history and whether patients are musical, scientific or artistic; whether they are sulky or rapidly angered; and so on. Homeopaths even note clients' hair and eye colour and their hopes and fears. In this way, homeopaths develop a detailed picture of their patients. Homeopaths then match a remedy to the profile. Cynics suggest that this intense interest increases the power of suggestion and enhances the placebo's potency.

You might think that scientific studies would settle the question of homeopathy's effectiveness. However, trials of homeopathy are extremely difficult to perform. Unlike studies using drugs, where a single medicine is prescribed to all patients, homeopathic treatment is individualised. No two patients have exactly the same personality, lifestyle and medical history. So people with different diseases may take the same homeopathic treatment, while people suffering from the same disease may take different homeopathic remedies.

Nevertheless, the few strictly controlled scientific studies that have been performed give homeopathy some credence. In 1986 a group of doctors from Glasgow compared the effects of a placebo and a homeopathic preparation of grass seed pollen in 144 hayfever sufferers. Neither the doctors nor the patients knew whether they had received the placebo or the homeopathic preparation. Nevertheless, patients who received the homeopathic preparation reported fewer symptoms – an observation confirmed by physicians' evaluation.

Eight years later, the same group of doctors reported that homeopathy alleviated asthma more effectively than a placebo. Asthmatics taking the homeopathic preparation reported fewer and less intense symptoms. The improvement emerged a week after starting treatment and persisted for eight weeks. Their lung function also improved. However, the effect was relatively modest compared to modern anti-asthma medications. A summary of more than 100 studies investigating homeopathy's effectiveness found that patients benefited in 77 trials. Homeopathy is also successfully used to treat animals. It seems that homeopathy's benefits cannot be dismissed as simply 'the placebo effect'.

Homeopathy and stress

As homeopathy treats the whole person and takes into account your temperament, personality and emotions, you are likely to get

the best results by going to a qualified homeopath. Most homeopaths are experienced in treating stress and emotional disturbances: around a quarter of patients consult a homeopath for
emotional problems. In many more – perhaps half – psychological disturbances contribute to their disease.

However, a number of homeopathic remedies are available
from chemists and health food shops that may help you deal with
specific stress-related disorders. But even off-the-shelf homeopathic remedies need to personalised. For example, a blue-eyed,
fair-haired woman going through the stress of the menopause
may benefit from pulsatilla nigricans. Her dark-haired friend may
need sepia. Likewise, if stress leaves you tossing and turning in
bed and unable to sleep, try aconite. If you can't sleep and yawn
frequently, try ignatia amara. The box may give you some idea of
where to start.

Homeopathic help for stress
* Aconite: insomnia, anxiety, restlessness, fear, grief, bereavement
* Ignatia amara: fright, prolonged grief, piercing headache,
  especially for emotional, sensitive people
* Kalium phosphoricum: mental and nervous exhaustion
* Natrum muriaticum: PMS, migraine, especially for insecure people
  who worry about the future
* Nux vomica: nervous indigestion, PMS, especially for thin, dark
  people who are impatient and irritable
* Pulsatilla nigricans: tinnitus and PMS, especially for people with
  fair hair, blue eyes and fair complexions who are easily moved to
  laughter or tears

Using homeopathic remedies
Homeopathic tablets are chewed or sucked on an empty stomach.
For rapid relief you may need to take tablets up to six times a day.
In chronic ailments, you take the remedy three times daily for a
week. Most homeopaths suggest treating yourself with the 6th
potency. But if you consult some homeopaths you may receive a
single dose and then return after a month to assess your progress.

Many people find that their symptoms initially get worse after
starting homeopathic treatment. Homeopaths regard this initial
worsening as a sign that the remedy is working. The Glasgow study
of hayfever sufferers confirmed that patients who suffered an initial

aggravation of symptoms were those most likely to improve. During this aggravation of symptoms, homeopaths suggest stopping the remedy and beginning again when the feeling passes.

This attitude towards symptom severity marks a crucial difference in opinion between conventional and homeopathic practitioners. Many doctors regard an upsurge in symptoms as a reason to review treatment and possibly increase the dose until patients are either symptom-free or develop side-effects. In contrast, homeopathy does not suppress symptoms, but works with the body. After the initial worsening, the symptoms should start improving. If the improvement is maintained you can stop taking the tablets.

Finding a homeopath

Your GP can refer you to a homeopathic hospital or a local qualified homeopath for treatment on the NHS. Around 600 NHS doctors hold a postgraduate qualification in homeopathy, and many more use some homeopathic remedies or refer patients for treatment. Your GP needs to send a referral letter to the nearest hospital – based in London, Glasgow, Liverpool, Bristol and Tunbridge Wells. Some GPs are also qualified to provide homeopathic treatment either privately or on the NHS. The British Homeopathic Association* and the Society of Homeopaths* can provide a list of homeopaths in your area, and the Homeopathic Trust* a list of medically qualified doctors who are also qualified homeopaths.

The cynicism surrounding homeopathy may mean your GP is reluctant to refer you. Many GPs do not realise – or choose to ignore – homeopathy's availability on the NHS. Theoretically, fundholding and the patients' charter should make referral easier. Nevertheless, some GPs pay only lip service to patient empowerment – especially when it means agreeing to something they don't believe in. You may have to stand your ground or consider a private consultation.

Hypnosis

For centuries, hypnotism was dismissed as a stage trick, with its benefits confined to the gullible. Then towards the end of the last century a French physician, A Liébeault, offered to treat people free – provided they allowed him to hypnotise them. After putting his peasant volunteers into a hypnotic trance, Liébeault used hypnotism to suggest their headaches, stomach pains or aches and pains would resolve. His success rate was high enough for his fame to spread. Later, another French doctor, Jean-Martin Charcot, found that patients with 'hysteria' could, under hypnosis, mimic symptoms of other illnesses. Moreover, before the introduction of chloroform, major operations – including amputations and removing large scrotal tumours – were performed under hypnosis, apparently without patients experiencing pain. However, the UK medical profession refused to take hypnotism seriously – although it was more widely accepted among their European colleagues.

However, the tide changed in the 1950s, when the *British Medical Journal* reported that hypnotism cured ichthyosis, a disfiguring disease where the skin appears rough and horny. A young boy was put into a hypnotic trance and told which areas of his skin would clear. These areas became almost normal. Most doctors now accept that hypnosis alleviates stress-related diseases. Nevertheless, some scientists retain a lingering cynicism. Even today, some scientists claim subjects fake trances to please the hypnotist and audience. However, it is hard to believe that a disfiguring skin disease would clear because the patient wanted to please the doctor. It is even harder to believe someone would endure the pain of a scrotal operation to please the surgeon.

The mystery of hypnotism

Not everyone is easily hypnotised. You have to want to be hypnotised. The best subjects tend to be people who immerse themselves in imaginary worlds – books, films and plays – and strongly identify with imaginary characters. Nevertheless, no one really understands how hypnotism works. It is clearly not a form of sleep. Most people feel tired, lethargic and drowsy during hypnosis, but while the brain's electrical activity changes during a hypnotic trance, it does not resemble sleep. Indeed, the brain's electrical activity suggests that the subject is fully awake during hypnosis. According to the scientists' favoured theory, the brain shuts off nerves supplying sensory information. This leaves subjects susceptible to certain suggestions. Certainly, during hypnosis subjects become very relaxed and compliant, which is why stage hypnotists can make people act as dogs or chickens.

However, medical hypnotism is far removed from the antics of stage hypnotists. Hypnotism is very relaxing, which benefits patients in its own right, but a growing number of studies show that hypnotism also alleviates a wide range of stress-related ailments and forms of behaviour (see box). For lists of qualified hypnotists contact the Central Register of Advanced Hypnotherapists* or the National Register of Hypnotherapists and Psychotherapists*.

Hypnotism for stress-related diseases
* addictions including gambling, nicotine, and alcohol * bed-wetting * eating and weight problems * fear of dentists * general anxiety * headaches, including migraines and tension headaches * hyperventilation and asthma * irritable bowel syndrome, diarrhoea, constipation * muscular problems, such as low back pain * palpitations * phobias and obsessions (severe symptoms may need treatment with drugs before hypnotherapy) * regression (re-living the situation under hypnosis often alleviates stress) * skin diseases, including eczema, psoriasis and urticaria * sexual problems, including impotence and frigidity * social problems such as stammering, blushing, nail-biting, etc.

Massage

Massage is one of the oldest stress-relieving techniques – and remains one of the most effective. Massage relieves muscle tension and promotes a sense of well-being. As a result, masseurs claim that massage alleviates a number of stress-related diseases, including tension headaches, fatigue and joint pain. But, perhaps most importantly, massage forces you to take time out for yourself – which contributes to its stress-beating properties.

Depending on the technique, massage may improve blood circulation, stimulates nerves and muscles, promotes healthy skin and relieves muscle tension and spasm. Using essential oils seems to enhance the benefits. There are plenty of well-illustrated books available showing various massage techniques for relaxation and health. However, the benefits of do-it-yourself massage are unlikely to be as pronounced as a session with a trained masseur (contact the British Massage Therapy Council*). Nevertheless, you can also use the books to explore the erotic possibilities of massage. Certainly, intimate massage can help overcome sexual problems in both men and women.

Shiatsu

Japanese massage – shiatsu – shares its origins with acupuncture. However, shiatsu is a relatively new technique fusing traditional Japanese massage and osteopathy. Shiatsu masseurs use fingers, elbows, knees and feet to massage the meridians and balance the flow of chi around the body. While this can relieve stress-related disorders, shiatsu tends to prevent – rather than treat – disease.

A shiatsu session takes about an hour and each point is pressurised for around seven seconds. You may feel a certain amount of discomfort at first. Shiatsu masseurs believe stagnant chi causes this discomfort and it usually disappears after a few sessions. Moreover, most shiatsu practitioners point out that the massage should form part of an overall review of your lifestyle – including diet and mental attitudes. The Shiatsu Society* is an umbrella organisation for UK practitioners.

Meditation

Meditation is undoubtedly one of the most effective ways to relax and build your defences against the daily onslaught of stress. Furthermore, meditation may alleviate a number of stress-related diseases including hypertension, insomnia, addictions and asthma. It also enhances mind-body co-ordination. Meditators often report an improvement in their academic performance, interpersonal relationships and marital satisfaction. Some studies even suggest that meditation boosts IQ, increases creativity and improves sensory acuity.

People from all ages, backgrounds and religions meditate. So far, more than 150,000 UK people and over four million people worldwide have learnt Transcendental Meditation* (TM). Classically, meditation involves sitting serenely, eyes closed, legs crossed, on a mat, focusing on your breathing or a saying for 20 or 30 minutes a couple of times a day. TM uses slightly shorter sessions of between 15 and 20 minutes. While this may seem a considerable commitment of time in a busy life, meditators argue that taking 40 or 60 minutes a day to meditate helps you achieve more with less effort. After a while, meditation becomes part of the coping strategies that you call on when stressed.

Does meditation work?

Meditation – especially TM – is one of the best-studied complementary medicines. Over the last 20 years, over 500 scientific papers have highlighted TM's efficacy against anxiety, mild depression, insomnia, tension headaches, migraine, high blood pressure, irritable bowel syndrome, post-natal depression and a number of other stress-related diseases. One study followed over 2,000 TM practitioners for at least five years. Meditators made fewer than half the number of visits to their doctor than non-meditators. Hospitalisations among the TM group also fell. The largest reduction was in the over-40s. Compared with non-meditators, young adult TM practitioners spent 50 per cent less time in hospital and made 55 per cent fewer visits to their doctor. In the 40-plus group, TM practitioners spent almost 70 per cent less time in hospital and made 74 per cent fewer visits to their doctor. Even children benefited – spending 50 per cent less time in hospital and making 47 per cent fewer doctor visits.

One major Dutch health insurance company offers reduced premiums to regular TM practitioners. It seems that meditators may be more likely to live otherwise healthy lives, which contributes to their reduced use of healthcare resources. For example, TM seems to reduce the need for artificial stimulants – a finding put to good use in the treatment of addiction. A recent paper combined the results of 19 studies investigating TM's effects on alcohol abuse, cigarette smoking and illicit drug use. TM emerged as up to:

- eight times more effective than other methods, including education and relaxation, at reducing alcohol abuse
- six times more effective than training addicts to resist peer pressure in reducing drug abuse.
- five times more effective than relaxation, hypnosis, counselling and acupuncture in reducing smoking.

Furthermore, TM produced overall abstinence rates of between 51 and 89 per cent over 18 months. The other techniques showed relapse rates of between 70 and 80 per cent in the first year. TM undoubtedly produces impressive results – even within the rigours of scientific studies. But does meditation offer any advantages over relaxation?

Meditation or relaxation?

Meditation and progressive relaxation produce a biological response directly opposed to the fight-or-flight response. However, several studies suggest that TM may be more effective than relaxation. A recent study compared the ability of TM and progressive muscle relaxation to lower high blood pressure. After three months, the blood pressure of subjects was compared to that of a group who followed a healthy lifestyle – for example, taking exercise, reducing salt consumption and eating a low-calorie diet.

Compared to the healthy lifestyle group, TM reduced systolic blood pressure by 11mmHg and diastolic blood pressure by 6mmHg – similar to the reduction produced by antihypertensive drugs. Comparing the effects of TM with the benefits of antihypertensive drugs suggests that a fall in systolic and diastolic blood pressure of 11mmHg and 6mmHg respectively would reduce deaths from heart disease and stroke by around 30 per cent. Progressive muscle relaxation reduced systolic and diastolic blood pressure by 5mmHg and 3mmHg respectively. In other words, TM was twice as effective as progressive muscle relaxation. However, the study was performed in older American-Africans. Whether TM is as effective in other groups of people with high blood pressure is less clear, but there is no good reason to suspect that TM would not be as effective in Caucasians or Asians.

Another study compared meditation and progressive relaxation in 154 employees of a New York Telephone company who claimed to suffer from stress. Another group practised neither meditation nor progressive relaxation. After almost six months, all groups reported fewer stress symptoms. Nevertheless, the meditation group showed the most pronounced reductions. The effect of progressive relaxation was no different to that seen among the group that used neither technique.

The reduction in stress symptoms among subjects who neither meditated nor practised progressive relaxation is worth noting. These subjects heard a motivating talk about the benefits of meditation and relaxation. Moreover, they were told they would be trained in stress management at the end of the study. It seems this expectation alone markedly reduced their levels of stress and anxiety. However, many of these patients may have treated themselves with stress-relieving techniques including counselling and exercise.

In this study, subjects benefited even if they meditated only occasionally. This contradicts several TM studies which suggest you need to meditate regularly. The difference may reflect symptom severity. Infrequent meditation may alleviate mild anxiety. Regular sessions are required to control deeply entrenched problems, such as addiction. Moreover, over 88 per cent of the New York subjects used 'mini-meditations' during the day. So whether missing the full meditation session counts as 'irregular' is questionable. In any event, you are the final arbiter. Some people may not need regular meditation to alleviate stress, while others need to meditate two or three times daily.

How to meditate

To learn meditation correctly, you need instruction from a teacher, but you can try it for yourself before investing time and money on a course. Find somewhere quiet. Beginners find meditation especially difficult where there are too many distractions. Sit comfortably. This doesn't need to be the full cross-legged 'lotus' position – a chair is fine. You will need to sit still for around 20 minutes without the distractions of cramps and other aches.

Now breathe deeply. Meditation teachers emphasise that most people tend to breathe into their chests instead of their abdomens. By concentrating we can learn to breathe slowly and evenly in highly stressful situations. This focus on breathing also means that meditation helps people with respiratory problems such as asthma.

You now need to focus your attention. TM uses a mantra – a personal phrase or saying given to you by your teacher. But for this trial choose your own. A mantra doesn't have to be exotic – any simple non-emotive word will do – even if it's nonsense. Other techniques encourage mindful meditation, where you maintain moment-to-moment awareness of the motion of your breath in and out of your nose and mouth. You can also focus on a candle flame, crystal or icon. These all have the same effect: they concentrate your mind and exclude distractions.

However, maintaining concentration for 20 minutes is far harder than it sounds. You will probably find that your mind wanders off. Just accept these ramblings and re-focus your attention on the subject. Try not to be annoyed with yourself.

Finding a teacher

TM* is taught at 50 centres across the UK. You go to four sessions on consecutive days and a further session three months later. However, TM isn't the only form of meditation – although it is the best studied. The Buddhist Society* can put you in touch with teachers of traditional Buddhist or Zen meditation. More recently, Clinically Standardized Meditation* was developed by the psychologist Dr Patricia Carrington. You can learn this technique from tapes and books. Finally, meditation is an integral part of yoga. Contact the British Wheel of Yoga* for further information.

Muscular relaxation

Relaxation means more than curling up with a good book or watching your favourite television programme. Relaxation involves down-regulating the sympathetic nervous system that controls the fight-or-flight reflex. As the mind and body are linked, you cannot be mentally tense and have a relaxed body and vice versa: relaxing the body relaxes the mind.

Muscle tension is a common stress symptom. Our necks feel stiff. Our jaw muscles clench. We frown. Our poor postures, while we work in sedentary jobs in poorly designed offices only make matters worse. Often only our fingers are exercised on our keyboards and mice. This creates muscle tension and exacerbates stress. So take steps to make your working environment stress-free (see box).

Working in a stress-free zone
- Maintain good posture. When you sit, try to keep your shoulders and head in a straight line and drop your shoulders. Sit upright at your desk with your feet on the floor.
- Try placing a cushion at the base of your spine.
- Adjust your computer screen so you can see it when looking straight ahead.
- Move your keyboard so that you aren't hunching or lifting your arms.
- If you use the phone a lot, use a headset instead of clamping the phone between head and shoulder.

- Take a break every half-hour: use tension-relaxation to ease stiff shoulders and neck.
- Watch for muscle tension. At the first sign of tension, use tension-relaxation exercises.

Relaxation's golden rules

Whichever technique you choose, following a few simple rules helps you make the most of your relaxation sessions.

- Try to relax every day. The best time may be first thing in the morning if the house is quieter then. Try setting your alarm half-an-hour earlier.
- Avoid relaxation exercises last thing at night. You probably won't be able to concentrate as well and you could fall asleep rather than relax.
- Shut your eyes.
- Either take the phone off the hook or switch on the answer-phone.
- Don't relax on a full stomach. After a meal, blood diverts from your muscles to your stomach. Trying to relax tense muscles on a full stomach can cause cramps. Moreover, relaxation exercises increase your awareness of your body's functions. A full stomach can be a distraction.
- Find a quiet room where you can sit in a comfortable chair or lie down. The chair should support your back. If you lie down to relax, you may want to put cushions under your neck and knees.
- Make yourself comfortable. Take your shoes off and wear loose-fitting clothes. Switch off any bright lights. The room shouldn't be too hot or too cold.
- Play a favourite piece of music. Many people find music helps them relax and minimises interruptions. However, the music shouldn't be too loud.
- Be passive: don't worry about whether you are relaxed enough yet.
- Think about your breathing. Most of us breathe shallowly using the upper parts of our lungs. However, to relax you need to breathe deeply and slowly without gasping. Put one hand on your chest and the other on your abdomen. Breathe

normally. You may find – especially if you're tense – that the hand on your chest moves, while the hand on the abdomen remains almost still. The hand on your stomach should rise and fall while the one on your chest hardly alters.

● Don't quit. Some days you'll find it easier to relax than others. After a while, relaxation sessions will become part of your everyday life. But you have to give them a chance.

Progressive muscular relaxation

Progressive muscular relaxation aims to relax each part of your body in turn. After a few deep breaths, start at your toes. Then say to yourself: 'My toes are tingling. They're becoming numb ...They are feeling heavier and heavier ... My toes are feeling increasingly relaxed ... The tension is draining away' and so on. When your toes feel relaxed move on to your calves. Say to yourself: 'My calves are relaxed ... They are feeling softer and heavier ... My calves are feeling numb and more relaxed ...' And then move on to your thighs. When you've worked to your forehead lie still for a few minutes before standing up.

Tension-relaxation

Tension-relaxation tenses a muscle for around ten seconds before relaxing. Each exercise is repeated three times, slowly, gently and gradually. Remember, you're not body building, you're trying to relax. Rest for a couple of minutes. Repeat the set twice – nine repetitions of the tension-relaxation for each group of muscles. Then rest for 20 to 30 minutes. Most teachers advise mastering one muscle group at a time, so it could take two or three months before you can tense and relax your whole body.

For example, put your hands by your side. Now clench your fists as hard as you can. Hold the fist for ten seconds. Now slowly relax your fist and let your hands hang loosely by your sides. Then shrug your shoulders as high as possible. Hold for ten seconds and then slowly relax. Then arch the back as high as you can, leaving only your head and buttocks touching the chair or floor. Tense your muscles when you inhale. During the tension don't hold your breath, but breathe slowly and rhythmically. Then exhale as you relax.

After practising tension-relaxation exercises for a few months, you'll come to recognise when your muscles are tense. Most of us have lived for years with considerable muscle tension, so our bodies become used to a certain level of muscle tension, but this means that we cannot tell if our muscles are relaxed or tense. Tension-relaxation exercises familiarise us with our muscles. However, if you suffer from back problems or any other serious medical problem you should talk to your doctor or physiotherapist before performing tension-relaxation exercises.

Tension-relaxation at work

You can use tension-relaxation exercises to alleviate aches and pains at work. If you are working at a keyboard and using a mouse you should take a break every half-hour or so. Try the hand tension-relaxation exercises. Many people hunch forward when they type, and this puts the neck muscles – which evolved to balance rather than support the head – under considerable strain, so it's perhaps no wonder that the neck and shoulders ache. Try the shoulder shrug exercise. You can also drop your head forward until it touches your chest and then to each side – slowly – towards your shoulder. Avoid putting the head right back as this can damage the spine. Again, hold each position for about ten seconds.

Music

Music's power to relieve mental torment was recognised in Biblical times: David's harp playing soothed Saul's madness. Later the Greek philosopher Pythagoras, who lived around 500 BC, used music to alleviate mental disorders. During the Middle Ages, music was used to treat fever, alleviate mania, prevent the plague and restore harmony between mind and body. Since the last century, when German health resorts used music to cure stress-related illnesses, music therapy has found a role in mainstream medicine to treat mental handicap and illness. Some residential homes for the elderly find that music therapy helps Alzheimer's disease sufferers. Music also provides a welcome distraction from the torment of chronic pain, and every day, people play or listen to music to relieve stress.

But musical tastes vary widely. Your teenage son's musical tastes may sound like a cacophony to you – and he probably can't stand your Bach concertos. Moreover, musical tastes vary with mood. Cheerful music is grating if you've got the blues, and you don't want to listen to a fugue at a party. Nevertheless, don't underestimate music's abilities to lift mood and alleviate stress. Switch the light off. Put on the headphones, and let your favourite music wash over you. Music also provides a soothing background to relaxation and other stress-relieving techniques.

Music therapy

There are two types of music therapy. Passive music therapy involves listening to music either live or recorded. Active music therapy means playing improvised music reflecting the client's personality, which can have a dramatic effect, especially among handicapped children.

> TONY is an autistic child. During his first music therapy session he played without rhythm or order. The chaotic music reflected his inner turmoil. The therapist played along on the piano, at first chaotically, but gradually introducing rhythms and stable beats. Over the months, Tony's drumming became more rhythmic, reflecting his growing feeling of inner order.

The nature of music therapy makes its benefits difficult to assess in scientific studies. Nevertheless, it seems to help disturbed children to interact with and relate to the world around them. Music's form and structure bring order and security to disabled and distressed children. Music helps them understand their moods and encourages communication, self-awareness and co-ordination. In this way, music therapy improves quality of life. Adults also benefit: after all, everyone responds to music, irrespective of handicap, injury or illness. Music therapy helps you examine your emotions. Why do you dislike certain music? Does it remind you of something or someone? Exploring your reaction to music can put you in touch with some of your hidden emotions.

Music therapists are musicians who take a post-graduate course in music therapy. Referrals come from health professionals – community psychiatric nurses, social workers, paediatricians, psychiatrists and GPs. Hospitals sometimes run music therapy sessions. Otherwise contact the Association of Professional Music Therapists*, the British Society for Music Therapy* or the Nordoff-Robbins Music Therapy Centre*.

Naturopathy

Naturopathy aims to promote health by stimulating and supporting the body's innate healing power. To do this, naturopaths help patients adopt a healthier lifestyle and increase their vitality by following principles established by the Greek physician Hippocrates who lived around 400 BC on Crete.

Disease as an imbalance

Naturopaths believe that disease arises following a disturbance in the body's internal environment. For example, toxic metabolic by-products and environmental poisons gradually kill cells, which may be the prelude to disease. The emerging role of free radicals – toxic metabolic by-products in heart disease, allergies, cancer and other diseases – lends some credence to this.

Symptoms result from the body's attempts to overcome chemical, mechanical or psychological obstructions that lead to the disturbance. Chemical obstructions are imbalances in the body's biochemistry – a dietary deficiency, eating to excess, poor circulation or inadequate kidney, lung or bowel function. Mechanical obstructions include muscle tension, strained ligaments and stiff joints. Psychological obstructions may result from stress, pressure and anxiety.

'Only nature heals'

Naturopaths create the right environment for the body to heal itself. Many modern drugs do not cure disease: they alleviate symptoms. Antihypertensives, for instance, lower blood pressure without resolving the underlying disorder. Naturopathy gives nature the opportunity to heal by 'unblocking' the life force through a combination of fasting, hydrotherapy, herbs and manipulation. Most naturopaths also encourage their clients to reduce stress using yoga, meditation and psychotherapy and by developing a positive outlook on life. Poor posture, naturopaths believe, may block the body's vital energy. So they use osteopathy, chiropractic, postural re-education and other techniques to realign the body. We all know the stress-beating value of a long soak in a hot bath. Naturopaths use hydrotherapy – including baths, compresses, sprays and douches – to alleviate stress-related ailments.

'Let food be your medicine'

Naturopaths teach good nutrition and advocate controlled fasts that, they believe, allow your body to concentrate on healing rather than digestion. Short fasts – a day or so – are harmless provided you are physically healthy, the fast is controlled and you drink plenty of water. Naturopaths believe that fasting helps a number of ailments including obesity, hypertension and arthritis. Naturopaths also encourage their clients to eat a balanced, wholesome, natural diet including drinking pure water, eating organic food, preferably raw, and limiting animal protein.

Naturopaths help patients prevent a recurrence. Once the body's balance has been restored using a combination of techniques, naturopaths encourage the patient to stick to a healthy lifestyle. However, in seriously ill patients, the elderly or those overwhelmed by stress, treatment may need to be continuous and naturopaths work alongside conventional doctors.

The General Council and Register of Naturopaths* can provide details of your nearest practitioner. Naturopaths may also use nutritional supplements and a number of other techniques such as homeopathy, osteopathy and herbalism. Ensure that your therapist is qualified to perform these additional treatments.

Osteopathy

Osteopathy has a long heritage. Healers have used manipulation to treat spinal and back problems for over 2,000 years. Then in 1874 the founder of osteopathy, the US physician Dr Andrew Taylor Still, developed a system of manipulation that alleviated a number of other disorders including headaches, migraines and painful joints. Cranial osteopathy followed when, in the 1930s, doctors realised that bones making up the skull could move slightly. Cranial osteopaths very gently manipulate the bones in the skull to alter tissues in the rest of the body. Practitioners suggest that cranial osteopathy alleviates a number of stress-related diseases including migraine and dizziness.

Osteopathy emphasises the importance of the interactions between muscles, ligaments and skeletons in maintaining health. Like many 'complementary' practitioners, Still believed in the body's innate ability to heal itself – provided the nerve and blood supply are uninterrupted. However, problems with the musculoskeletal system can block this healing process. So osteopaths use manipulation to realign structural deviations and abnormalities, including muscle spasms, spinal curvature and problems caused by poor posture (see also chiropractic, page 188). However, as abnormalities in the musculoskeletal system are not the only factors in disease, osteopathy cannot help diseases caused by genetics, environmental factors and infections, for example.

Osteopaths begin by asking you to describe the factors that exacerbate and alleviate your symptoms, so you might like to keep a diary for a couple of weeks before visiting an osteopath. Osteopaths also review your posture and the way you move and examine each vertebra for areas of tenderness, stiffness or abnormal shape.

Treatment includes manipulation, massage, rhythmic stretching and joint mobilisation. Osteopaths may stretch soft tissues, rhythmically move joints or apply a high velocity thrust to improve a joint's range of movement. These techniques aim to 'balance' the musculoskeletal system, and so alleviate tension and stress in other parts of the body. As osteopathy aims to resolve the cause of your problems, the treatment may be some distance from the site of the complaint. Furthermore, two patients with apparently the same symptom may be treated differently.

Usually osteopathy is not painful. You may feel tired, light-headed, stiff or ache for a couple of days afterwards. However, many people have no ill-effects at all and find osteopathy a good way to relax. Osteopathy aims to prevent the problem recurring, so osteopaths educate their clients about correct posture and emphasise the value of exercise in keeping the spine supple. They may also advise on diet.

Both physicians and politicians have given osteopathy their blessing. The UK's 2,500 osteopaths hold around five million consultations annually. Around a quarter of these patients attend with their doctor's blessing. Ten per cent are directly referred by a conventional physician. In 1993 Parliament passed the Osteopaths Act that will ensure state registration, probably by 1997. Until that time, anyone can set up in practice as an osteopath. You can contact a registered practitioner through the Osteopathic Information Service*, which represents osteopaths allied to a number of organisations.

Pets

The UK is a nation of animal lovers. Together we own around six million pet dogs, a similar number of pet cats and around two million budgerigars. And that's not counting hamsters, rabbits, fish or the menagerie of other domestic animals. Aggressive dogs and fouled footpaths notwithstanding, owning pets is probably good for the health of the nation. American studies suggest that pet owners are less likely to visit their doctor than people who don't own pets. Pets alleviate stress, provide companionship and, in some cases, oblige the owner to take some exercise. Pets can also provide a creative and rewarding hobby. Keeping tropical fish or a pedigree dog often entails considerable work.

However, pets are probably most beneficial for children and the elderly. Children with pets develop a sense of responsibility and a respect for nature. Some studies suggest that pet-owning families have better parent-child relationships and a happier atmosphere than non-pet owners. A contented family life lays the foundations for a healthy, happy adult life. At the other end of the generation gap, pets partly fill the void left by a spouse's death, providing day-to-day companionship. Dogs, especially, prevent older people from becoming house-bound and provide a sense of security.

Even people with severe mental disorders benefit from owning pets. Withdrawn, self-centred and uncommunicative patients can form strong bonds with animals. Agitated, restless patients can burn off some stress by exercising an energetic dog. The responsibility imposed by having a pet encourages self-confidence and self-reliance.

Another recent study assessed the impact of pet ownership on survival after a heart attack. People who had high levels of social support and those that owned dogs were less likely to die during the year following a heart attack than those people with less social support or those who didn't own dogs. However, cat owners were no more likely to survive than people who didn't own pets. Partly this reflects the fact that dogs need their owners to exercise them, while cats are quite happy taking themselves for a walk. But this doesn't seem to be the whole explanation. For example, other studies suggest that owning pets – not only dogs – seems to ameliorate the effects of stress. Pets also seem to reduce anxiety and lower arousal.

You don't need to be a life-long animal lover to benefit. Your health seems to improve within a few months of buying a pet, but choose a pet that complements your personality and fits in with your budget. It's not only food: most animals need vaccinations, fall ill or get into accidents. You may like to take out insurance.

Psychotherapy

Psychotherapy explores the unconscious causes of the clients' problems and emotions. This may enhance the client's sense of well-being and may alleviate stress and anxiety. There are around 250 types of psychotherapy – most offering variations on behavioural therapy, cognitive therapy, and psychoanalysis. Some may help clients gain an insight into their problems and their past and present relationships by exploring the subconscious causes. Others offer practical help for specific problems, without exploring the subconscious.

JUNE was engaged to get married – for the fourth time. While she looked forward to her new life, June realised that she was responsible, at least partly, for the failure of her previous marriages. A psychoanalyst argued that June needed to understand her feelings about men generally, and her father in particular, before marrying again. A behavioural therapist encouraged June to develop practical ways to better relate to men and overcome the self-destructive feelings that caused problems in her previous marriages.

Many therapists integrate a number of techniques that seem to be the most effective for a particular problem. A therapist's experience and relationship with the client are probably more important than the theoretical underpinnings, but your attitudes are just as important. Psychotherapy is hard work. You need to want to change and believe that therapy will help. In some cases, you'll make a considerable investment of time and money, so ensure you are comfortable with your therapy.

Psychoanalysis

Psychoanalysts believe that the roots of our psychological illness lie in our unconscious. The roots are often so deeply buried that we are unaware of the cause of our distress. Psychoanalysis exposes the roots, which may help you understand your problems, subconscious motivations and repressed desires.

You've seen psychoanalysis in the movies. The analyst sits outside the line of vision, while the client relaxes on a couch and says the first thing that comes into his or her head – free associates – without worrying that the comment is foolish, obscene or insulting. If you are relaxed, the conscious weakens its hold on the subconscious. Suppressed thoughts rise to the surface. Analysts pay particular attention to thoughts that seem to be blocked or that trigger anxiety. Analysts may also analyse your dreams, which may reveal hidden – especially sexual – conflicts. But psychoanalysis is a long, difficult and often painful experience. You may need to take several sessions a week – or even daily – for between three and five years.

Freudian analysts

Freudian analysts follow the principles laid down by Sigmund Freud around 100 years ago – albeit updated to the 1990s. Freudian analysts today recognise that their founder's views on children and women were somewhat simplistic. Nevertheless, Freudian analysis may provide some profound insights into our natures and motivations.

For example, Freud divided the personality into the id, ego and superego. The id represents our instincts: sexuality, aggression and so on. The ego is our logical, conscious mind. The superego is our judge and jury. Stress and anxiety, Freudians believe, arise when the id's primeval impulses place us in danger or when the superego threatens disapproval or punishment. The ego attempts to deal with the source of the stress. So, for example, the ego drives us to gratify the id's urges. We may explode with anger – and then face our superego's retribution. In other words, we feel guilty. But if the superego is too harsh we may repress the aggression – leaving us passive and uncompetitive.

Some people banish anxiety-provoking thoughts and desires from their consciousness – a strategy known as repression. But if the ego cannot control the superego, repressed thoughts and desires may re-surface, causing stress, guilt and anxiety. Alternatively, the repressed thoughts and desires re-emerge in dreams, when the person is under the influence of drugs or alcohol, or as irrational thoughts. By exploring these repressed desires and the relationship between the id, ego and superego, Freudian analysts may resolve the conflicts, which some clients find alleviates stress and anxiety. The British Psycho-Analytical Society* represents most Freudian psychoanalysts.

Jungian analysts

Carl Jung founded the most important psychoanalytical school to follow in Freud's footsteps. Originally a Freudian, Jung believed Freud overemphasised sexuality's role. In contrast, Jung emphasised the role of cultural, intellectual and spiritual dimensions. He highlighted the role that society and our environment play in the development of anxiety and other mental problems.

Jung believed that 'neuroses' draw attention to a side of our personality that has been neglected or repressed. Neuroses can signal that the person has been unable to move to a new stage in his or her personal development. Jungian analysts – known as analytical psychoanalysts – help their clients explore their neglected or repressed side or ease them into the next stage of development. This alleviates stress-related symptoms, anxiety and other neuroses. Contact the Society of Analytical Psychology*.

Humanistic psychotherapy

Jung was an optimist. He believed that humanity was essentially positive, idealistic and heroic. This view laid the foundation for humanistic psychotherapy. Humanistic psychotherapists believe that we are driven to fulfil our goals, hopes and ambitions and live peaceful and happy lives. They argue that everyone would grow constructively – if only our circumstances would allow. This view is almost directly opposed to Freud, who believed that our essential drive was to fulfil the id's base desires.

Humanistic psychotherapy examines our self-image – which may be radically different to how other people view us.

JOHN, a successful businessman, owned a chain of shops across the Midlands. He lived in a beautiful village just outside Manchester, with an attractive wife. His two daughters studied at Oxford. But John couldn't shake the feeling that he was an abject failure – despite the evidence surrounding him every day. John grew up in a family that disapproved of almost everything he did and never appreciated his achievements. They heaped praise on his brother, who went to medical school and ended up a divorced, bored, rural GP. Humanistic psychotherapy allowed John to explore the reasons for his self-delusion. He emerged happier and more content.

Humanistic psychotherapists suggest that, in some ways, John's problems were inevitable. They believe children should be raised in environments where they are trusted, respected and loved for who they are – even when they do something that their parents don't approve of. Most parents only approve of certain thoughts and actions. The disapproval surrounding the forbidden thoughts and actions can cause stress and anxiety.

Humanistic psychotherapists alleviate stress by examining and modifying this self-image. First, they help clients understand those feelings and desires they previously denied even to themselves. Secondly, clients explore the cause of their problems. Finally, they learn to act more positively and develop a new, more realistic self-image that adapts to new experiences.

Psychodynamic psychotherapists and brief psychotherapy
Like psychoanalysts, psychodynamic psychotherapists believe that the roots of anxiety and stress lie in unresolved childhood conflicts. Psychodynamic psychotherapists analyse these conflicts. Sessions are usually weekly, the client sits opposite the therapist, and the analysis extends to the person's work, family and social

life. Psychodynamic psychotherapists take a more active role than the passive Freudian observer.

Many psychodynamic psychotherapists use a variation of classical psychoanalysis, called brief psychotherapy. This has more limited – but for many people perhaps more realistic – aims than classical psychoanalysis. Brief psychotherapy doesn't attempt to chart the entire subconscious: rather, it provides an insight into clients' specific problems, conflicts and anxieties in order to resolve symptoms rapidly. In many cases this approach is as effective as the traditional analysis.

Behavioural therapy

Behavioural therapy replaces unhelpful coping strategies – such as avoidance – with behaviour and attitudes that don't provoke anxiety, without necessarily gaining an insight into the cause of the problem. For specific problems, behavioural therapy can be more effective than drugs. In panic disorder, for example, 87 per cent of sufferers who underwent behavioural therapy were attack-free. This compares with half of those receiving a tranquilliser and around a third who were either untreated or who took a placebo.

At the start of treatment, behavioural therapists analyse unhelpful coping strategies. This reveals behaviours that the person should aim to change. The analysis also uncovers the conditions that trigger, maintain and exacerbate the unhelpful coping strategies. Behavioural therapy encourages positive behaviour – rather than uncovering repressed motives – by using several techniques including:

- Gradual desensitisation – the exposure gets more intense and frightening at each session. An agoraphobic may walk down the road, then walk to the local supermarket, then take a bus ride, and so on.
- Flooding – the client learns relaxation techniques and then confronts a situation that normally triggers anxiety. The client tries to relax and remains in the fear-provoking situation until the anxiety decreases.
- Aversion therapy and extinction – clients are punished if they perform a certain act. Combined with positive approaches, this can break unpleasant habits. Smokers, for example, may

sit in a room surrounded by cigarette adverts. Each time they light a cigarette they receive an electric shock. Eventually, the electric shock becomes associated with smoking and may lead to the extinction of the habit.

- Learning simple social skills, such as how to start a conversation, can help you fell relaxed and confident in company. Social skills training usually means role-playing in front of a video camera. Watching the tape gives patients an insight into how they appear – rather than how they think they appear.

Behavioural therapy in practice

If you're a parent you probably use behavioural therapy every day – you reward good and punish bad behaviour. In some mental hospitals, inmates once received tokens for dressing, eating and behaving correctly. They exchanged the tokens for privileges, such as renting televisions and radios, or buying cigarettes and sweets. However, these schemes are not widely used today. A similar idea was successful in schools for mentally handicapped or emotionally disturbed children.

However, behavioural therapy can be counterproductive. In one study, psychologists split nursery school children into two groups. When the first group mastered drawing with felt tip pens they received a certificate and badge. The second group drew for fun. Once the first group received their rewards they tended to lose interest. The second group continued drawing. In another study, a monkey watched an experimenter place a piece of banana under one of two containers. A screen was placed between the monkey and the container. The researcher replaced the banana with lettuce – which monkeys don't regard as quite so succulent a delicacy – and removed the screen. The monkey headed for the container hiding the food – and was outraged when it found the lettuce rather than the banana. If you don't get the expected reward, behavioural therapy can backfire.

Cognitive therapy

Cognitive therapy – or cognitive-behavioural therapy – replaces a destructive thought pattern with a more realistic, positive and enjoyable approach to life. Cognitive therapists argue that anxiety and depression arise when a person learns negative ideas early in life. For example, a bereavement early in life can undermine self-esteem and alter a person's view of the past, present and future. Furthermore, people selectively remember depressing or negative memories that fuel and maintain their negative view of life. Cognitive therapy may help clients take responsibility for their behaviour by changing their attitudes, ideas and expectations.

First, clients keep a diary identifying and recording negative thoughts. They learn how these relate to their symptoms of anxiety and depression, for example. Next they look at the evidence for and against their negative thoughts and replace them with ideas more firmly rooted in reality. After a while, the person may learn to identify, ignore and, ultimately, change deep-seated negative beliefs.

So does cognitive-behavioural therapy work in practice? In one study, 76 per cent of panic disorder sufferers gradually reduced and eventually stopped using tranquillisers during cognitive therapy. Most patients were still off the tablets three months later. During therapy, patients learnt to identify the symptoms of panic and withdrawal and replace their negative interpretation with a more positive view. They also learnt relaxation techniques, such as muscle relaxation and correct breathing, and were exposed to situations likely to trigger anxiety – so they could rehearse their coping strategies. Their success rate compares with only 25 per cent among those who tried to stop tranquilliser use by reducing the dose alone.

Who benefits from psychotherapy?

Different therapies suit different people and you need to find the therapy that suits you. Psychoanalysis and psychodynamic psychotherapy tend to benefit:

- those suffering from specific problems – anxiety, depression, family difficulties, marital problems or failure at work
- those who are unable to adjust to change or disability
- those who are articulate and able to see the historical roots of their problems
- those who are able to invest the time and money
- those who are able to cope with an analysis that may delve into painful areas.

Behavioural therapy benefits people suffering:

- specific phobias, anxieties or sexual problems
- social skill problems, e.g. aggression, sexually inappropriate behaviour, lack of assertiveness
- obsessive or compulsive behaviour
- eating disorders, alcoholism, drug abuse
- bed-wetting
- sleep disorders
- unpleasant habits e.g. nail-biting, hair-pulling
- old age disabilities, including dementia
- chronic diseases, including pain, raised blood pressure, asthma, migraine
- disease-related behavioural problems, such as not taking medication prescribed by a doctor
- people preparing for or recovering from surgery.

Cognitive therapy benefits people suffering:

- depression
- generalised anxiety
- panic disorder – especially hyperventilation
- drug abuse
- benzodiazepine withdrawal
- eating disorders.

Finding a psychotherapist

Finding a psychotherapist can be difficult. There is no statutory register. This means that poorly trained – or even untrained – people can set up as analysts.

In response, the British Confederation of Psychotherapists* publishes a register of over 1,200 qualified therapists from a number of organisations, including the Association of Child Psychotherapists*, the British Association of Psychotherapists*, the British Psycho-Analytical Society*, the Lincoln Centre & Institute for Psychotherapy*, the Scottish Association of Psychoanalytical Psychotherapists*, the Scottish Institute of Human Relations*, the Northern Ireland Association for the Study of Psycho-Analysis*, the Tavistock Clinic* and the Society of Analytical Psychology*. The British Confederation of Psychotherapists* also publishes a free booklet called *Finding a therapist* for childhood, adolescent and adult problems.

You can also be referred on the NHS. If you wish to undergo assessment for psychotherapy, contact your GP. Many therapists work in general and psychiatric hospitals, child and family clinics and voluntary organisations. However, consultant psychotherapists are relatively rare in the NHS. Around half the NHS districts do not employ a single consultant psychotherapist.

Reflexology

Reflexology assumes that the 72,000 nerve endings in the sole and upper foot are connected to organs in the rest of the body. While there is no anatomical basis for this, reflexologists claim the connection allows diseases to be detected by examining the patient's feet. If an organ is functioning below par, that area of the foot is tender or the person reports feeling as if they are walking on sand. Some reflexologists suggest that this 'grainy' feeling reflects an accumulation of calcium and lactic acid crystals.

Reflexology's principles are similar to those of shiatsu and acupuncture. Reflexologists believe energy flows along meridians ending in the feet. They aim to encourage a healthy flow of energy along these meridians by massaging, kneading, stroking, rotating and pressurising the foot. This alleviates tension, encourages relaxation and nurtures a sense of well-being. Whether, as reflexologists claim, foot massage alleviates more serious conditions – beyond promoting a 'feel good factor' – is less well established. However, reflexologists claim that they can successfully treat migraine, constipation and other stress-related ailments. Contact the British Complementary Medicine Association* or the Association of Reflexologists*.

Spiritual and faith healing

Each year, thousands of people make a pilgrimage to Lourdes. Most come away feeling better – if not cured. Many more visit spiritual and faith healers in the UK. Often they hope to find cures for intractable diseases, such as multiple sclerosis or cancer, but many consult spiritual and faith healers for stress-related problems including depression, alcoholism and anxiety. Even among people suffering from terminal illness, healers can help patients feel less stressed and anxious, more relaxed and more positive about life – which benefits both sufferers and their families. You don't have to be religious.

On a superficial level, healers believe that everyone naturally draws on the power of healing. Massage, positive thinking and lending a sympathetic ear are all examples of healing. Parents know the value of tender loving care when their children fall ill, and doctors and nurses know the therapeutic benefits of touching their patients. All help relieve anxiety and stress linked to minor physical, mental and emotional complaints. However, healers believe they were born with a special gift that allows them to help people suffering from more severe diseases.

Differences between faith and spiritual healing

There are more similarities than differences between spiritual and faith healing. In both cases it is thought that by going into a relaxed but conscious state, healers channel a higher power into the patient. In both cases this power is believed to penetrate into the deepest levels of the body and mind. Usually, the healers channel their healing power by laying their hands on or above the patient. Healing can be also performed some distance from the patient. Healing relies heavily on prayer – especially for distance healing – and meditation.

The fundamental difference between spiritual and faith healing rests in the 'source' of the healer's power. Faith healers believe that the recipient must believe in divine grace. Spiritual healers, in contrast, say that the person's beliefs are irrelevant. They point out that spiritual healing often helps hardened cynics – although many are converted by their experiences – and faith healing fails to alleviate the suffering of many deeply religious people.

Despite an enormous body of anecdotal evidence, healing remains controversial – especially when cures seem miraculous. Critics point out that 'spontaneous remissions' of serious diseases, such as cancer, can occur – albeit rarely. Other miraculous cures are explained away as mistaken diagnosis, suggestion or even, in one case, that an entire tumour was removed during the diagnostic biopsy.

Healing and conventional medicine

Nevertheless, conventional medicine increasingly recognises healing's benefits – even if it remains sceptical of miraculous cures. Healers now work alongside conventional doctors and nurses in around 200 hospitals, pain clinics, hospices and general practices.

However, this move towards medical respectability means that healing has evolved into a 'complementary' rather than 'alternative' therapy. Healers traditionally rely on intuition to diagnose the patient's problem, but modern healers leave the diagnosis of physical ailments to doctors and aim to restore patients' internal harmony and balance. Conventional doctors may diagnose 'irritable bowel syndrome' or 'chronic pain'. A healer may describe the essence of the problem as, for example, guilt, loneliness and despair. Alleviating the underlying problem, healers argue, resolves many symptoms of physical illness.

Through symptomatic relief and by reducing stress, healing may lessen patients' need for painkillers, tranquillisers and sleeping tablets. Healing – especially if backed by other relaxation techniques – alleviates anxiety, encourages a feeling of inner calm, reduces stress and encourages self-confidence. During one study, a healer worked in a GP's practice. Patients could choose to consult the healer or be referred by a member of the medical team. A third of patients consulted the healer for physical problems, a quarter for both physical and psychological problems and the remainder for a variety of physical, psychological and spiritual problems. Seventy-one per cent said they benefited from the healing sessions and 83 per cent thought that healing would help people with similar problems.

Finding a healer

There are around 8,500 healers practising in the UK. The National Federation of Spiritual Healers* runs a healer referral service and the College of Healing* can provide a register of practitioners. Most healers offer their services irrespective of a patient's ability to pay. Indeed, many healers feel that money sullies their healing gift and do not charge for their services – although donations are sometimes welcome. However, the increasing demand for healing has led some practitioners to practise full-time and so charge for their services. Most make concessions in cases of financial hardship.

Supplements against stress

Living under siege from stress takes its toll physically and mentally, so your body needs an adequate intake of vitamins and minerals to cope. But stress also takes its toll on your diet. You may skip breakfast, drink several cups of coffee, grab a sandwich at your desk for lunch and warm up a TV dinner in the microwave for dinner. The first casualties are the vitamins and minerals that may protect you from the ravages of stress.

Many of us take supplements to make up nutritional deficits. Taking a multivitamin daily acts as an insurance policy against our poor diets. However, supplements paper over cracks in our lifestyle. Taking a handful of vitamin and mineral supplements cannot replace a healthy, balanced diet.

Moreover, very high doses of some vitamins – so-called megadosing – can cause side-effects. Zinc, for example, strengthens the immune system in small doses, but at higher doses can be an immunosuppressant. Mega-dosing can also create imbalances in ratios between vitamins. Nevertheless, provided you're careful, taking vitamin supplements can bolster your stress defences. Whether supplements do this better than eating a healthy diet is debatable. But it is extremely difficult to get some of the high doses advocated by vitamin enthusiasts from food.

Vitamin advocates believe that the government's Reference Nutrient Intake (RNI) for many vitamins and minerals is too low. The aim is to prevent deficiency diseases in 97 per cent of the population. The RNI for vitamin C, for example, aims to protect you from scurvy. However, RNIs do not account for differences in vitamin and mineral requirements in people suffering from disease. Moreover, an RNI that prevents a deficiency disease may not be the same as the dose needed to keep you in the best of health. Around 25 years ago Nobel-prize winner Linus Pauling argued that differences in metabolism mean that our personal optimal intake of many vitamins and minerals may be different from the RNI. For example, certain metabolic reactions occur ten times faster in some individuals than others – even if they are the same sex, age and weight.

However, you may be slightly deficient in certain vitamins without developing classic deficiency diseases, such as beriberi. For example, recent research suggests that some people with marginal deficiencies develop psychological changes such as feeling anxious, depressed or pessimistic. However, these psychological changes are not as marked or as serious as those experienced by people suffering from anxiety disorders or depression.

These marginal deficiencies may be relatively common. A study of 113 women in their early 20s found that a fifth had a marginal thiamine intake. These women tended to have a poorer mood. They then received either a thiamine supplement or an inactive placebo. Neither the women nor their doctors knew who had taken the supplements and who the placebos. After three months, women taking the supplement reported that their mood improved – provided their thiamine intake was marginal at the beginning of the study. Mood worsened among women whose thiamine levels further declined.

If you suffer from any serious diseases it is probably sensible to consult your doctor before taking mega-doses of vitamins and minerals, although daily multivitamins are safe. Mega-doses of vitamin E can decrease diabetics' insulin requirements and increase blood pressure. However, you should also remember that most doctors receive, at best, a few hours of nutritional education in medical school. A few years ago most doctors would have treated the ideas that evening primrose oil alleviates breast pain or folic acid prevents birth defects with scorn.

Experimenting with supplements is generally safe, but treat them with respect and follow these simple rules:

- Never take mega-doses of vitamins if you are pregnant. However, you should consider taking one of the special supplements for pregnant women – at least for the first three months.
- You can give children a single multivitamin daily, perhaps with additional vitamin C during the winter. But do not try megadosing, unless under medical supervision.
- Always increase – and decrease – the dose of vitamin and minerals slowly.
- You may have to wait several weeks before the maximum benefits emerge.

- Spread large doses over the day.
- If you suffer side-effects reduce the dose until symptom resolves. You should especially watch for pain, weakness, rashes, changes in bowel habits or digestive problems.

Supplements for stress

B vitamins

These may alleviate a number of stress-related disorders including PMS, fatigue, depression, nervousness and anxiety. In a recent study, healthy volunteers took a capsule containing either 10 vitamins or inactive placebo daily. After a year, women receiving the multivitamin tended to feel more 'composed' and 'agreeable'. The improvement was most marked in women who had marginal intakes of riboflavin (vitamin B2) and pyridoxine (vitamin B6). Men benefited less – although they reported feeling more 'agreeable'. However, subjects' mood changes were most marked after a year of taking supplements – although blood levels of vitamins were stable after three months. In other words, the B vitamins' benefits don't reflect correction of a dietary deficiency.

The B vitamins work together and the ratio between the various vitamins in the complex is critical. The anti-stress B vitamins are found in certain foods. However, vitamin enthusiasts suggest intakes higher than those you could easily obtain from diet. So start with a B-complex supplement (25mg increasing to 50mg). You can then add various single supplements, depending on your symptoms:

- Vitamin B3 – also called niacin – may improve memory and act as a general tonic against stress. High protein foods such as meat, eggs and certain cereals are rich in vitamin B3. However, more than 50mg niacin may produce flushing, itching and skin-tingling.
- People with a low intake of vitamin B6, also called pyridoxine, may experience depression. Up to 15 per cent of women may suffer from mild vitamin B6 deficiency. Taking 100 to 200mg – no more – of vitamin B6 can alleviate symptoms of depression. Vitamin B6 is found in meat, fish, nuts, bananas, potatoes, bran and dairy products. Very high doses – several grams – of B6 can cause nerve problems.

- Vitamin B12 helps relieve stress and fatigue and may improve memory. B12 deficiency causes pernicious anaemia – the symptoms of which include fatigue. Vitamin B12 is found only in animal products. Beef, fish, chicken and dairy products are good sources of vitamin B12. So vegetarians – and especially vegans – may receive inadequate amounts. However, more than 1mg of folic acid daily can mask B12 deficiency. In other words, high levels of folic acid may mask the symptoms of pernicious anaemia.

Chromium

This partly controls sugar and fat metabolism. Physical and mental stress – including a high sugar diet, strenuous exercise, physical trauma and some infection – can deplete chromium stores. Furthermore, chromium helps stabilise blood sugar levels. Fluctuating blood sugar levels may underlie some cases of fatigue.

Many of us get inadequate amounts of chromium. The current international recommended daily intake is 50-200 micrograms. However, the average northern European diet contains just 35 micrograms. You can boost your chromium levels by eating more meat, wholemeal foods, shellfish and brewer's yeast. Alternatively, try taking a supplement containing around 100 micrograms of chromium daily. Chromium interacts with insulin to control blood sugar fluctuations, so diabetics changing their chromium consumption may find their insulin requirements alter.

Co-enzyme Q10

Millions of people worldwide swear by Q10's energy-boosting properties. Around ten million Japanese and a million Danes and Swedes take supplements containing Q10 every day and it is growing in popularity in the UK. Also called ubiquinone, Q10 is found in mitochondria, cells' power stations, which convert food into energy. Q10 regulates a critical step in this reaction and low levels mean you don't get the maximum amount of energy from your food.

The liver makes Q10 from the amino acid phenylalanine. Diet only provides between 5mg and 15mg a day. Meat, offal, poultry, nuts, mackerel, sardines, wholemeal products and eggs are all rich in Q10. However, our demand for Q10 may outstrip supplies from the liver and diet. Q10 production increases during exercise, but it is quickly used up, so some athletes have lower levels of Q10 than their couch potato friends. Supplements help make up the difference. Try taking 30-60mg Q10 as a supplement daily. You would have to eat about 0.8kg of sardines and over 1.5kg of beef to get 50mg of Q10. However, you may need to take Q10 supplements for up to three months before experiencing the full benefits. No side-effects have emerged even with large doses of Q10 (up to 200mg) taken for several months.

Evening primrose oil
Gammalinolenic acid is an oil found in a number of plants including evening primrose, medical borage and starflower. The body converts gammalinolenic acid into prostaglandins – chemical messengers controlling a number of biological processes including inflammation. As a result, gammalinolenic acid alleviates breast pain and probably other PMS symptoms. It may also help inflammatory conditions exacerbated by stress such as eczema, allergies and rheumatism and may act directly on the brain. Sixty-seven per cent of a group of depressed and hyperactive children improved after taking evening primrose oil compared to when they received olive oil.

Iron

JANINE, an advertising executive for a major magazine, felt tired, faint and breathless. She assumed she was suffering from stress. She believed her almost constant headaches were the by-product of her pressurised job. Her nails and hair were brittle – probably, she believed, because of her poor diet. Her lips felt sore. Eventually, Janine reluctantly went to her GP.

Janine's GP looked at her eyes and lips and took a blood sample. He also asked if Janine experienced heavy periods. She did, and the GP told Janine that her 'stress symptoms' were caused by iron-deficiency anaemia. He prescribed iron supplements. After a week or so, Janine began to feel better.

Janine isn't alone. Mild iron deficiency is common among menstruating women. Around 14 per cent of women have low blood ferritin levels – which reflect depleted iron stores. Anaemia can cause a range of symptoms that mimic stress signals. Try taking up to 24mg of iron daily.

Choosing a supplement

In any health food shop, supermarket or chemist you will face an almost bewildering choice of vitamins and supplements. So how can you choose? Taking a multivitamin is the backbone of using vitamins and minerals to bolster your stress defences. Choose one from a reputable manufacturer.

Even supplements containing the same active ingredient can vary. For example, the formulation can alter the amount of active chemical released from the supplement and taken up into the body – known as the bioavailability. For instance, Q10's bioavailability is higher from soft gelatine capsules than from tablets or capsules containing granules or powders. If in doubt, ask the pharmacist or shop owner.

Tai chi

Tai chi, the graceful, dance-like exercise performed by millions of people throughout the Far East, is rapidly growing in popularity in the West. It is easy to see why: there is something beautiful and serene in the graceful movements, something far removed from the hectic pace of modern life.

Tai chi looks an undemanding way to unwind – until you try it. Tai chi is mentally, physically and spiritually challenging: mentally, because the forms – the complex series of movements – can involve 100 postures; physically, because our unruly bodies are difficult to control; spiritually, because tai chi is a form of moving meditation rooted deep in Eastern philosophy.

Over 4,000 years ago, Chinese physicians suggested that living in damp, humid conditions stagnates your blood and spirits. They added that you can alleviate this stagnation by performing breathing exercises and a dance that imitated the movements of animals. The tai chi practised today developed in the 19th century, when Grandmaster Yang Lu-Ch'an founded the Yang style. His grandson and other teachers reorganised the forms into one long slow series aimed at improving students' health. Since then four other tai chi schools have emerged: Wu, Chen, Woo and Sun. Each differs in the style of the postures and how they link into a form. The Yang style, for example, uses large, open postures. The Chen style uses rapid, coiling movements interspersed with slower gentle ones.

Most tai chi styles have two main forms. The short form contains around 30 postures, takes three to ten minutes to perform and can be learnt in about 12 lessons. The longer, more complex form may contain over 100 postures, take up to 30 minutes to perform and a lot longer to learn. However, teachers bring their own interpretation to each school. Some concentrate on the spiritual aspects, others emphasise the martial side. Nevertheless, all styles integrate three main aspects: meditation, self-defence and healing.

Tai chi and self defence
The fear of being mugged, raped or attacked causes considerable stress – often out of all proportion to the risk. Tai chi may help you gain the confidence to overcome this common cause of stress. After all, tai chi is a martial art. Its full name – tai-chi-chuan – reflects this. Chuan translates as fist.

Nevertheless, it seems strange that tai chi's slow, graceful movement might be effective against a mugger. Tai chi's gentle movements seem far removed from the high-kicking exploits of Bruce Lee. But what looks impressive on the screen may not work on the street. Tai chi's practitioners point out that you can defend yourself with a graceful movement – if you speed it up. A rising hand can deflect a blow to the head, a descending hand can deflect a kick to the groin.

Tai chi for health
Tai chi undoubtedly helps practitioners relax. The concentration needed to remember even the 30 moves of the short forms can distance you from the rat race. As with many complementary therapies, tai chi teachers stress the importance of correct breathing – which relieves stress. However, many tai chi practitioners believe that tai chi also alleviates chronic illness.

Since 1949 Chinese scientists have been amassing a growing body of evidence that chi kung – the various arts including tai chi that develop chi – alleviates a range of diseases including ulcers, ME, multiple sclerosis, cancer, polio, back problems, migraine and sports injuries. In the UK, the Pathgate Institute* uses chi kung and other related arts to treat serious illness, sometimes at the request of doctors and alternative practitioners. Certainly, tai chi's gentle exercises can help alleviate arthritis, sports injuries and other problems. Even older people benefit. The exercise keeps them healthy without making too many demands on their heart. Tai chi also improves flexibility and balance, which helps reduce the risk of falls. However, if you suffer from any medical illness you should consult your doctor before attempting any exercise programme.

If your body does not work at its peak, neither does your mind. Tai chi helps develop awareness and a calm mind that allows you to live in harmony and balance – again reducing stress. But tai chi is not a quick fix. It takes six months to a year to gain any proficiency. To gain a degree of mastery can take ten years or more.

A number of books and videos are now available that can give you a flavour of tai chi. These should be available from a martial arts shop, or you can try advertisements in a martial arts magazine. However, you should learn the forms from a teacher. Your local library, the National Tai Chi Chuan Association* or the British Council of Chinese Martial Arts* can put you in touch with a local teacher.

Yoga

Yoga brings millions of people worldwide some inner peace, relief from stress and improved health. Yoga may relieve a number of stress-related diseases and help wheelchair-bound people maintain their independence. Yoga keeps your mind and body supple. It relaxes and strengthens your stressed-out physique. In other words, yoga is far removed from the image of forcing your body into strange positions in a drafty church hall. Yoga is a complete system that helps you manage your life.

In common with most other complementary techniques, yoga practitioners see every aspect of our lives – consciousness, mind, energy and body – as intertwined. Yoga aims to harmonise these aspects – the Indian root of the word yoga means 'to unite'. Yoga seeks to achieve this unity in three ways.

Posture
Yoga is perhaps best known for the postures that improve our control of our bodies. Known as asanas, these postures are more than

physical exercises. Correctly performed, asanas involve mental control, correct breathing and using the body with the minimum effort and tension. The postures gently stretch and contract muscles and joints. This allows you to move more freely and improves stamina, flexibility and strength. Practitioners claim asanas train the mind and raise consciousness.

Mental

Yoga practitioners claim that yoga bolsters your stress defences and prevents the stress-driven drift towards ill health. Many of the events that stress us haven't happened yet – and probably never will. We worry about the future instead of devoting our energy to the present. Yoga and meditation help practitioners to 'let go' of stress and live in the present.

Energy

Like many other complementary medicines, yoga emphasises correct breathing. When you are tense your breaths tend to be shallow and centre on the upper chest. Using breathing exercises that retrain and control the breath, yoga practitioners learn to use the entire lung. Yoga practitioners believe breath control allows them to control their physical and mental processes and helps them attain the ultimate goal of yoga self-enlightenment. However, breathing exercises may also bring some more mundane benefits, especially to patients with asthma and other respiratory disorders.

Unlike many complementary medicines, yoga's benefits have been scientifically studied. Some studies suggest, for example, that yoga may slow the progression of heart disease. Yoga's postures and relaxation techniques alleviate back pain and help patients maintain a healthy back. Likewise the asanas allow arthritis patients to remain active. Yoga can also alleviate depression. However, patients should continue to take their drugs. When their symptoms seem to be under control they can discuss their medication with their doctor.

Like meditation, you should perform yoga in a quiet, well-ventilated and warm room. Wear comfortable and light clothes and don't practise on a full stomach. You will need to attend classes to learn yoga correctly. However, apart from the classes you must be prepared to set aside some time to practise each day – ideally 20 to 30 minutes. The benefits aren't instant. It takes time to learn how to train your body.

A wide range of books and videos can provide you with a basic understanding of yoga and its benefits. However, you should learn yoga from a teacher. The British Wheel of Yoga* can provide further details. The Yoga for Health Foundation* runs yoga retreats. Your library or adult education centre may also have details of local courses.

ANSWERS TO QUIZ ON PAGES 30/31

ANXIETY SCORES

1. I feel tense or wound up:

Most of the time	3
A lot of the time	2
From time to time, occasionally	1
Not at all	0

2. I get a sort of frightened feeling as if something awful is about to happen:

Very definitely and quite badly	3
Yes, but not too badly	2
A little, but it doesn't worry me	1
Not at all	0

3. Worrying thoughts go through my mind:

A great deal of the time	3
A lot of the time	2
From time to time, not too often	1
Only occasionally	0

4. I can sit at ease and feel relaxed:

Definitely	0
Usually	1
Not often	2
Not at all	3

5. I get a sort of frightened feeling like 'butterflies' in the stomach:

Not at all	0
Occasionally	1
Quite often	2
Very often	3

6. I feel restless as if I have to be on the move:

Very much indeed	3
Quite a lot	2
Not very much	1
Not at all	0

7. I get sudden feelings of panic:

Very often indeed	3
Quite often	2
Not very often	1
Not at all	0

DEPRESSION SCORES

1. I still enjoy the things I used to enjoy:

Definitely as much	0
Not quite so much	1
Only a little	2
Hardly at all	3

2. I can laugh and see the funny side of things:

As much as I always could	0
Not quite so much now	1
Definitely not so much now	2
Not at all	3

3. I feel cheerful:

Not at all	3
Not often	2
Sometimes	1
Most of the time	0

4. I feel as if I am slowed down:

Nearly all the time	3
Very often	2
Sometimes	1
Not at all	0

5. I have lost interest in my appearance:

Definitely	3
I don't take as much care	2
I may not take quite as much care	1
I take just as much care as ever	0

6. I look forward with enjoyment to things:

As much as ever I did	0
Rather less than I used to	1
Definitely less than I used to	2
Hardly at all	3

7. I can enjoy a good book or radio or TV programme:

Often	0
Sometimes	1
Not often	2
Very seldom	3

ADDRESSES

Action on Smoking and Health (ASH)
Devon House, 12-15 Dartmouth Street
London SW1H 9BL
0171-314 1360

African-Caribbean Mental Health
Association
35-37 Electric Avenue
London SW9 8JP
0171-737 3603

Age Concern Cymru
4th Floor, Transport House
1 Cathedral Road
Cardiff CF1 9SD
(01222) 371566

Age Concern England
Astral House, 1268 London Road
London SW16 4ER
0181-679 8000

Age Concern Northern Ireland
3 Lower Crescent
Belfast BT7 1NR
(01232) 245729

Age Concern Scotland
113 Rose Street
Edinburgh EH2 3DT
0131-220 3345

Al-Anon
61 Great Dover Street
London SE1 4YF
0171-403 0888 (24-hour helpline)

Alcoholics Anonymous (AA)
PO Box 1, Stonebow House
Stonebow, York YO1 2NJ
(01904) 644026 (office)
0171-352 3001 (helpline 9am-5pm)
or see local phone book

Alcohol Concern
Waterbridge House
32-36 Loman Street
London SE1 0EE
0171-928 7377

Aleph One Ltd
The Old Courthouse, Bottisham
 Cambridge CB5 9BA
(01223) 811679

Alexander Teaching Network
PO Box 53, Kendal LA9 4UP

Alexander Technique International
142 Thorpedale Road
London N4 3BS
0171-281 7639

Anxia – Anxiety Disorders Association
20 Church Street
Dagenham RM10 9UR
0181-491 4700 (office)
0181-270 0999 (helpline)

Aromatherapy Organisations Council
3 Latymer Close, Braybrooke
Market Harborough LE16 8LN
(01858) 434242

Arthritis & Rheumatism Council for
Research
Copeman House
St Mary's Court, St Mary's Gate
Chesterfield S41 7TD
(01246) 558033

Arthritis Care
18 Stephenson Way
London NW1 2HD
0171-916 1500

Association of Child Psychotherapists
120 West Heath Road
London NW3 7TU
0181-458 1609

Association for Post-Natal Illness
25 Jerdan Place
London SW6 1BE
0171-386 0868

Association of Professional Music
Therapists
38 Pierce Lane
Fulbourn CB1 5DL

Association of Reflexologists
27 Old Gloucester Street
London WC1N 3XX
(0990) 673320

BACUP
3 Bath Place, Rivington Street
London EC2A 3JR
(0800) 181199/0171-613 2121 (info)
0171-696 9000/0141-553 1553
(counselling)

Black Carers Support Group
Annie Wood Resource Centre
129 Alma Way, Lozells
Birmingham B19 2LS
0121-554 7137

BM Families
London WC1N 3XX

Breast Cancer Care/Breast Care and
Mastectomy Association of Great Britain
Kiln House, 210 New Kings Road
London SW6 4NZ
0171-384 2984 (office)
(0500) 245345 (helpline)

British Acupuncture Council
Park House, 206 Latimer Road
London W10 6RE
0181-964 0222

British Association for Applied
Chiropractic
The Old Post Office, Cherry Street
Stratton Audley
Nr Bicester OX6 9BA
(01869) 277111

British Association for Autogenic
Training
Heath Cottage, Pitch Hill
Ewhurst GU6 7NP

British Association of Counselling
1 Regent Place
Rugby CV21 2PJ
(01788) 578328

British Association of Psychotherapists
37 Mapesbury Road
London NW2 4HL
0181-452 9823

British Association for Sexual and
Marital Therapy
PO Box 63, Sheffield S10 3TS

British Chiropractic Association
29 Whitley Street
Reading RG2 0EG
(01734) 757557

British Complementary Medicine
Association
39 Prestbury Road
Pittville, Cheltenham GL52 2PT
(01242) 226770

British Confederation of
Psychotherapists
37 Mapesbury Road
London NW2 4HJ
0181-830 5173

British Council of Chinese Martial Arts
46 Oaston Road
Nuneaton CV11 6JZ

British Digestive Foundation
PO Box 251
Edgware HA8 6HG

British Heart Foundation
14 Fitzhardinge St
London W1H 4DH
0171-935 0185

British Homeopathic Association
27A Devonshire Street
London W1N 1RJ
Send s.a.e. for list of registered doctors

British Hypnosis Research (BHR)
Page House
164 West Wycombe Road
High Wycombe HP12 3AE
(01494) 539559

British Massage Therapy Council
Greenbank House
65a Adelphi Street
Preston PR1 7BH
(01772) 881063

British Migraine Association
178a High Road, Byfleet
West Byfleet KT14 7ED
(01932) 352468

British Psycho-Analytical Society
Mansfield House
63 New Cavendish Street
London W1M 7RD
0171-580 4952

British Snoring and Sleep Apnoea
Association (BSSAA)
1-5 How Lane, Chipstead CT5 3LT
(01737) 557997

British Society for Music Therapy
25 Rosslyn Avenue
East Barnet EN4 8DH

British Tinnitus Association
14-18 West Bar Green
Sheffield S1 2DA
(0114) 279 6600

British Wheel of Yoga
1 Hamilton Place, Boston Road
Sleaford NG34 7ES
(01529) 306851

Buddhist Society
58 Eccleston Square
London SW1V 1PH
0171-834 5858

Cancer Care Society
21 Zetland Road
Redland BS6 7AH
(0117) 942 7419

Cancerlink
17 Britannia Street
London WC1X 9JN
0171-833 2451

Carers National Association
Ruth Pitter House
20/25 Glasshouse Yard
London EC1A 4JS
0171-490 8818 (administration)
0171-490 8898 (carers line)

Central Register of Advanced
Hypnotherapists
28 Finsbury Park Road
London N4 2JX
0171-359 6991

Childline
Freepost 1111, London N1 0BR
(0800) 1111

City of London Migraine Clinic
22 Charterhouse Square
London EC1H 6DX
0171-251 3322

Clinically Standardized Meditation
Learning for Life Ltd
PO Box 2280
Bournemouth BH9 2ZE
(01202) 547444

College of Healing
Runnings Park, Croft Bank
West Malvern WR14 4DU
(01684) 566450

Compassionate Friends
53 North Street
Bristol BS3 1EN
(0117) 9665202 (administration)
(0117) 9539639 (helpline)

Council for Complementary and
Alternative Medicine
Park House, 206/208 Latimer Road
London W10 6RE
0181-968 3862

Cruse – Bereavement Care
Cruse House, 126 Sheen Road
Richmond TW9 1UR
0181-940 4818 (office)
0181-332 7227 (helpline)

Cry-sis
BM Cry-sis
London WC1N 3XX
0171-404 5011 (helpline)

Defeat Depression – see The Royal
College of Psychiatrists

Depression Alliance
PO Box 1022
London SE1 7QB
0171-721 7672

Dr Edward Bach Centre
Mount Vernon, Baker's Well
Brightwell-cum-Sotwell
Wallingford OX10 0PZ
(01491) 834678

Eating Disorders Association
Sackville Place, 44 Magdalen Street
Norwich NR3 1JU
(01603) 621414 (adult helpline)
(01603) 765050 (youth helpline)

Enuresis Resource and Information
Centre
65 St Michael's Hill
Bristol BS2 8DZ
(0117) 9264920 (helpline)

Families Anonymous
Unit 37, Doddington and Rollo
Community Association
Charlotte Despard Avenue
London SW11 5JE
0171-498 4680

Families Need Fathers
134 Curtain Road
London EC2A 3AR
0181-886 0970

General Council and Register of
Naturopaths
Goswell House, 2 Goswell Road
Street BA16 0JG
(01458) 840072

Gingerbread (Association for One
Parent Families)
16 Clerkenwell Close
London EC1R 0AA
0171-336 8184 (advice line)
0181-514 1177 (careline)

Helping Parents
CCCES – Centre for Children's
Counselling and Educational Support
Centre House, 14 Basil Avenue
Armthorpe, Doncaster DN3 2AT
(01302) 832760 (office)
(01302) 833596 (helpline)

Help the Aged
16/18 St James's Walk
London EC1R 0BE
0171-253 0253 (administration)
(0800) 650065 (advice line)

Hodgkin's Disease and Lymphoma
Association
PO Box 275, Haddenham
Aylesbury HP17 8JJ
(01844) 291500

Homeopathic Trust
2 Hahnemann House, 2 Powis Place
Great Ormond Street
London WC1N 3HT
0171-837 9469

IBS Network
St John's House, Hither Green Hospital
Hither Green Lane
London SE13 6RU
0181-698 4611 ext 8194

Impotence Association
0181-767 7791

Institute for Complementary Medicine
PO Box 194
London SE16 1QZ

Institute for Family Therapy
43 New Cavendish Street
London W1M 7RG
0171-935 1651

International Federation of
Aromatherapists
Stamford House,
2/4 Chiswick High Road
London W4 1TH
0181-742 2605

Leukaemia Care Society
14 Kingfisher Court
Venny Bridge, Pinhoe
Exeter EX4 8JN
(01392) 464848

Lifeskills
Bowman House, 6 Billetfield
Taunton TA1 3NN
(01823) 451771

Lincoln Centre & Institute for
Psychotherapy
19 Abbeville Mews
88 Clapham Park Road
London SW4 7BX
0171-978 1545

Manic Depression Fellowship
8/10 High Street
Kingston-upon-Thames KT1 1EY
0181-974 6550

McTimoney Chiropractic Association
21 High Street, Eynsham OX8 1HE
(01865) 880974

ME Association
Stanhope House, High Street
Stanford-le-Hope SS17 0HA
(01375) 642466 (office)
(01375) 361013 (information)

Migraine Trust
45 Great Ormond Street
London WC1N 3HZ
0171-278 2676

MIND – National Association for
Mental Health
Granta House, 15/19 Broadway
London E15 4BQ
0181-519 2122

National Association for Premenstrual
Syndrome
PO Box 72, Sevenoaks
Kent TN13 1XQ
(01732) 741709

National Asthma Campaign
Providence House, Providence Place
London N1 0NT
0171-226 2260 (office)
(0345) 010203 (helpline)

National Back Pain Association
16 Elmtree Road
Teddington TW11 8ST
0181-977 5474

National Childbirth Trust
Alexandra House, Oldham Terrace
London W3 6NH
0181-992 8637

National Drugs Helpline
(0800) 776600

National Eczema Society
163 Eversholt Street
London NW1 1BU
0171-388 4097 (office)
0171-388 4800 (advice line)

National Federation of Solo Clubs
Room 8, Ruskin Chambers
191 Corporation Street
Birmingham B4 6RY
0121-236 2879

National Federation of Spiritual Healers
Old Manor Farm Studio, Church Street
Sunbury-on-Thames TW16 6RG
(01932) 783164 (office)
(01891) 616080 (healer referral service)

National Institute of Medical Herbalists
56 Longbrook Street
Exeter EX4 6AH
(01392) 426022

National Missing Persons Helpline
Roebuck House
284/286 Upper Richmond Road West
London SW14 7JE
0181-392 2000 (office)
(0500) 700700 (helpline)
(0500) 700740 (message home service)

National Register of Hypnotherapists
and Psychotherapists
12 Cross Street, Nelson
Lancashire BB9 7EN
(01282) 699378

National Schizophrenia Fellowship
28 Castle Street
Kingston-upon-Thames KT1 1SS
0181-547 3937 (office)
0181-974 6814 (advice line)

National Tai Chi Chuan Association
PO Box 8627
London E11 1UQ
0181-556 6393

Nordoff-Robbins Music Therapy Centre
2 Lissenden Gardens
London NW5 1PP
0171-267 4496

Northern Ireland Association for the
Study of Psycho-Analysis
75 Ballybentragh Road
Muckamore BT41 2HJ
(01232) 648038

Open University
PO Box 188, Walton Hall
Milton Keynes MK7 6DH
(01908) 653231

Osteopathic Information Service
PO Box 2074, Reading RG1 4YR
(01734) 512051

Parentline
Endway House
Endway, Hadleigh
Benfleet SS7 2AN
(01702) 554782 (office)
(01702) 559900 (helpline)

Pathgate Institute
PO Box 100
Newcastle upon Tyne NE7 7YZ

Phobic Society
4 Cheltenham Road
Chorlton cum Hardy
Manchester M21 9QN
0161-881 1937

Quitline
Victory House
170 Tottenham Court Road
London W1P 0HA
(0800) 002200 (helpline)
0171-388 5775 (office)

Registered Nursing Homes Association
Calthorpe House, Hagley Road
Edgbaston B16 8QY
0121-454 2511

Relate – National Marriage Guidance
Herbert Gray College
Little Church Street
Rugby CV21 3AP
(01788) 573241 (office)
For local centres, look in telephone book
under 'R'

Release
388 Old Street
London EC1V 9LT
0171-729 9904 (advice line 10am-6pm)
0171-603 8654 (advice line 6pm-10am)

Research Into Ageing
Baird House, 15/17 St Cross Street
London EC1N 8UN
0171-404 6878

Re-Solv
30a High Street
Stone ST15 8AW
(01785) 817885

Royal College of Psychiatrists
17 Belgrave Square
London SW1X 8PG
0171-235 2351

Royal National Institute for Deaf People
(RNID)
19-23 Featherstone Street
London EC1V 8SL
0171-296 8000

Samaritans
10 The Grove
Slough SL1 1QP
(01753) 532713 (office)
(0345) 90 90 90 (helpline)

SANE
(Schizophrenia – A National Emergency)
199/205 Old Marylebone Road
London NW1 5QP
0171-724 6520 (office)
(0345) 678000 (helpline)

Save Our Sons (testicular cancer)
Tides Reach, 1 Kite Hill
Wootton Bridge
Isle of Wight PO33 4LA
(01983) 882876

Scottish Association of Psychoanalytical
Psychotherapists
56 Albany Street
Edinburgh EH1 3QR
0131-556 0924

Scottish Institute of Human Relations
56 Albany Street
Edinburgh EH1 3QR
0131-556 0924

Seasonal Affective Disorder Association
PO Box 989
London SW7 2PZ

SeniorLine
(0800) 650065
(0800) 289404 (winter warmth line, Oct-
March)

Shiatsu Society
31 Pullman Lane
Godalming GU7 1XY
(01483) 860771

Society of Analytical Psychology
1 Daleham Gardens
London NW3 5BY
0171-435 7696

Society of Homoepaths
2 Artizan Road
Northampton NN1 4HU
(01604) 21400
Send an S.A.E. for list of registered
members

Society for the Promotion of Nutritional
Therapy
PO Box 47, Heathfield TN21 8ZX
(01435) 867007

Society of Teachers of Alexander
Technique
20 London House
266 Fulham Road
London SW10 9EL
0171-351 0828

Standing Conference on Drug Abuse
(SCODA)
Waterbridge House, 32/6 Loman Street
London SE1 0EE
0171-928 9500

Stroke Association
CHSA House, 123/7 Whitecross Street
London EC1Y 8JJ
0171-490 7999

Tavistock Clinic
120 Belsize Lane
London NW3 5BA
0171-435 7111

Tenovus Cancer Information Centre
College Buildings, Courtney Road
Splott, Cardiff CF2 2JP
(0800) 526527

Tranquilliser Advice and Support Project
Philipson House
5 Philipson Street, Walker
Newcastle-upon-Tyne NE6 4EN
0191-234 3486

Transcendental Meditation
Freepost, London SW1P 4YY
(0800) 269303

Triumph over Phobia (TOP UK)
PO Box 1831
Bath BA1 3YX
(01225) 330353

Universal Colour Healers Research
Foundation
67 Farm Crescent, Wrexham Court
Slough SL2 5TQ

Women's Health Concern (WHC)
93-99 Upper Richmond Road
London SW15 2TG
0181-780 3007 (helpline)
0191-272 2694 (helpline)
(01733) 893586 (helpline)

Yoga for Health Foundation
Ickwell Bury, Ickwell
Biggleswade SG18 9EF
(01767) 627271

INDEX